101 MICROPROCESSOR SOFTWARE AND HARDWARE PROJECTS

Acknowledgments

Much of the material in this book is reprinted by permission of Intel Corporation, copyright 1982.

No.1333
$16.95

101 MICROPROCESSOR SOFTWARE AND HARDWARE PROJECTS

BY FRANK P. TEDESCHI & GARY KUECK

TAB BOOKS Inc.
BLUE RIDGE SUMMIT, PA. 17214

FIRST EDITION

FIRST PRINTING

Printed in the United States of America

Library of Congress Cataloging in Publication Data

Tedeschi, Frank P.
101 microprocessor software and hardware projects.

Includes index.
1. Microcomputers—Amateurs' manuals. I. Kueck, Gary. II. Title. III. Title: One hundred one microprocessor software and hardware projects. IV. Title: One hundred and one microprocessor software and hardware projects.
TK9969.T42 001.64 81-9253
ISBN 0-8306-0030-2 AACR2
ISBN 0-8306-1333-1 (pbk.)

Contents

Introduction

This book is for anyone who wants to understand the fundamentals of microcomputer programming and interfacing by performing projects rather than reading and writing programs. Any time microprocessor or microcomputer programming are mentioned, a particular set of instructions (programming material), technical data and hardware must be defined. In this book, we employ the INTEL SDK-85 microcomputer trainer. You are furnished information for purchase of the trainer in Chapter 1. Chapters 2, 3, 4, 5, and the Appendix furnish the hardware information, technical data, and instruction set of the SDK-85 trainer.

Projects in Chapters 1, 6, 7, 8, 9, and 10 are software and hardware oriented. This feature is not offered in most microprocessor project books. However, a number of software-only projects are offered for the software purist.

The first chapter includes hardware modifications to the basic SDK-85 microcomputer in order to work the projects in Chapters 7, 8, 9, and 10. The electronics buff will enjoy wiring and assembling power supplies and switches to expand the SDK-85 trainer.

Chapter 6 illustrates basic software projects performable on the basic SDK-85 microcomputer without modifications. The programs illustrate addition, subtraction, multiplication, bit testing, parity checking and rotation in assembly language.

Chapter 7 includes projects that can be performed on the basic SDK-85 microcomputer and projects that need additional hardware as outlined in Chapter 1. The programs illustrate memory copy, division, combination lock, number guess game, a game called 21, random number generator, seven segment movable displays, clocks, D/A conversion and many more enjoyable projects.

Chapter 8 requires interface between the SDK-85 and a teletype (TTY). You are furnished purchase information of the TTY at a surprisingly low cost. The TTY can be used as an inexpensive printer in expanding your microcomputer system. The programs employed with the TTY include data design projects for your enjoyment.

Chapter 9 shows how to interface the SDK-85 with an oscilloscope. Interfacing projects include stationary and moving data designs displayed on the oscilloscope.

Chapter 10 includes five projects that interface the SDK-85 with electronic circuitry to simulate electronic dice, random number generator, 24-hour clock, stop clock, and a metronome.

We would like to express our sincere thanks to three persons who have helped in making this book possible: Mr. Larry English, an application engineer for Allen Bradley Corp.; Mr. Douglas Passey, a design engineer for Allen Bradley Corp.; and Mr. David Gill, an engineer for General Motors Corp.

Chapter 1 SDK-85 Microcomputer and Hardware Projects

1.1 INTRODUCTION

Everyone in today's modern society has been or will be affected by a computer. The electronic hobbyist must know about computers, especially microprocessors, microcomputers, and microcomputer systems. This book will help the electronic buff understand the workings of a microprocessor by allowing he/she to build a microcomputer employing an 8085 microprocessor, experimenting with microprocessor programs, and interfacing with peripheral devices to develop a small microcomputer system.

The term microprocessor has been used loosely among people in the electronic field. A microprocessor is usually a single chip containing the digital logic of a central processing unit (CPU) plus other logic directing the flow of data IN, OUT, and AROUND the CPU. A block diagram of the 8085A CPU shows the flow of the data in Fig. 1-1. The 8085A CPU will be employed throughout this book. The explanation of *how* the 8085A CPU chip functions requires an entire chapter in this book. The microprocessor chip is the brain and nervous system of the microcomputer system.

The basic microcomputer we will be using is the MCS-85 System Design Kit, normally called the SDK-85. The SDK-85 can be purchased at your favorite electronic hobby store, but if you cannot find it there, write or call:

INTEL CORPORATION
3065 Bowers Ave.
Santa Clara, CA. 95051
Phone: (408) 987-8080

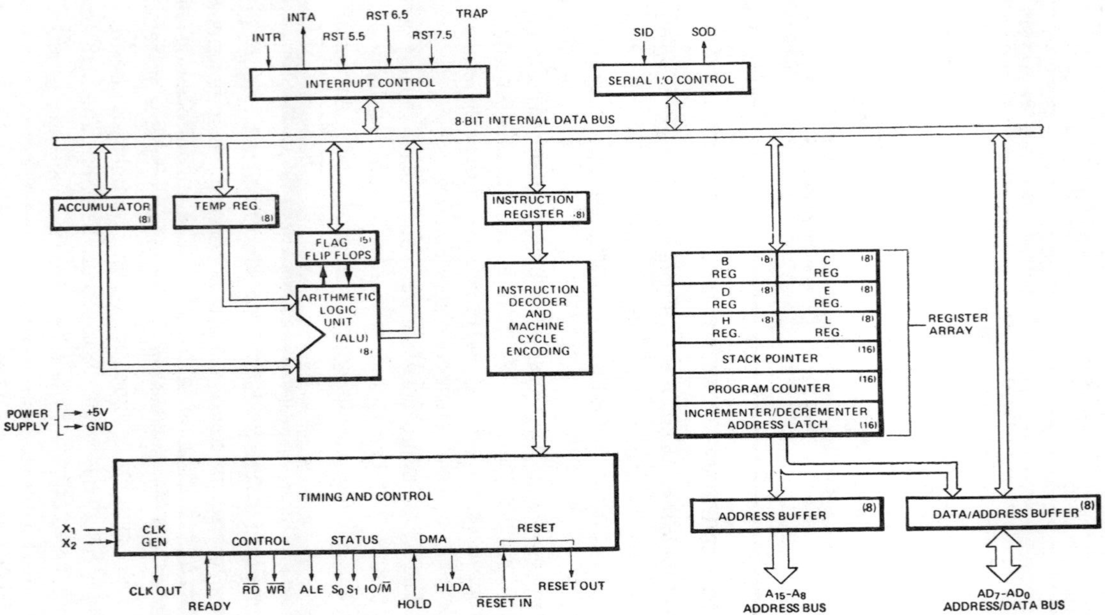

Fig. 1-1. 8085A CPU functional block diagram.

The programs furnished in this book can be used with the BASIC SDK-85 KIT. The programs are written at a basic level, intermediate level, and game level. In addition, programs have been written which require an expansion of the BASIC SDK-85 KIT, along with external hardware and/or instrumentation. The advanced programs include teletypewriter (TTY) communication between the SDK-85 and a TTY, oscilloscope displays, and sound effect circuits. The advanced programming illustrates the concept of building a microprocessor into a microcomputer system through programming and hardware development. This technique is not usually illustrated in most literature, which generally highlights programming and only talks about hardware interfacing with the programming.

1.2 DESCRIPTION OF THE SDK-85

In order to employ the projects in this book, you must purchase the MCS-85 System Design Kit (SDK-85), either from your favorite electronic store, or by contacting INTEL CORP. (see Section 1.1). The SDK-85 contains all the parts with which you can build a complete 8085 microcomputer system on a single board, and with which you can execute all the basic software projects in Chapter 6 and most of the intermediate software projects in Chap-

Fig. 1-2. Basic SDK-85 trainer (courtesy of Intel Corporation).

ter 7. In order to execute the gaming projects, TTY projects, oscilloscope displays, and other advanced programs, you will be required to assemble other hardware besides what is furnished to you in the BASIC SDK-85 KIT. The authors assure you that hardware projects necessary to execute advanced programs will be furnished at the appropriate time.

The BASIC SDK-85 KIT is shown in finished form in Fig. 1-2. The expanded model will include more hardware than shown in Fig. 1-2. You can assemble the kit in 3 to 5 hours, depending upon your skill and experience at building electronic kits. Only a 5 Volt DC power source capable of delivering 1.3 Amperes is needed to make the computer operate, using its built-in display and keyboard. However, a larger current capacity supply is necessary to operate the advanced programs presented in this book. The authors recommend that a 2 Ampere supply be used. If the reader doesn't have the 5 Volt, 2 Ampere DC supply, the next section offers the complete circuitry necessary for the assembly of the 5 Volt, 2 Ampere DC supply.

The finished SDK-85 computer has the following built-in features:

1. High-performance 3-MHz 8085 CPU (1.3 μs instruction cycle).
2. 8085A Instruction set.
3. Direct Teletypewriter (TTY) Interface.
4. Large Wire-Wrap Area for Custom-Designed Circuit.
5. System Monitor Software in ROM.

The SDK-85 Specifications are listed below:

CENTRAL PROCESSOR:
8085A
1.3 μs Instruction Cycle
Instruction Cycle: 1.3 microsecond
T_{cy}: 330 ns
Memory
ROM: 2K bytes (expandable to 4K bytes)
8355 or 8755
RAM: 256 bytes (expandable to 512 bytes) 8155
Addressing: ROM 0000-07FF (expandable to OFFF with an additional 8355 or 8755) RAM 2000-20FF (2800-28FF available with an additional 8155)
Input/Output
Parallel: 38 lines (expandable to 76 lines).

Serial: Through SID/SOD ports of 8085. Software generated baud rate.

Baud Rate: 110

Interfaces

Bus: All signals TTL compatible.

Parallel I/O: All signals TTL compatible.

Serial I/O: 20 mA current loop TTY.

Note: By populating the buffer area of the board, you have access to all bus signals which enable you to design custom system expansions into the kit's wire-wrap area.

- Microcomputer Systems Databook
- MCS-85 User's Manual
- 8080/8085 Assembly Language Programming Manual

Physical Characteristics

Width: 12.0 in.

Height: 10 in.

Depth 0.50 in.

Weight: approx. 12 oz.

Electrical Characteristics (DC Power Required)

V_{cc}: +5V ± 5%   1.3A

V_{TTY}: −10V ± 10%   0.3A

(V_{TTY} required only if teletypewriter is to be connected to the kit)

Environmental

Operating Temperature: 0-55°C

Interrupts

Three Levels: (RST 7.5) - Keyboard Interrupt
(RST 6.5) - TTL Input
(INTR) - TTL Input

DMA

Hold Request: Jumper selectable. TTL compatible input.

Software

System Monitor: Preprogrammed 8755 or 8355 ROM

Addresses: 0000-07FF

I/O: Keyboard/Display or TTY (serial I/O)

Literature

Design Library (Provided with kit):

- SDK-85 User's Manual

If you wish to interface a TTY to the SDK-85, you will also

need a –10 Volt DC power supply, whose construction is shown in Section 1.10 of this chapter.

After you have completed the basic kit, you may expand both memory and I/O by adding more RAM-I/O or ROM-I/O devices in the spaces provided for that purpose. More hardware can also be wired into the SDK-85 as the user deems necessary. The authors have included in this chapter necessary hardware projects that expand the SDK-85 into a microcomputer system which can execute the programs shown in later chapters.

1.3 PROJECT 1: SDK-85 CUSTOM DC POWER SUPPLY

The +5 V, 1.3 A DC power supply needed to operate the SDK-85 trainer is shown in Fig. 1-3. Once the power supply has been assembled, adjust potentiometer R3 so that the output voltage is +5 V. After this adjustment is made, connect the power supply to the SDK-85 trainer at the top of the trainer marked +5 V for the PLUS side of the supply and connect the MINUS side of the supply to the terminal marked GND on the top of the trainer.

After the power supply has been connected to the trainer measure the output of the power supply and adjust R3 so the output of the DC supply is +5 V. Now press the RESET key and the characters 8085 should appear on the SDK-85 display. If 8085 doesn't appear, refer to the SDK-85 readers manual.

This power supply is also used in projects shown in Chapters 7 and 9.

1.4 PROJECT 2: LED ASSEMBLY FOR OUT PORT 22 AND IN PORT 21

The SDK-85 trainer must be modified to execute the programs in Chapters 7, 8, 9 and 10. Figure 1-4 shows the top view of the SDK-85 trainer. In this section we will show the reader the necessary modifications that need to be made in order to wire and install 16 LEDs and their driver circuits.

Figure 1-5 illustrates the necessary wiring of the 16 LEDs to their driver circuits. Also included on the wiring diagram is the parts list for the wiring project. Besides the 16 LEDs, 16 resistors (270 Ohms, ¼W), and three ICs (SN7416) with three DIP sockets must be used. Figure 1-5 includes the part numbers of the LEDs and DIP sockets from Radio Shack. The ICs can be purchased from your local TI distributor.

Figure 1-6 shows the location of the LEDs, Resistors, DIP sockets, and ICs on the SDK-85 trainer. The reader must put the

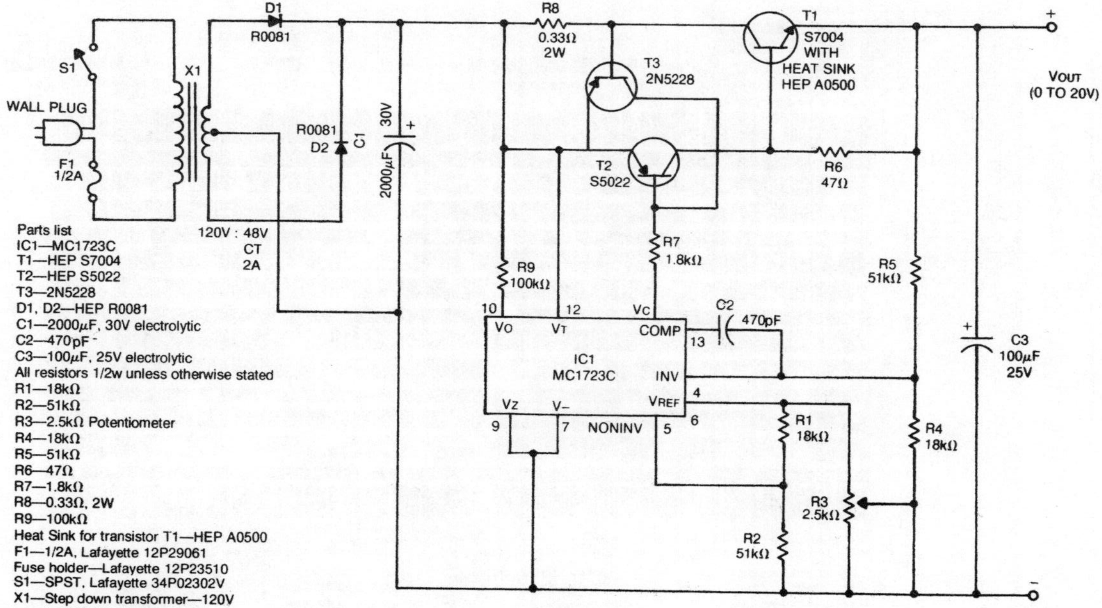

Parts list
IC1—MC1723C
T1—HEP S7004
T2—HEP S5022
T3—2N5228
D1, D2—HEP R0081
C1—2000μF, 30V electrolytic
C2—470pF
C3—100μF, 25V electrolytic
All resistors 1/2w unless otherwise stated
R1—18kΩ
R2—51kΩ
R3—2.5kΩ Potentiometer
R4—18kΩ
R5—51kΩ
R6—47Ω
R7—1.8kΩ
R8—0.33Ω, 2W
R9—100kΩ
Heat Sink for transistor T1—HEP A0500
F1—1/2A, Lafayette 12P29061
Fuse holder—Lafayette 12P23510
S1—SPST, Lafayette 34P02302V
X1—Step down transformer—120V
to 48V, 2A; Stancor Type
P-8618 Newark 5F1437
Regulated DC power supply variable 0 to 20 V, at 2A.

Fig. 1-3. SDK-85 regulated DC custom power supply schematic (+5V at 2A).

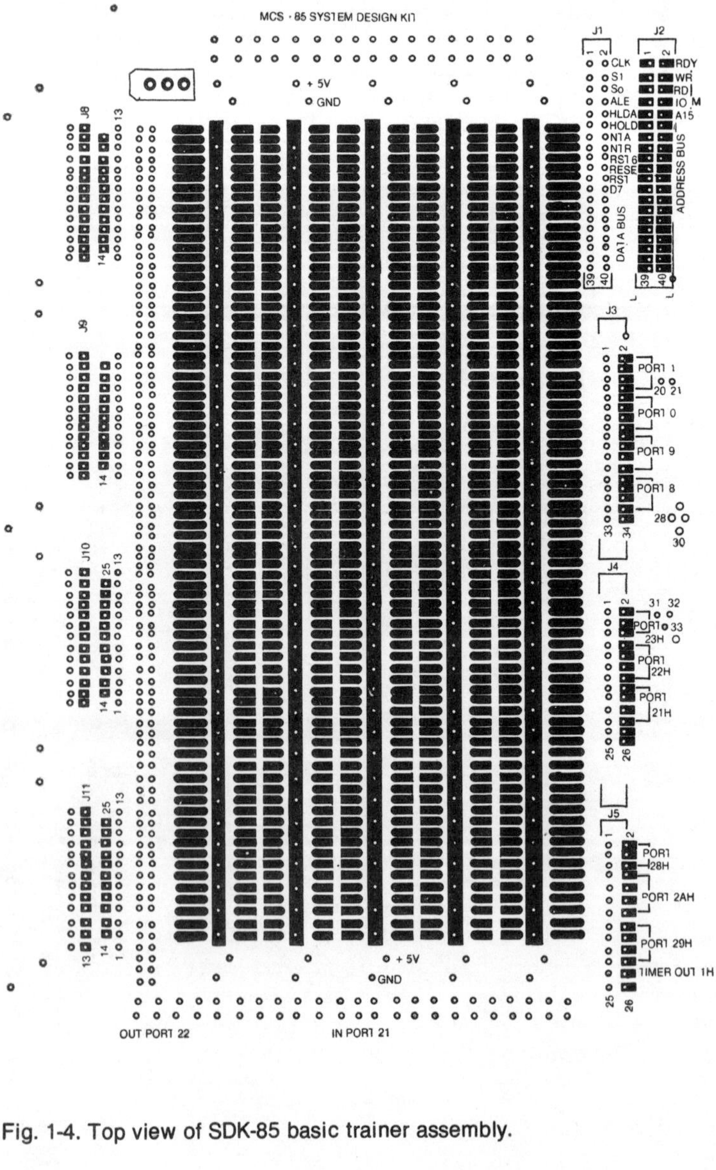

Fig. 1-4. Top view of SDK-85 basic trainer assembly.

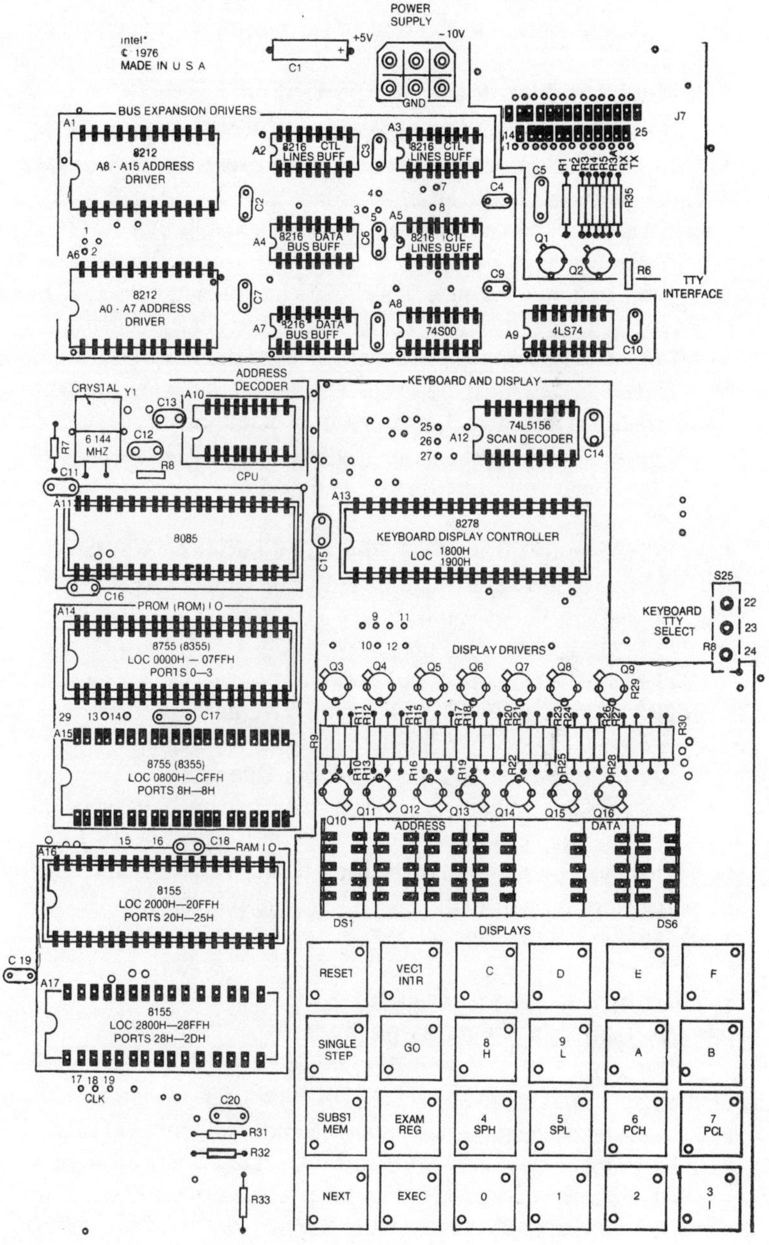

intel*
© 1976
MADE IN U S A
POWER SUPPLY
+5V
-10V
GND
C1
BUS EXPANSION DRIVERS
8212
A8 - A15 ADDRESS DRIVER
8216 CTL LINES BUFF
8216 DATA BUS BUFF
8212
A0 - A7 ADDRESS DRIVER
74S00
4LS74
J7
TTY INTERFACE
ADDRESS DECODER
CRYSTAL
6 144 MHZ
CPU
8085
KEYBOARD AND DISPLAY
74L5156
SCAN DECODER
8278
KEYBOARD DISPLAY CONTROLLER
LOC 1800H 1900H
PROM (ROM) I O
8755 (8355)
LOC 0000H — 07FFH
PORTS 0—3
8755 (8355)
LOC 0800H—CFFH
PORTS 8H—8H
RAM I O
8155
LOC 2000H—20FFH
PORTS 20H—25H
8155
LOC 2800H—28FFH
PORTS 28H—2DH
CLK
KEYBOARD TTY SELECT
DISPLAY DRIVERS
ADDRESS
DATA
DISPLAYS
RESET
VECT INTR
C
D
E
F
SINGLE STEP
GO
8 H
9 L
A
B
SUBST MEM
EXAM REG
4 SPH
5 SPL
6 PCH
7 PCL
NEXT
EXEC
0
1
2
3 I

components in the exact location as indicated in Fig. 1-6 so that the trainer can accommodate the remaining projects in this chapter.

1.5 PROJECT 3: DUAL-IN-LINE (DIP) SWITCH ASSEMBLY

The location of the DIP switch on the SDK-85 trainer is shown on Fig. 1-6 of the preceding section. The reader must place the components in the exact location as indicated in Fig. 1-6 so the trainer can accommodate the remaining projects in this chapter.

Figure 1-7 illustrates the necessary wiring of the Dual-In-Line package of switches to the driver circuits installed in Project 2. In other words, the ICs (SN7416) employed in Project 2 are also used in this project. Besides the DIP switches and the ICs, 8 resistors (470 Ohms, ¼ W) must be used. Figure 1-7 includes the part numbers of the DIP switch package from Radio Shack.

Figure 1-8 is the schematic diagram of the LED assembly of the LEDs connected to PORTs 21 and 22.

1.6 PROJECT 4: OPTIONAL CHIP AND LOGIC CIRCUIT EXPANSION

The five different IC chips needed for this project are shown in Fig. 1-9 and are listed below:

INTEL 8155 RAM: One unit
INTEL 8212 Address Drive: Two units
INTEL 8216 Data Buss and Control: Five units
TI SN 74S00 Quad-Two Input Nand Gate: One unit
TI SN 74LS74 Dual D-Type Flip-Flop: One unit

The SDK-85 trainer has positions indicated on its basic board for each of the chips listed above, and also the 8 capacitors (0.1 μF, 50 V) that must be soldered to the basic board. The capacitors may be purchased through Radio Shack, and the ICs through INTEL Corp. and Texas Instruments.

1.7 PROJECT 5: INSTALLATION OF A PROTO-BOARD EXPERIMENTATION AREA

The Proto-Board is needed for the wiring of discrete component circuits not contained on the SDK-85 trainer. Chapters 8, 9, and 10 have projects which interface external circuits to the SDK-85 trainer from the Proto-Board. The Proto-Board location of the SDK-85 trainer is shown in Fig. 1-10. The board can be glued to the trainer by any silicon glue purchased at your local electronic hobby store.

The Proto-Board is manufactured by Global Specialities Corp. The name of the board is called Experimentor (Model No. 300).

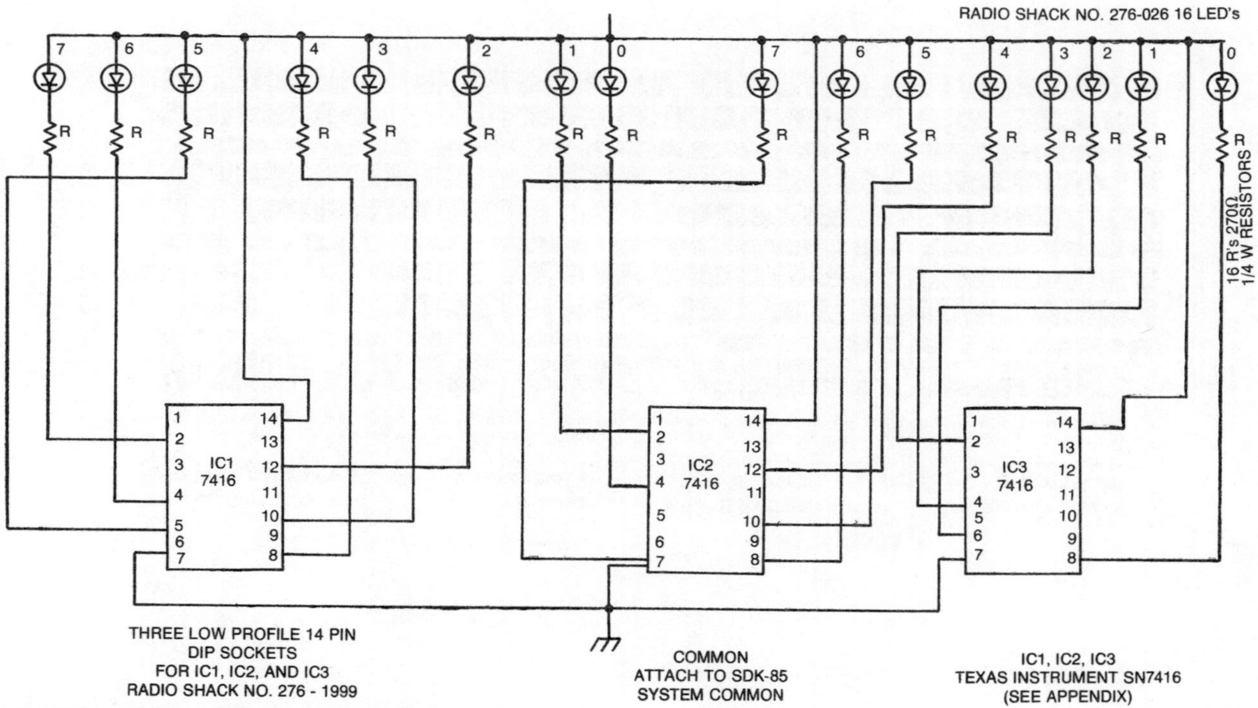

Fig. 1-5. Wiring of LED display assembly (top view).

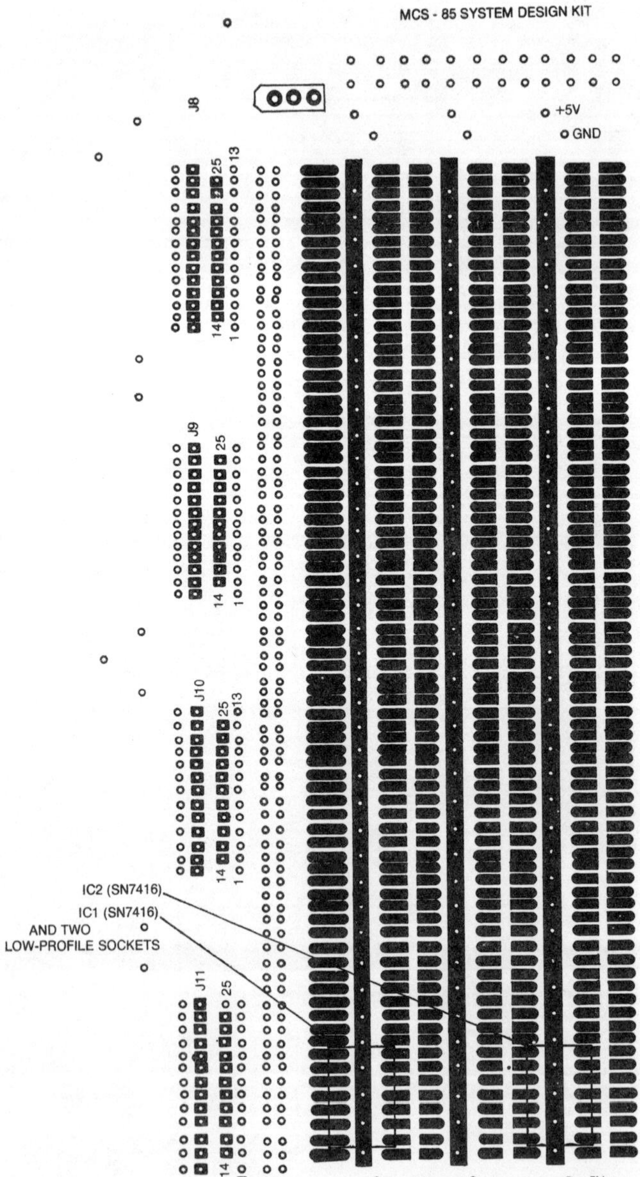

Fig. 1-6. Part placement for LED display assembly and dual-in-line (DIP) switches on SDK-85 trainer (top view).

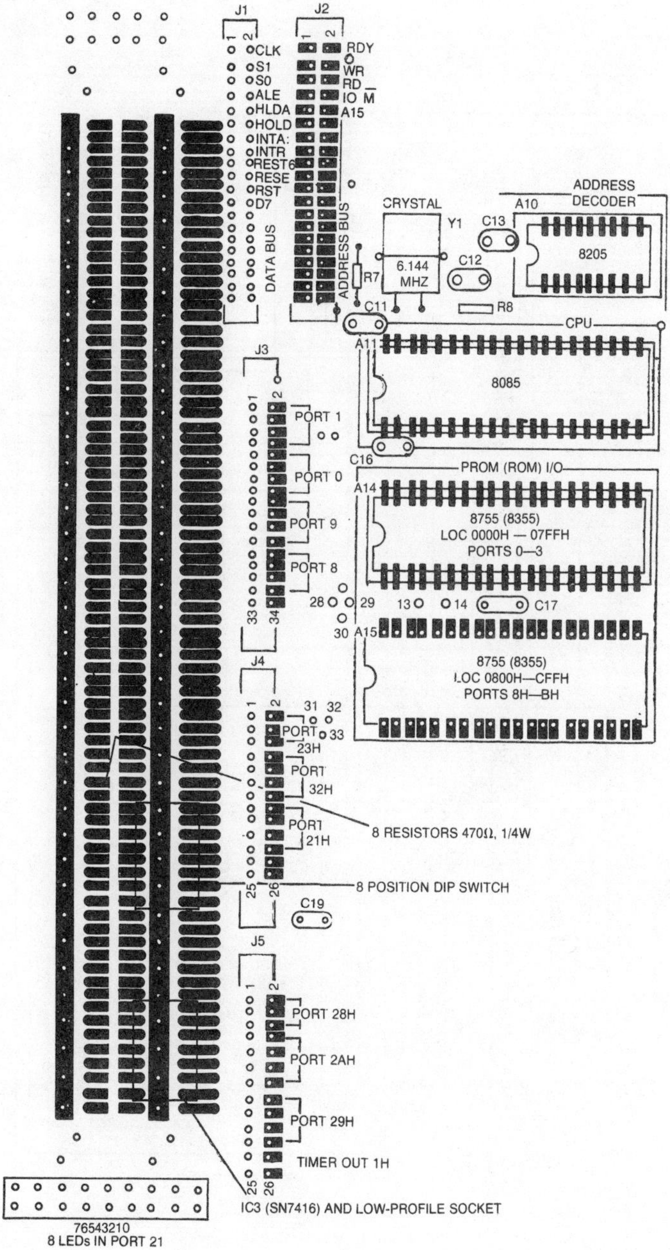
J1
J2
CLK
S1
S0
ALE
HLDA
HOLD
INTA:
INTR
REST6
RESE
RST
D7
DATA BUS
RDY
WR
RD
IO M
A15
ADDRESS BUS
CRYSTAL
Y1
6.144 MHZ
R7
C13
C12
ADDRESS DECODER
A10
8205
C11
R8
CPU
A11
8085
C16
PROM (ROM) I/O
A14
8755 (8355)
LOC 0000H — 07FFH
PORTS 0—3
28
29
30
13
14
C17
A15
8755 (8355)
LOC 0800H—CFFH
PORTS 8H—BH
J3
PORT 1
PORT 0
PORT 9
PORT 8
33
34
J4
31
32
33
PORT 23H
PORT 32H
PORT 21H
8 RESISTORS 470Ω, 1/4W
25
26
8 POSITION DIP SWITCH
C19
J5
PORT 28H
PORT 2AH
PORT 29H
TIMER OUT 1H
IC3 (SN7416) AND LOW-PROFILE SOCKET
76543210
8 LEDs IN PORT 21

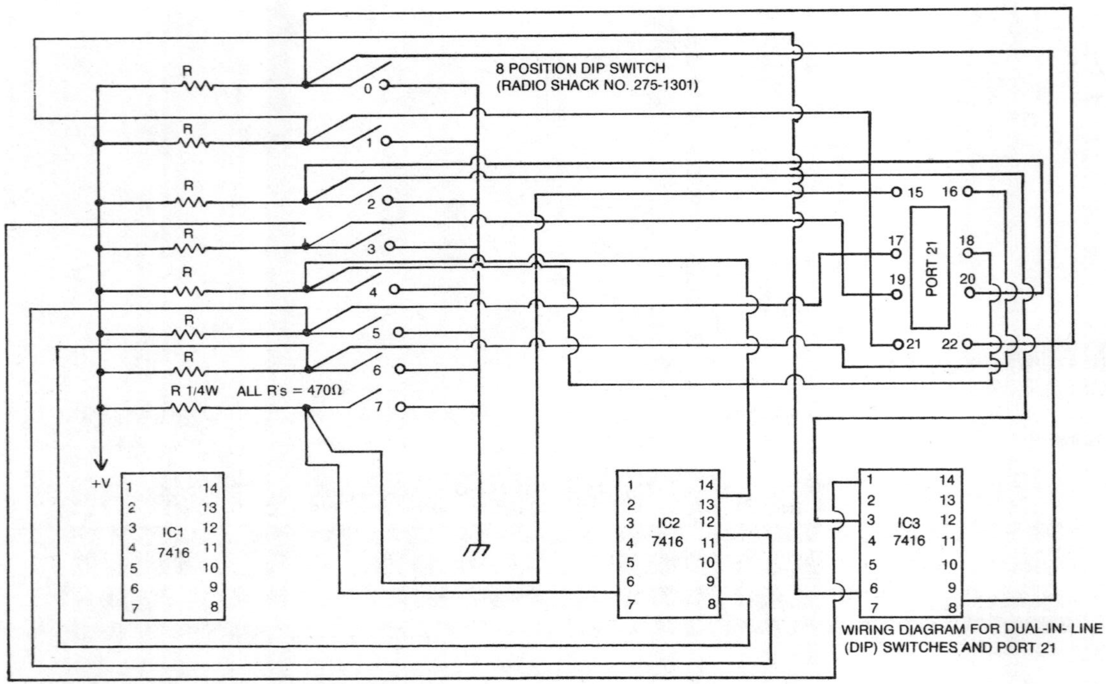

Fig. 1-7. Wiring diagram for DIP switches and PORT 21.

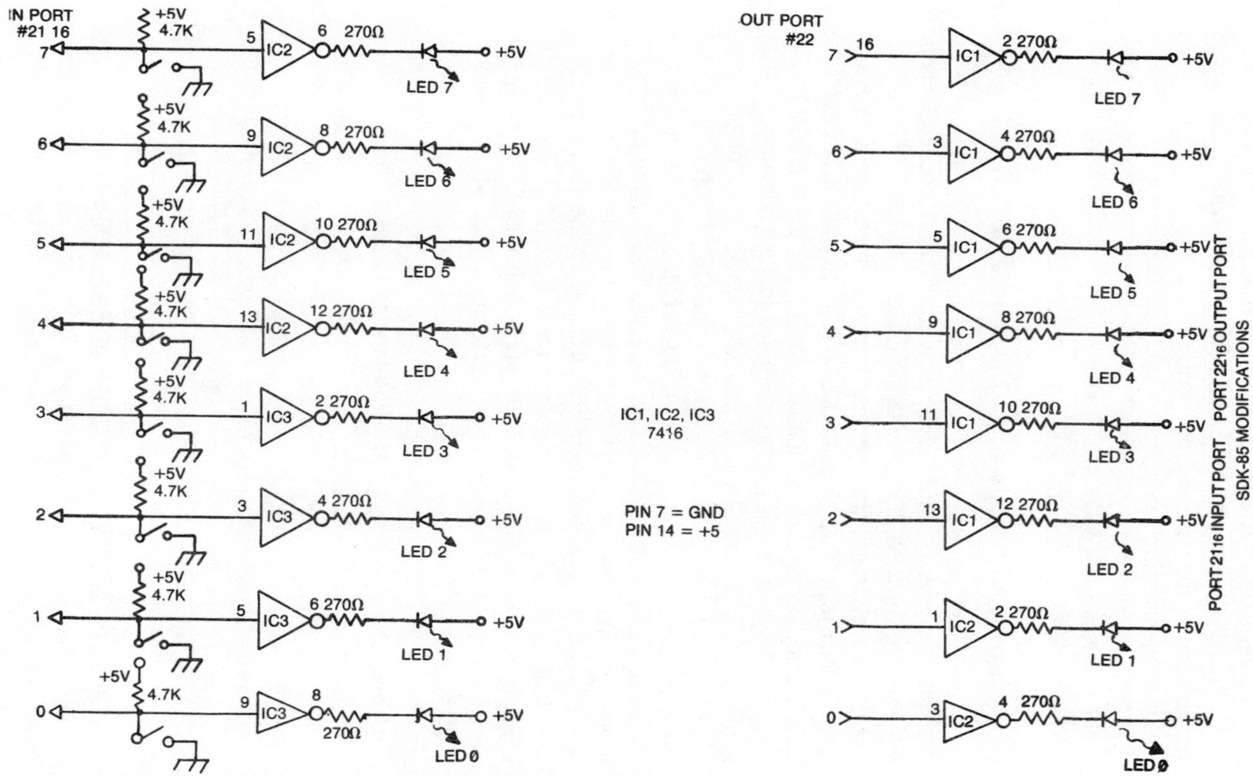

Fig. 1-8. Schematic of LED display assembly and PORT 21.

Two sections of the Experimentor must be purchased and glued in the location shown in Fig. 1-10. If the reader cannot find the Proto-Board at his/her favorite electronic store, write to the following address for purchase information:

Global Specialities Corp.
70 Fulton Terr. P.O. Box 1942
New Haven CT. 06509
Phone: (203) 624-3103

1.8 PROJECT 6: VECTOR INTERRUPT DEBOUNCE CIRCUIT

The vector interrupt is used frequently to begin programs. When the user presses the vector interrupt key the user expects the key to close ONCE and send ONE signal to the CPU (8085 chip). However, the vector interrupt key could send MORE THAN ONE signal to the CPU, because of built in bounce by the key itself. This bounce occurrence is similar to relay chatter in electronic systems. To temper this key bounce condition, but not completely eliminate it, a Debounce Circuit can be wired between the vector interrupt key and the CPU. The schematic and wiring of the Debounce Circuit is shown in Fig. 1-11 and Fig. 1-12. The reader is cautioned to carefully look at Fig. 1-11 and Fig. 1-12 in order to properly make the necessary changes on the SDK-85 trainer, which requires opening a trace connection from the vector interrupt key to the CPU in order to correctly wire the Debounce Circuit. The reader is also advised that the Debounce Circuit is not necessary in order to make the remaining projects in this book perform properly.

1.9 PROJECT 7: TELETYPE (TTY) SWITCH ASSEMBLY

In order for the reader to operate a Teletype (TTY) from the SDK-85, a Single Pole Double Throw (SPDT) Switch must be soldered into the position shown in Fig. 1-13. The switch can be purchased at Radio Shack. If the reader does not wish to employ the TTY, place a jumper wire from point NO. 23 to NO. 24 on the SDK-85 board in order to operate the other projects in the book.

1.10 PROJECT 8: TELETYPE CUSTOM DC POWER SUPPLY

In order to operate the Teletype (TTY) projects, the reader must employ the power supply shown in Fig. 1-14. When the power supply is assembled, check the output of the supply to insure a −10 V output. The power supply should not be connected to the top of

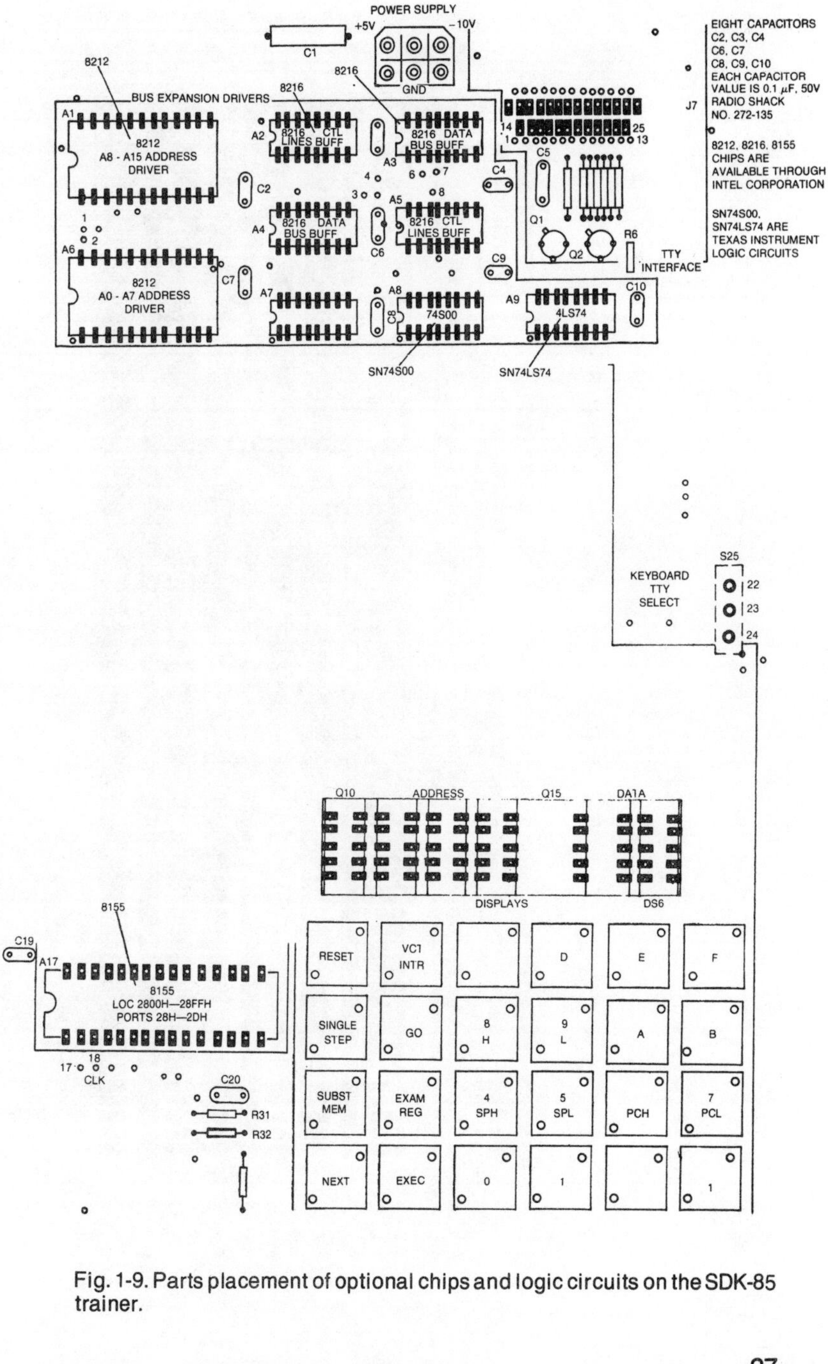

Fig. 1-9. Parts placement of optional chips and logic circuits on the SDK-85 trainer.

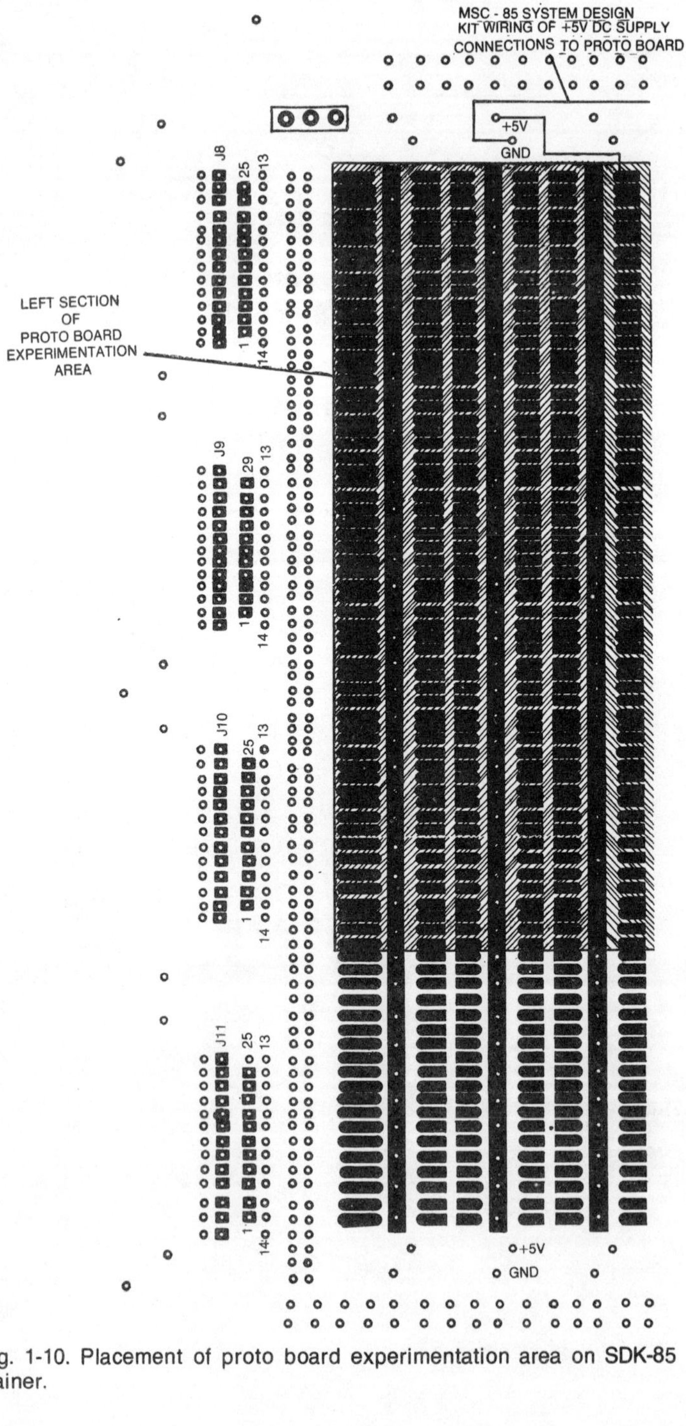

Fig. 1-10. Placement of proto board experimentation area on SDK-85 trainer.

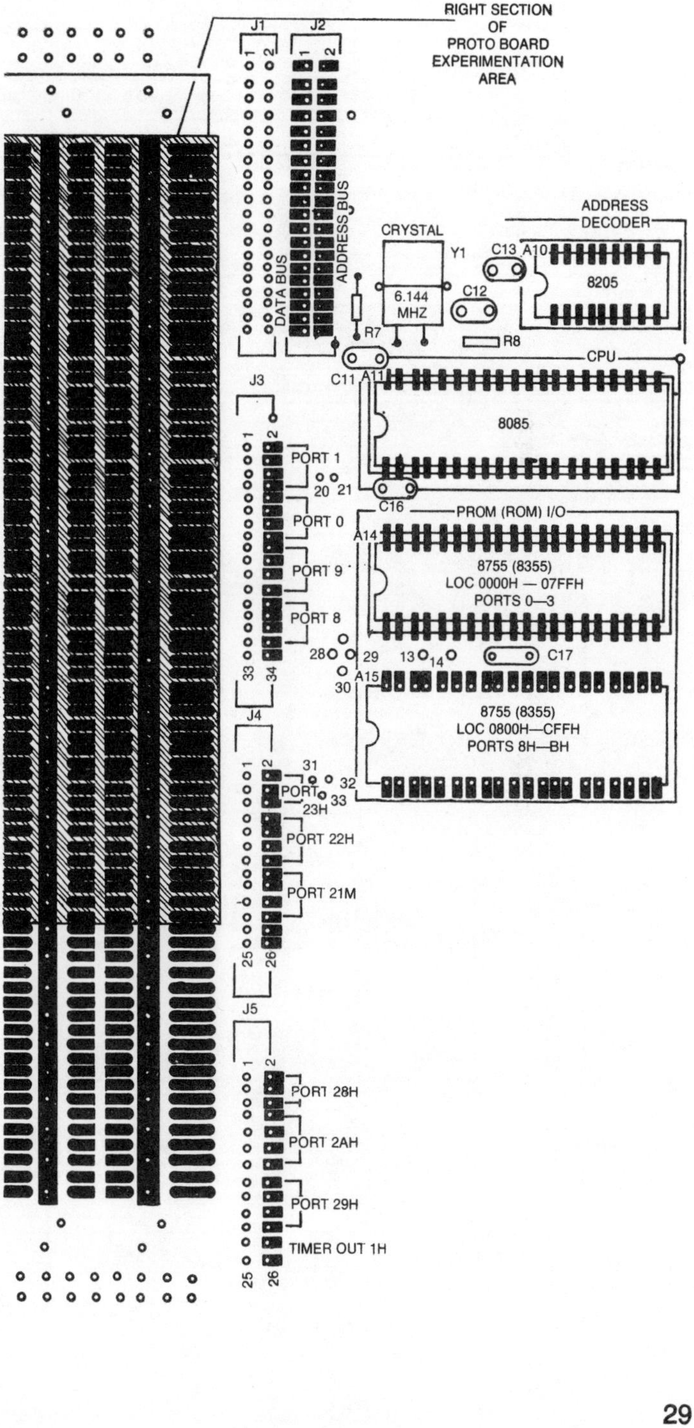
RIGHT SECTION
OF
PROTO BOARD
EXPERIMENTATION
AREA
J1
J2
DATA BUS
ADDRESS BUS
CRYSTAL
Y1
6.144
MHZ
R7
ADDRESS
DECODER
C13
A10
8205
C12
R8
CPU
C11
A11
8085
J3
PORT 1
20
21
C16
PORT 0
PROM (ROM) I/O
A14
PORT 9
8755 (8355)
LOC 0000H — 07FFH
PORTS 0—3
PORT 8
28
29
13
14
C17
30
A15
J4
8755 (8355)
LOC 0800H—CFFH
PORTS 8H—BH
31
32
PORT
23H
33
PORT 22H
PORT 21M
J5
PORT 28H
PORT 2AH
PORT 29H
TIMER OUT 1H

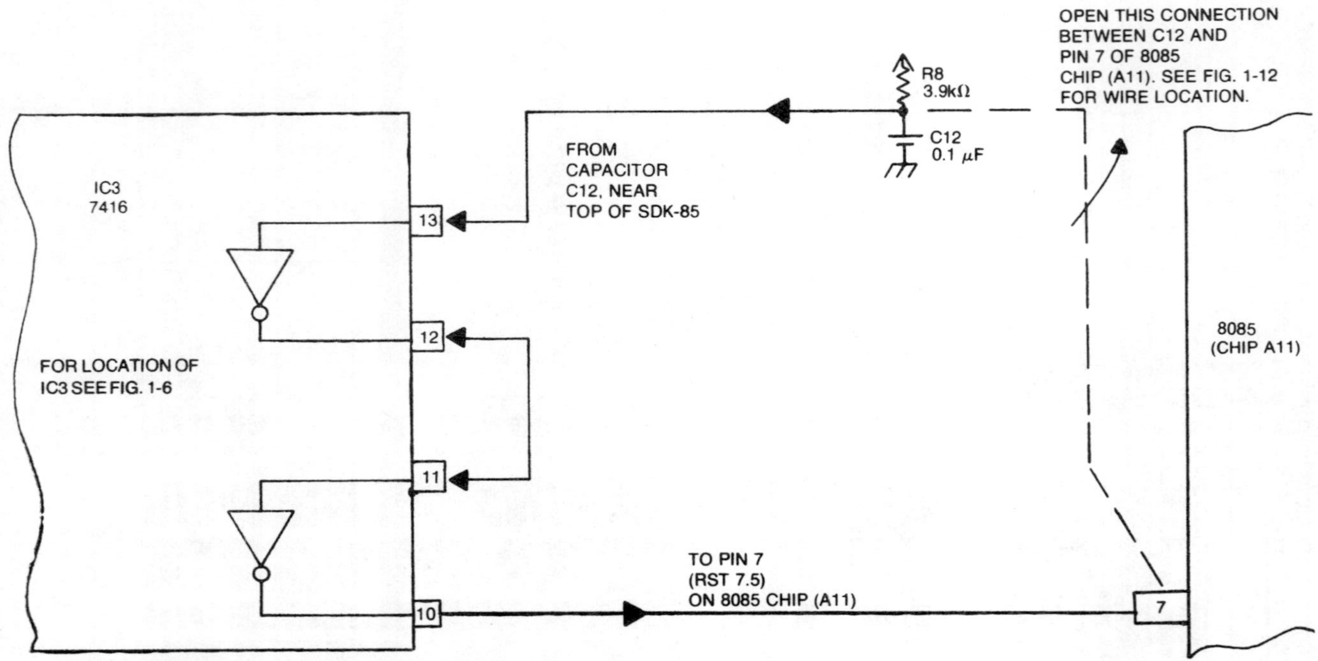

Fig. 1-11. Schematic and wiring diagram for vector interrupt debounce circuit.

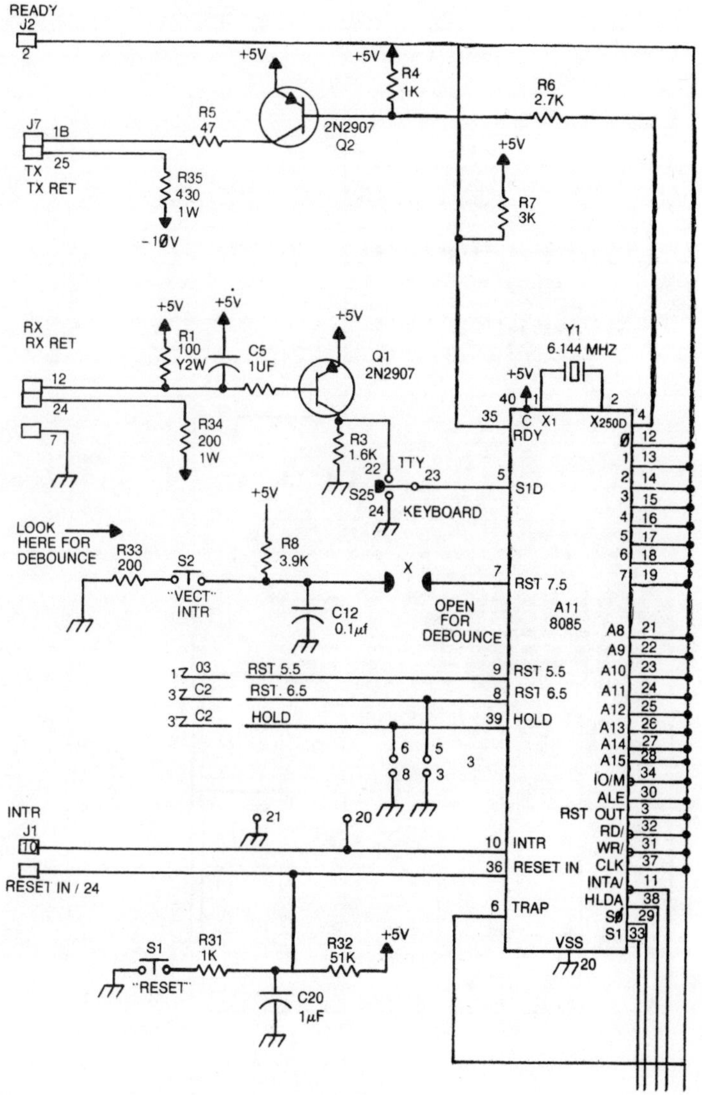

Fig. 1-12. Location of connection to OPEN for wiring of debounce circuit.

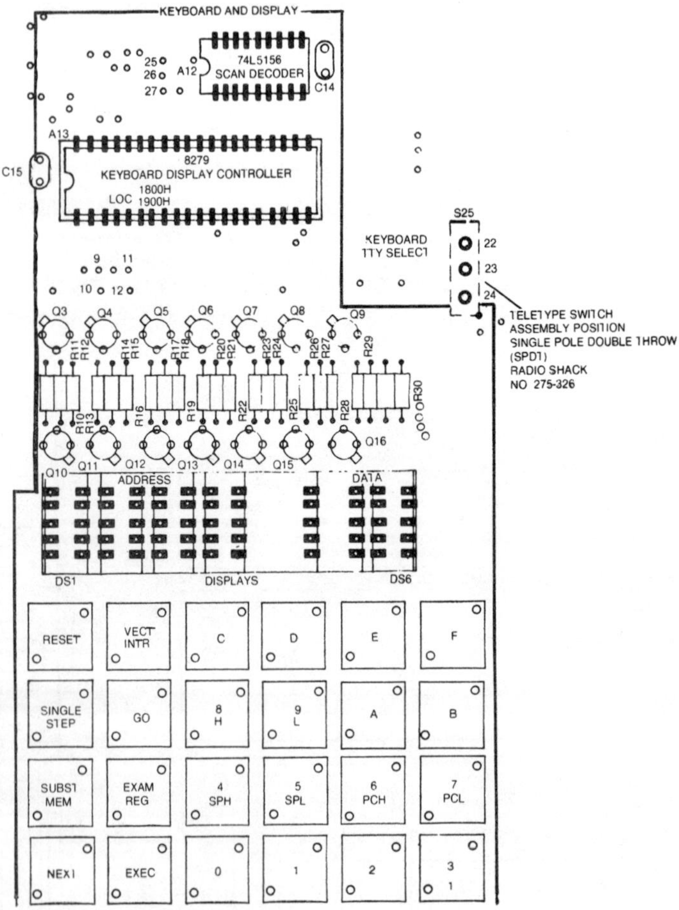

Fig. 1-13. Placement of teletype (TTY) switch assembly on SDK-85 trainer.

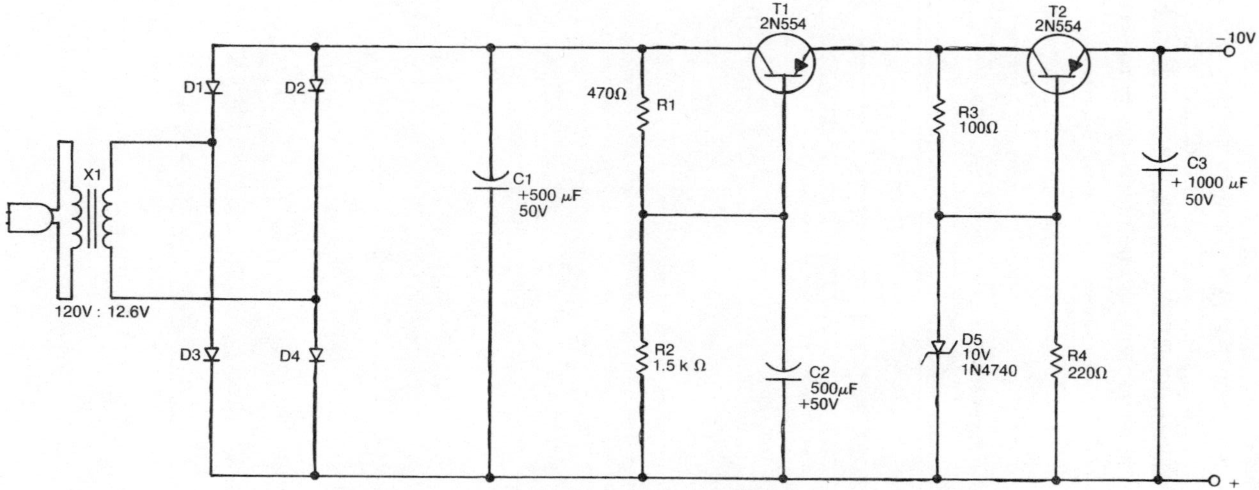

PARTS LIST
X1 - TRANSFORMER (120V to 12.6V)
RADIO SHACK CAT. NO. 273-1505
T1, T2 - 2N554 (MOTOROLA TRANSISTORS)
D1, D2, D3, D4 - HEP R0052
D5 - 10V, 1W ZENER DIODE (MOTOROLA)

C1, C2 - 500 μF, 50V ELECTROLYTIC
C3 - 1000 μF, 50V ELECTROLYTIC
R1 - 470Ω, 1/2W
R2 - 1.5kΩ, 1/2 W
R3 - 100Ω, 1/2W
R4 - 200Ω, 1/2W

Fig. 1-14. The-10V custom power supply for the teletype (TTY).

the SDK-85 trainer until the TTY projects of Chapter 8 Section 8.1 are read and performed.

The −10 V power supply is connected to the top of the SDK-85 trainer. The −10 V side of the supply is connected to the terminal marked −10 V on the SDK-85, and the +10 V side of the supply is connected to GND terminal on the top of the trainer.

Chapter 2

SDK-85 System Operation

2.1 INSTRUCTION TIMING

If you were to observe the operation of the 8085A, you would notice that the execution of any program consists entirely of a sequence of READ and WRITE operations, where each READ or WRITE operation transfers a byte of data between the 8085A and a particular memory or I/O address. While the 8085A will vary the address, data, type, and sequence of the operations, it is nevertheless capable of performing only READ or WRITE operations. With the exception of a few special control lines, these READ and WRITE operations are the only communication between the processor and the other components, and are all that is necessary to execute any instruction or program.

Each READ or WRITE operation of the 8085A is referred to as a MACHINE CYCLE. The execution of each instruction by the 8085A consists of a sequence of from one to five machine cycles, and each machine cycle consists of a minimum of from three to six CLOCK CYCLES (also referred to as T states). Consider the case of the Store Accumulator Direct (STA) instruction, shown in Fig. 2-1. The STA instruction causes the contents of the accumulator to be stored at the direct address specified in the second and third bytes of the instruction. During the first machine cycle (M_1), the CPU puts the contents of the program counter (PC) on the address bus and performs a MEMORY READ cycle to read from memory the opcode of the next instruction (STA). The M_1 machine cycle is also referred to as the OPCODE FETCH cycle, since it fetches the operation code of the next instruction. In the fourth clock cycle (T_4) of M_1, the CPU interprets the data read in and recognizes it as the opcode of the STA instruction. At this point the CPU knows that it must do three machine cycles (two MEMORY reads and one MEMORY WRITE) to complete the instruction.

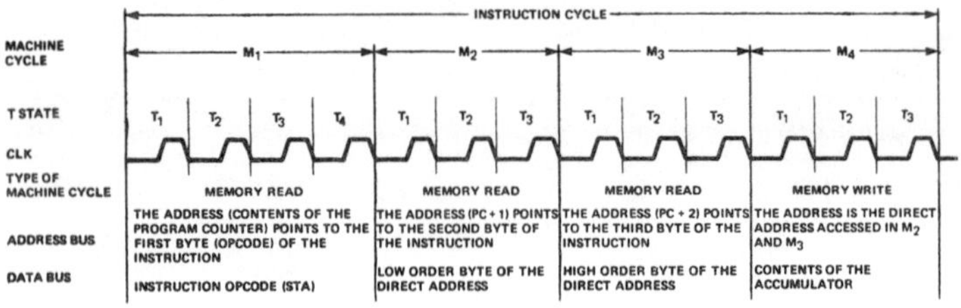

Fig. 2-1. CPU timing for store accumulator direct (STA) instruction.

The 8085A then increments the program counter so that it points at the next byte of the instruction and performs a MEMORY READ machine cycle (M_2) at the address (PC+1). The accessed memory places the addressed data on the data bus for the CPU. The 8085A temporarily stores this data (which is the low order byte of the direct address) internally in the CPU. The 8085A again increments the program counter (PC+2) and reads from memory (M_3) the next byte of data, which is the **high-order** byte of the direct address.

At this point, the 8085A has accessed all three bytes of the STA instruction, which it must now execute. The execution consists of placing the data accessed in M_2 and M_3 on the address bus, then placing the contents of the accumulator on the data bus, and then performing a MEMORY WRITE machine cycle (M_4). When M_4 is finished, the CPU will fetch (M_1) the first byte of the next instruction and continue from there.

State Transition Sequence

As the preceding example has shown, the execution of an instruction consists of a series of machine cycles, whose nature and sequence is determined by the opcode accessed in the M_1 machine cycle. While no one instruction cycle will consist of more than five machine cycles, every machine cycle will be one of the seven types listed in Fig. 2-2A. These seven types of machine cycles can be differentiated by the state of the three status lines ($IO/\overline{M}$, S0, and S1) and the three control signals ($\overline{RD}$, $\overline{WR}$, and $\overline{INTA}$).

Every machine cycle normally consists of three clock cycles (also referred to as T states), with the exception of OPCODE FETCH, which normally has either four or six clock cycles. The actual number of states required to execute any instruction de-

MACHINE CYCLE		STATUS			CONTROL		
		$IO/\overline{M}$	S1	S0	$\overline{RD}$	$\overline{WR}$	$\overline{INTA}$
OPCODE FETCH	(OF)	0	1	1	0	1	1
MEMORY READ	(MR)	0	1	0	0	1	1
MEMORY WRITE	(MW)	0	0	1	1	0	1
I/O READ	(IOR)	1	1	0	0	1	1
I/O WRITE	(IOW)	1	0	1	1	0	1
INTR ACKNOWLEDGE	(INA)	1	1	1	1	1	0
BUS IDLE	(BI): DAD	0	1	0	1	1	1
	INA(RST/TRAP)	1	1	1	1	1	1
	HALT	TS	0	0	TS	TS	1

0 = Logic "0" 1 = Logic "1" TS = High Impedance X = Unspecified

Fig. 2-2A. 8085A machine cycle chart.

pends on the instruction being executed, the particular machine cycle within the instruction cycle, and the number of WAIT and HOLD states inserted into each machine cycle through the use of the READY and HOLD lines. The state transition diagram in Fig. 2-3 illustrates how the 8085A proceeds from state to state in the course of a machine cycle. The state of various status and control signals, as well as the system buses, is shown in Fig. 2-2B for each of the ten possible machine states that the processor can be in.

Machine State	Status & Buses				Control		
	S1,S0	$IO/\overline{M}$	A_8-A_{15}	AD_0-AD_7	$\overline{RD},\overline{WR}$	$\overline{INTA}$	ALE
T_1	X	X	X	X	1	1	1†
T_2	X	X	X	X	X	X	0
T_{WAIT}	X	X	X	X	X	X	0
T_3	X	X	X	X	X	X	0
T_4	1	0*	X	TS	1	1	0
T_5	1	0*	X	TS	1	1	0
T_6	1	0*	X	TS	1	1	0
T_{RESET}	X	TS	TS	TS	TS	1	0
T_{HALT}	0	TS	TS	TS	TS	1	0
T_{HOLD}	X	TS	TS	TS	TS	1	0

0 = Logic "0" 1 = Logic "1" TS = High Impedance X = Unspecified

†ALE not generated during 2nd and 3rd machine cycles of DAD instruction.

*$IO/\overline{M}$ = 1 during T_4-T_6 states of RST and INA cycles.

Fig. 2-2B. 8085A machine start chart.

Figure 2-3 also shows when the READY, HOLD, and interrupt signals are sampled, and how they modify the basic instruction sequence (T_1-T_6 and T_{WAIT}). In the present discussion we are concerned only with the basic sequence; the functions of HOLD, HALT, RESET, and the interrupts will be discussed later. We will

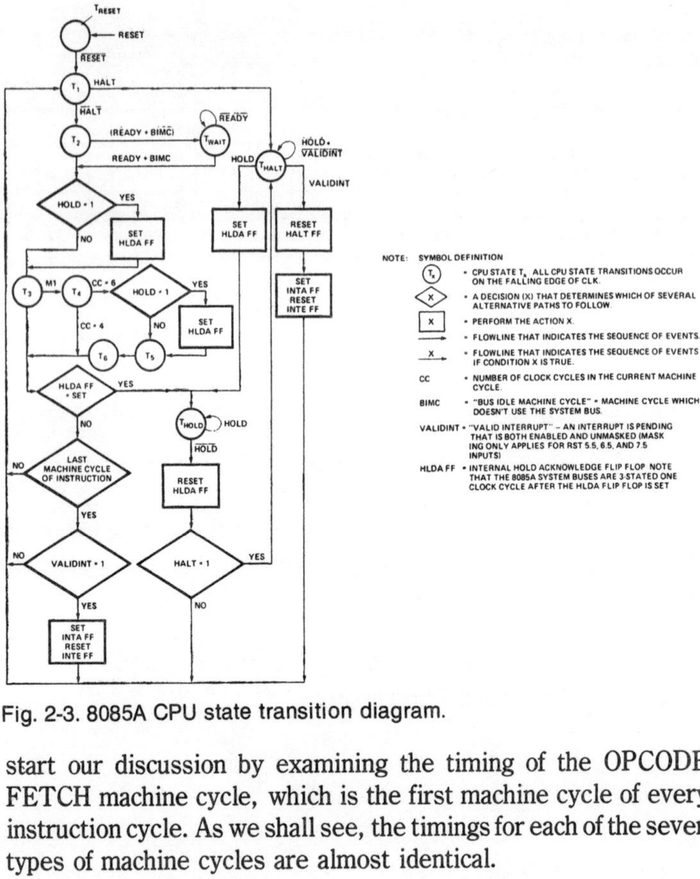

Fig. 2-3. 8085A CPU state transition diagram.

start our discussion by examining the timing of the OPCODE FETCH machine cycle, which is the first machine cycle of every instruction cycle. As we shall see, the timings for each of the seven types of machine cycles are almost identical.

2.2 OPCODE FETCH (OF):

Recall that the 8085A passes through at least three states in each machine cycle, with each state defined by successive high to low transitions of CLK. In fact, the OPCODE FETCH (OF) machine cycle is unique in that it is the only machine cycle that has more than three clock cycles. This is because the CPU must interpret the opcode accessed in T_1, T_2, and T_3 before it can decide what to do next.

Figure 2-4 shows the timing relationships for an OF machine cycle. The particular instruction illustrated is DCX, whose timing for OF may differ from other instructions only in that it has six T states, while some instructions have only four T states for OF. In this discussion, as well as the following discussions, only the relative timing of the signals will be discussed; for the actual A.C. timings, please refer to the data sheets of the individual parts.

The first thing that the 8085A does at the beginning of every machine cycle is to send out three status signals ($IO/\overline{M}$, S1, S0) that define what type of machine cycle is about to take place. The $IO/\overline{M}$ signal identifies the machine cycle as being either a memory reference or input/output operation. The S1 status signal identifies whether the cycle is a read or write operation. The S0 and S1 status signals can be used together (see Fig. 2-2A) to identify READ, WRITE, or OPCODE FETCH machine cycles as well as the HALT state. Referring to Fig. 2-4, the 8085A will send out $IO/\overline{M} = 0$, S1 = 1, S0 = 1 at the beginning of the machine cycle to identify it as a read from a memory location to obtain an opcode; in other words, it identifies the machine cycle as an OPCODE FETCH cycle.

The 8085A also sends out a 16-bit address at the beginning of every machine cycle to identify the particular memory location or I/O port that the machine cycle applies to. In the case of an OF cycle, the contents of the program counter is placed on the address bus. The high order byte (PCH) is placed on the A_8-A_{15} lines, where it will stay until at least T_4. The low order byte (PCL) is placed on the AD_0-AD_7 lines, whose three-state drivers are enabled if they aren't already on. Unlike the upper address lines, however, the information on the lower address lines will remain there for only one clock cycle, after which the drivers will go to their high impedance state, indicated by a dashed line in Fig. 2-4. This is necessary because the AD_0-AD_7 lines are time multiplexed between the address and data buses. During T_1 of every machine cycle, AD_0-AD_7 output the lower 8-bits of address after which

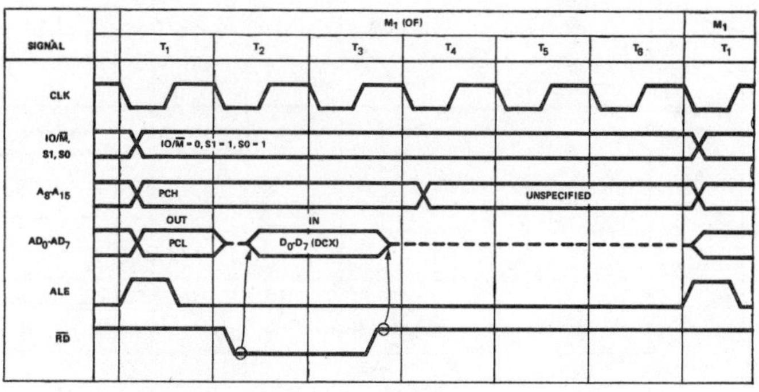

Fig. 2-4. Opcode fetch machine cycle (of DCX instruction).

AD_0-AD_7 will either output the desired data for a WRITE operation or (as is the case for the OF cycle) the drivers will float, allowing the external device to drive the lines for a READ operation. Since the address information on AD_0-AD_7 is of a transitory nature, it must be latched either internally in parts like the 8155 or externally in parts like the 8212 (see Fig. 2-18B). The 8085A provides a special timing signal, ADDRESS LATCH ENABLE (ALE), to facilitate the latching of A_0-A_7; ALE is present during T_1 of every machine cycle.

After the status signals and address have been sent out and the AD_0-AD_7 drivers disabled, the 8085A drops RD to enable the addressed memory device. This device will then start driving the AD_0-AD_7 lines; this is indicated by the dashed line turning into a solid line in Fig. 2-4. After a period of time (which is the access time of the memory) valid data will be present on AD_0-AD_7. The 8085A during T_3 will load the data on AD_0-AD_7 into its instruction register and then raise RD, disabling the addressed memory device. At this point, the 8085A will have finished accessing the opcode of the instruction. Since this is the first machine cycle (M_1) of the instruction, the CPU will automatically step to T_4, as shown in Fig. 2-3.

During T_4, the CPU will decode the opcode in the instruction register and decide whether to enter T_5 on the next clock or to start a new machine cycle and enter T_1. In the case of the DCX instruction shown in Fig. 2-4, it will enter T_5 and then T_6 before going to T_1.

During T_5 and T_6, of DCX, the CPU will decrement the designated register. Since the A_8-A_{15} lines are driven by the ad-

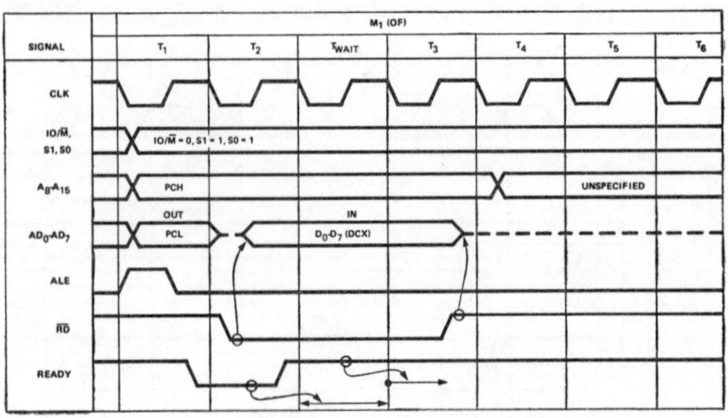

Fig. 2-5. Opcode fetch machine cycle with one wait state.

dress latch circuits, which are part of the incrementer/decrementer logic, and A_8-A_{15} lines may change during T_5 and T_6. Since the value of A_8-A_{15} can vary during T_4-T_6, it is most important that all memory and I/O devices on the system bus qualify their selection with RD. If they don't use $\overline{RD}$, they may be spuriously selected. Moreover, with a linear selection technique (see Fig. 2-17B), two or more devices could be simultaneously enabled, which could be potentially damaging. The generation of spurious addresses can also occur momentarily at address bus transitional periods in T_1. Therefore, the selection of all memory and I/O devices must be qualified with $\overline{RD}$ or $\overline{WR}$.

Figure 2-5 is identical to Fig. 2-4 with one exception, which is the use of the READY line. As we can see in Fig. 2-3, when the CPU is in T_2, it examines the state of the READY line. If the READY line is high, the CPU will proceed to T_3 and finish executing the instruction. If the READY line is low, however, the CPU will enter T_{WAIT} and stay there indefinitely until READY goes high. When the READY line does go high, the CPU will exit T_{WAIT} and enter T_3, in order to complete the machine cycle. As shown in Fig. 2-5, the external effect of using the READY line is to preserve the exact state of the processor signals at the end of T_2 for an integral number of clock periods, before finishing the machine cycle. This "stretching" of the system timing has the further effect of increasing the allowable access time for memory or I/O devices. By inserting T_{WAIT} states, the 8085 can accommodate even the slowest of memories. Another common use of the READY line is to SINGLE-STEP the processor with a manual switch.

2.3 MEMORY READ (MR):

Figure 2-6 shows the timing of two successive MEMORY READ (MR) machine cycles, the first without a T_{WAIT} state and the second with one T_{WAIT} state. The timing during T_1-T_3 is absolutely identical to the OPCODE FETCH machine cycle, with the exception that the status sent out during T_1 is IO/M = 0, S1 = 1, SO = 0, identifying the cycle as a read from a memory location. This differs from Fig. 2-4 only in that S0 = 1 for an OF cycle, identifying that cycle as an OPCODE FETCH operation. Otherwise, the two cycles are identical during T_1-T_3.

A second difference occurs at the end of T_3. As shown in Fig. 2-3, the CPU always goes to T_4 from T_3 during M1, which is always an OF cycle. During all other machine cycles, the CPU will always go from T_3 to T_1 of the next machine cycle.

The memory address used in the OF cycle is always the contents of the program counter, which points to the current instruction, while the address used in the MR cycle can have several possible origins. Also, the data read in during an MR cycle is placed in the appropriate register, not the instruction register.

2.4 I/O READ (IOR):

Figure 2-6 also shows the timing of two successive I/O READ (IOR) machine cycles, the first without a T_{WAIT} state. As is readily apparent, the timing of an IOR cycle is identical to the timing of an MR cycle, with the exception of $IO/\overline{M} = 0$ for MR and $IO/\overline{M} = 1$ for IOR; recall that $IO/\overline{M}$ status signal identifies the address of the current machine cycle as selecting either a memory location or an I/O port. The address used in the IOR cycle comes from the second byte (Port No.) of an INPUT instruction, which is duplicated onto both AD_0-AD_7 and A_8-A_{15}. The IOR cycle can occur only as the third machine cycle of an INPUT instruction.

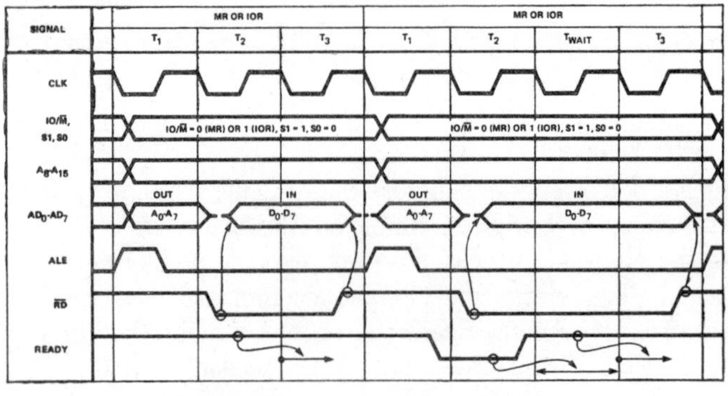

Fig. 2-6. Memory read (or I/O read) machine cycles.

Note that the READY signal can be used to generate T_{WAIT} states for I/O devices, as well as memory devices. By gating the READY signal with the proper status lines, one could generate T_{WAIT} states for only memory devices or for only I/O devices. By gating in the address lines, one can further qualify T_{WAIT} state generation by the particular devices being accessed.

2.5 MEMORY WRITE (MW):

Figure 2-7 shows the timing for two successive MEMORY WRITE (MW) machine cycles, the first without a T_{WAIT} state, and the second with one T_{WAIT} state. The 8085A sends out the status during T_1 in a similar fashion to the OF, MR and IOR cycles, except that $IO/\overline{M} = 0$, $S1 = 0$, and $SO = 1$, identifying the current machine cycle as being a write operation to a memory location.

The address is sent out during T_1 in an identical manner to MR. However, at the end of T_1, there is a difference. While the AD_0-AD_7 drivers were disabled during T_2-T_3 of MR in expectation of the addressed memory device driving the AD_0-AD_7 lines, the drivers are not disabled for MW. This is because the CPU must provide the data to be written into the addressed memory location. The data is placed on AD_0-AD_7 at the start of T_2. The $\overline{WR}$ signal is also lowered at this time to enable the writing of the addressed memory device. During T_2, the READY line is checked to see if a T_{WAIT} state is required. If READY is low, T_{WAIT} states are inserted until READY goes high. During T_3, the $\overline{WR}$ line is raised, disabling the addressed memory device and thereby terminating the write operation. The contents of the address and data lines is not changed until the next T_1, which directly follows.

Note that the data on AD_0-AD_7 is not guaranteed to be stable before the falling edge of $\overline{WR}$. The AD_0-AD_7 lines are guaranteed to be stable both before and after the rising edge of $\overline{WR}$.

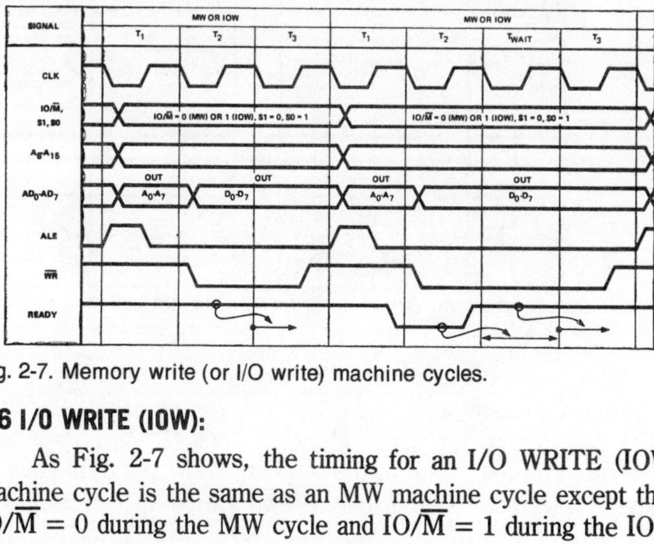

Fig. 2-7. Memory write (or I/O write) machine cycles.

2.6 I/O WRITE (IOW):

As Fig. 2-7 shows, the timing for an I/O WRITE (IOW) machine cycle is the same as an MW machine cycle except that $IO/\overline{M} = 0$ during the MW cycle and $IO/\overline{M} = 1$ during the IOW cycle.

AS with the IOR cycle discussed previously, the address used in an IOW cycle is the IO port number. In the case of IOW, the port number comes from the second byte of an OUTPUT instruction as the instruction is executed.

2.7 INTERRUPT ACKNOWLEDGE (INA):

Figures 2-8A and 2-8B depict the course of action the CPU takes in response to a high level on the INTR line if the INTE FF (interrupt enable flip flop) has been set by the E1 instruction. The status of the TRAP and RST pins as well as INTR is sampled during CLK of the T state preceding $M_1 \cdot T_1$. If INTR was the only valid interrupt and if INTE FF is set, then the CPU will reset INTE FF and then enter an INTERRUPT ACKNOWLEDGE (INA) machine cycle. The INA cycle is identical to an OF cycle with the exception that $\overline{INTA}$ is sent out instead of $\overline{RD}$. Although the contents of the program counter is sent out on the address lines, the address lines are ignored.

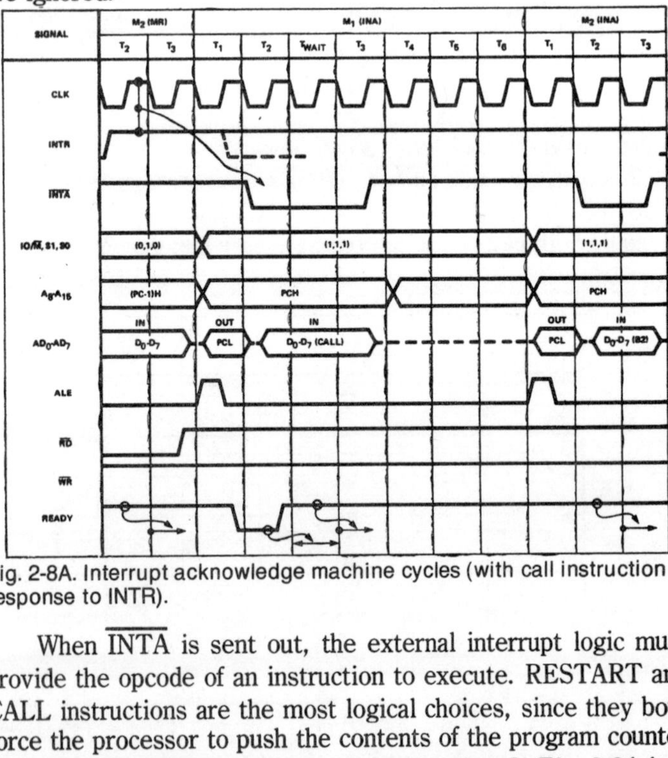

Fig. 2-8A. Interrupt acknowledge machine cycles (with call instruction in response to INTR).

When $\overline{INTA}$ is sent out, the external interrupt logic must provide the opcode of an instruction to execute. RESTART and CALL instructions are the most logical choices, since they both force the processor to push the contents of the program counter onto the stack before jumping to a new location. In Fig. 2-8A it is assumed that a CALL opcode is sent to the CPU during M_1. The CALL opcode could have been placed there by a device like the 8259, INTEL's PROGRAMMABLE INTERRUPT CONTROLLER. Note that a T_{WAIT} state can be inserted in an INA cycle, just as in other machine cycles.

After receiving the opcode, the processor then decodes it and determines, in this case, that the CALL instruction requires two more bytes. The CPU therefore performs a second INA cycle (M_2) to access the second byte of the instruction from the 8259. The timing of this cycle is identical to M_1, except that it has only three T states. M_2 is followed by another INA cycle (M_3) to access the third byte of the CALL instruction from the 8259.

Now that the CPU has accessed the entire instruction used to acknowledge the interrupt, it will execute that instruction. Note that any instruction could be used, but the RESTART and CALL instructions are the most logical choices. Also notice that the CPU inhibited the incrementing of the program counter (PC) during the three INA cycles, so that the correct PC value can be pushed onto the stack during M_4 and M_5.

During M_4 and M_5, the CPU performs MEMORY WRITE machine cycles to write the upper and then lower bytes of the PC onto the top of the stack. The CPU then places the two bytes accessed in M_2 and M_3 into the lower and upper bytes of the PC. This has the effect of jumping the execution of the program to the location specified by the CALL instruction.

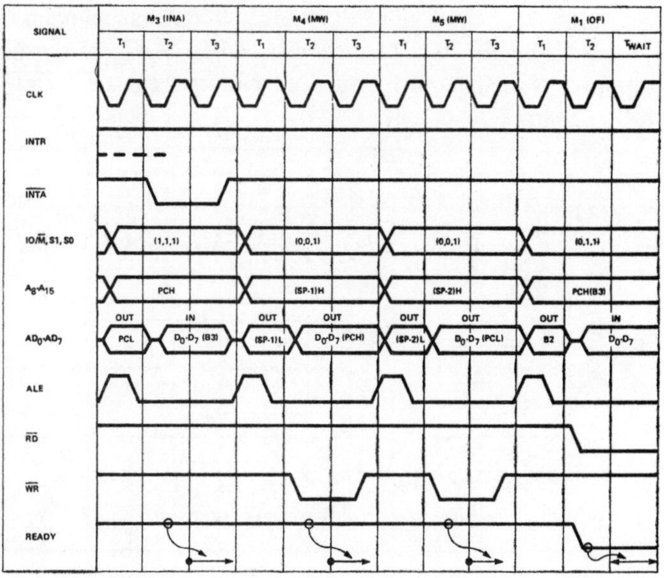

Fig. 2-8B. Interrupt acknowledge machine cycles (with call instruction in response to INTR).

2.8 BUS IDLE (BI):

Most machine cycles of the 8085A are associated with either a read or write operation. There are only two exceptions to this rule. The first exception takes place during M_2 and M_3 of the DAD instructions. The 8085A requires six internal T states to execute a DAD instruction, but it is not desirable to have M_1 be ten (four normal plus six extra) states long. Therefore, the CPU generates two extra machine cycles that don't access either the memory or the I/O. These cycles are referred to as BUS IDLE (BI) machine cycles. In the case of DAD, they are identical to MR cycles except $\overline{RD}$ remains high and ALE is not generated.

The only other example of the BUS IDLE machine cycle occurs during the internal opcode generation for the RST 5.5, RST 6.5, RST 7.5, or TRAP interrupts. FIGURE 2.9 illustrates the B1 cycle generated in response to RST 7.5. As the example illustrates, we will assume that a HALT instruction has just been executed and the CPU is the T_{HALT} state, with its various signals floating. There are only two ways the processor can completely exit the T_{HALT} state, as shown in FIGURE 2.3. The first way is for RESET to occur, which always forces the 8085A to T_{RESET}. The second way to completely exit T_{HALT} is for a valid interrupt to occur, which will cause the CPU to disable further interrupts by resetting INTE FF, and to then proceed to $M_1 \bullet T_1$ of the next instruction. Note that the pressure of HOLD will cause the CPU to exit T_{HALT} only temporarily.

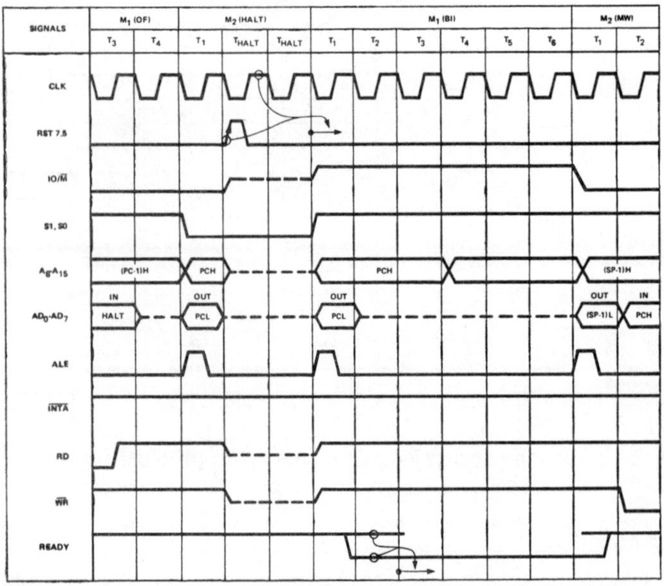

Fig. 2-9. Halt state and bus idle machine cycle RST 7.5 terminates T_{HALT} state.

In Fig. 2-9, note that the RST 7.5 line is pulsed during T_{HALT}. Since RST 7.5 is a rising edge triggered interrupt, it will set an internal latch which is sampled during CLK of every T_{HALT} state (as well as during CLK of the last T state before any $M_1 \cdot T_1$). The fact that the latched interrupt was high (assuming that INTE FF = 1 and the RST 7.5 mask = 0) will force the CPU to exit the T_{HALT} state at the end of the next CLK period, and to enter $M_1 \cdot T_1$.

At this point the CPU must generate its own RESTART type instruction to cause the program to vector to location $3C_{16}$. The easiest way to do this is to have a normal OF machine cycle, except without issuing RD; instead, generate a RESTART opcode internally. After M_1, the CPU continues execution as if nothing special has taken place. The only other unique feature of a BI cycle, is that the state of the READY line is ignored. As shown in Fig. 2-3, the CPU steps from T_2 to T_3 without examining the READY line.

This completes our analysis of the timing of each of the seven types of machine cycles. We will now examine more closely the timing involved in the $T_{HALT,}$ $T_{HOLD,}$ and T_{RESET} machine states.

Relationship of the Hold and Interrupt Functions:

The 8085A uses the T_{HOLD} state to momentarily cease executing machine cycles, allowing external devices to gain control of the buses and perform DMA cycles. The processor internally latches the state of the HOLD line and the unmasked interrupts during CLK of every T_{HALT} state. If the internal latched HOLD signal is high during CLK of any T_{HALT} state, the CPU will exit T_{HALT} and enter T_{HOLD} on the following CLK. As shown in Fig. 2-10, this will occur even if a valid interrupt occurred simultaneously with the HOLD signal.

The state of the HOLD and the unmasked interrupt lines is latched internally during CLK of each T_{HOLD} state as well as during T_{HALT} states. If the internal latched HOLD signal is low during CLK, the CPU will exit T_{HOLD} and enter T_{HALT} on the following CLK. This is also shown in Fig. 2-10.

When the CPU is not in T_{HALT} or T_{HOLD}, it internally latches the HOLD line only during CLK of the last state before T_3 (T_2 or T_{WAIT}) and during CLK of the last state before T_5 (T_4 of a Six t-state M_1). If the internal latched HOLD signal is high during the next CLK, the CPU will enter T_{HOLD} after the following CLK (T_3 or T_5). Furthermore, when the CPU is not in T_{HALT} or T_{HOLD}, it will internally latch the state of the unmasked interrupts only during CLK of the next to the last state before each $M_1 \cdot T_1$.

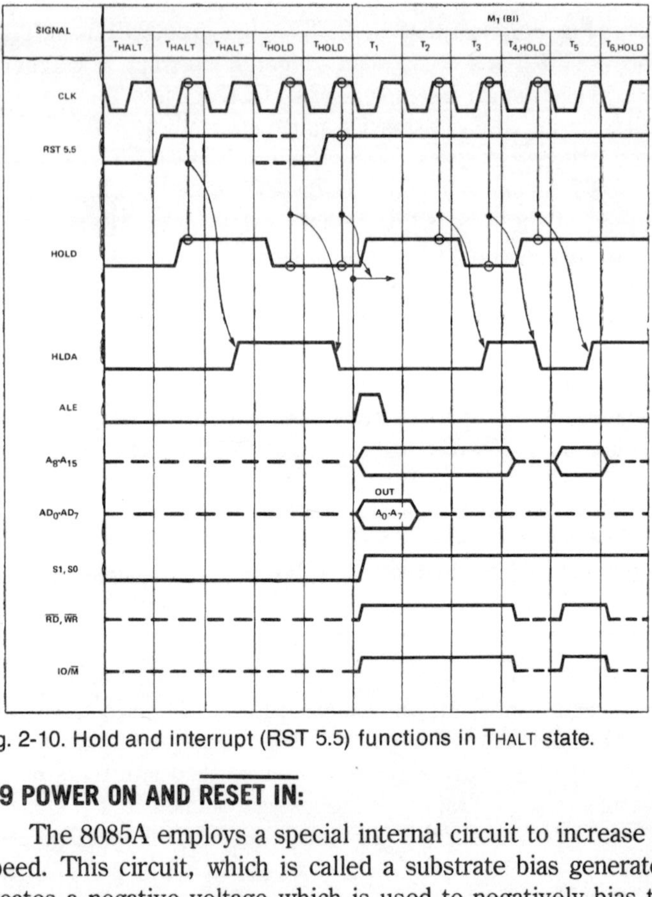

Fig. 2-10. Hold and interrupt (RST 5.5) functions in THALT state.

2.9 POWER ON AND $\overline{\text{RESET IN}}$:

The 8085A employs a special internal circuit to increase its speed. This circuit, which is called a substrate bias generator, creates a negative voltage which is used to negatively bias the substrate. The circuit employs a self-starting oscillator and a charge pump which require a certain amount of time after POWER ON to start functioning properly. This 8085A circuit is conservatively specified as requiring 500 μsec after V_{CC} reaches its specified limits (4.75V).

Taking this circuit into account, the 8085A is not guaranteed to work until 500 μsec after V_{CC} reaches 4.75V. For this reason, it is suggested that $\overline{\text{RESET IN}}$ be kept low during this period. A simple RC network, indicated by a dashed line in Fig. 2-11, (also see Fig. 2-14A), can satisfy this requirement.

The $\overline{\text{RESET IN}}$ line is latched every CLK. This latched signal is examined by the CPU during CLK of every T state. If it is low the CPU will issue RESET OUT and enter T_{HALT} for the next T state. $\overline{\text{RESET IN}}$ should be kept low for a minimum of three clock periods to insure the proper synchronization of the CPU. When the RESET IN signal goes high, the CPU will enter $M_1 \cdot T_1$ for the next T state. Note that the various signals and buses are floated in T_{RESET} as well as T_{HALT} and T_{HOLD}. It may therefore be desirable to provide pull-up resistors for the main control signals.

Specifically, the RESET IN signal causes the following actions:

RESETS	SETS
PROGRAM COUNTER	RST 5.5 MASK
INSTRUCTION REGISTER	RST 6.5 MASK
INTE FF	RST 7.5 MASK
RST 7.5 FF	
TRAP FF	
SOD FF	
MACHINE STATE FF's	
MACHINE CYCLE FF's	
INTERNALLY LATCHED FF's for HOLD, INTR, AND READY	

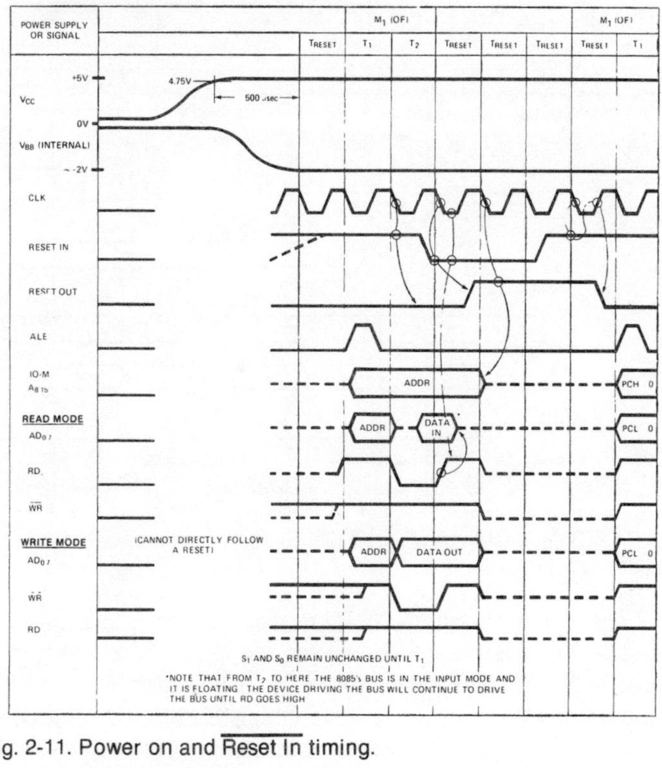

Fig. 2-11. Power on and Reset In timing.

$\overline{\text{RESET IN}}$ may also change the contents of the 8085A's registers (A,B,C,D,E,H,L) and the results are indeterminate. Therefore, the 8085A will be reset to start executing instructions at location 0 with the interrupt system disabled, as shown in Fig. 2-11.

Figure 2-11 shows the 8085A system bus entering a read mode following power on reset. The figure also shows a read operation and a write operation being terminated by a reset signal. Note that a reset may terminate prematurely any read or write operation in process when the reset occurs.

SID and SOD Signals:

Figure 2-12 shows the timing relationship of the SID and SOD signals to the RIM and SIM instructions. The 8085A has the ability to read the SID line into the accumulator bit 7 using RIM instruction. As we can see in Fig. 2-12, the state of the SID line is latched internally during $T_3 \bullet \overline{CLK}$ of every machine cycle, in order that it can be placed into the accumulator bit 7 during $M_1 \bullet T_1 \bullet \overline{CLK}$ of the instruction following RIM. The state of the interrupt pins and masks are transferred directly at that time.

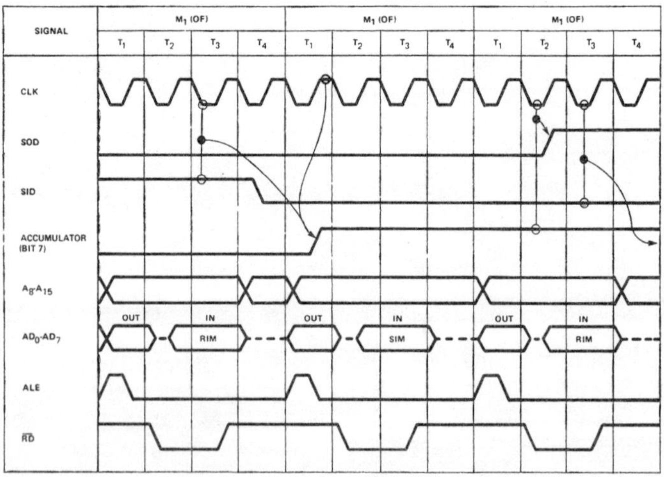

Fig. 2-12. Relationship of SID and SOD signals to RIM and SIM instructions.

The 8085A can set the SOD line from bit 7 of the accumulator using the SIM instruction. As we can see in Fig. 2-12, the data is transferred from the accumulator bit 7 to SOD during $M_1 \bullet T_2 \bullet \overline{CLK}$ of the instruction following SIM, assuming that the accumulator bit 6 is a 1. The interrupt masks will also be set at this time.

2.10 MCS-85™ SYSTEM BUS

When the MCS-85 system bus was being developed, the following major goals and restrictions were placed on the design team:

GOALS:

1. Ease of Use

One of the main goals in designing the 8085A was to provide the user with a system bus that was easy to use. The timing of the control signals should be simple and uniform, allowing the easy interface of standard memory and peripheral circuits. The DC characteristics of the various signals should have the proper voltage and current specifications to allow the direct bussed interconnection of a large number of MOS parts. The DC characteristics should also allow the direct connection of an MOS signal to a standard TTL, part, for applications where additional buffering or gating is required.

2. Efficiency

Another goal for the MCS-85 system was to provide an interconnection bus that made efficient use of its signals. The fewer the number of pins required to interface the MCS-85 parts, the more pins would be available on each part for other purposes. This in turn would allow more features to be added to each part, resulting in more features per square inch of printed circuit board.

RESTRICTIONS:

1. Compatibility

The MCS-85 system bus must be able to be easily modified to provide the same signals as the 8080A, 8224, and 8228 CPU GROUP, with the same (or better) timing. It must be easy to interface the 8085A to the MCS-80 peripheral circuits and to standard memories.

2. Speed

The nature of the system bus should not be a limiting factor of the clock of the 8085A. The system bus should be designed to allow the 8085A to run at its maximum possible speed. The bus should also be capable of being driven at speeds both faster and slower than that of the 8085A.

MCS-80™ and MCS-85™ Bus Comparison

The designers of the 8085A were able to design a system bus that met all of their goals, while satisfying the restrictions.

The MCS-85 system bus is an efficient, fast, and easy-to-use bus that is easily modified to interface to MCS-80 peripheral and memory circuits. Let us start our examination of the MCS-85 bus by comparing it to the MCS-80 bus. Figure 2-13 details the signals and general timing of the two buses; the timing diagrams are drawn to the same scale (8080A clock cycle = 480ns and 8085A clock cycle = 320ns) to facilitate comparison.

2.11 COMPARISON OF MCS-80™ AND MCS-85™ SYSTEM BUSES

MCS-80™ System Bus

The MCS-80 bus is terminated on one end by the CPU-GROUP (consisting of the 8080A, 8224, 8228) and on the other end by the various memory and I/O circuits. The following figure shows the major signals of the MCS-80 Bus.

MCS-85™ System Bus

The MCS-85 BUS is terminated on one end by the 8085A and the other end by various memory and I/O devices. The MCS-85 BUS may be optionally de-multiplexed with an 8212 eight bit latch to provide an MCS-80 type BUS. The following figure shows the major signals of the MCS-85 BUS.

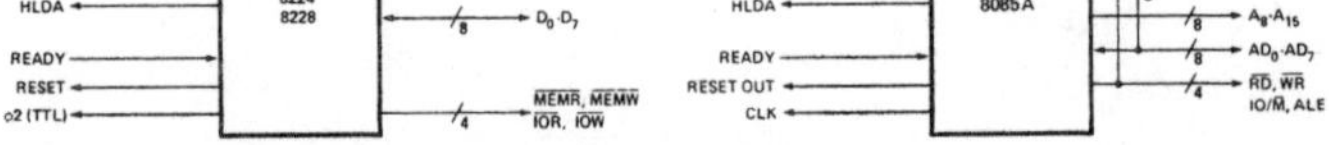

Fig. 2-13A. Comparison of system buses.

SIGNAL (S)	FUNCTION
A_0-A_{15}	The 16 lines of the address bus identify a memory or I/O location for a data transfer operation.
D_0-D_7	The 8 lines of the data bus are used for the parallel transfer of data between two devices.
$\overline{MEMR}$, $\overline{MEMW}$, $\overline{IOR}$, $\overline{IOW}$, $\overline{INTA}$	These five control lines (MEMORY READ, MEMORY WRITE, I/O READ, I/O WRITE, and INTERRUPT ACKNOWLEDGE) identify the type and timing of a data transfer operation.
READY, RESET, HOLD, HLDA ø2 (TTL), INT	These signals are used for the synchronization of slow speed memories, system reset, DMA, system timing, and CPU interrupt.

The basic timing of the MCS-80 BUS for a READ CYCLE is as follows:

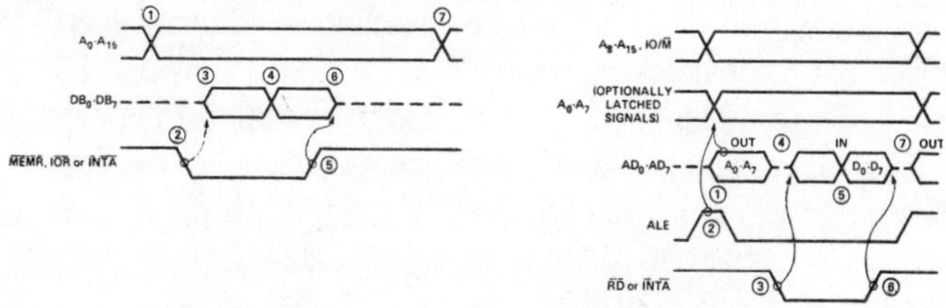

Fig. 2-13B. Basic timing for MCS-80 and MCS-85 buses on read cycle.

The MCS-80 first presents the address ① and shortly thereafter the control signal ②. The data bus, which was in the high impedance state, is driven by the selected device ③. The selected device eventually presents the valid data to the processor ④. The processor raises the control signal ⑤ which causes the selected device to put the data bus in the high impedance state ⑥. The processor then changes the address ⑦ for the start of the next data transfer.

SIGNAL (S)	FUNCTION
A_8-A_{15}	These are the high order eight bits of the address, and are used to identify a memory or I/O location for a data transfer cycle.
AD_0-AD_7	These eight lines serve a dual function. During the beginning of a data transfer operation, these lines carry the low order eight bits of the address bus. During the remainder of the cycle, these lines are used for the parallel transfer to data between two devices.
$\overline{RD}$, $\overline{WR}$, $\overline{INTA}$	These signals identify the type and timing of a data transfer cycle.
IO/$\overline{M}$	The I/O/$\overline{MEMORY}$ line identifies a data transfer as being in the I/O address space or the memory address space.
ALE	ADDRESS LATCH ENABLE enables the latching of the A_0-A_7 signals.
READY, RESET OUT, HOLD, HLDA, CLK, INTR	These signals are used for the synchronization of slow speed memories, system reset, DMA, system timing, and CPU interrupt.

At the beginning of the READ cycle, the 8085A sends out all 16 bits of address①. This is followed by ALE②which causes the lower eight bits of address to be latched in either the 8155/56, 8355, 8755A, or in an external 8212. RD is then dropped③by the 8085A. The data bus is then tri-stated by the 8085A in preparation for the selected device driving the bus④; the selected device will continue to drive the bus with valid data⑤, until RD is raised⑥by the 8085A. At the end of the READ CYCLE⑦, the address and data iines are changed in preparation for the next cycle.

The basic timing of the MCS-80 BUS for a WRITE CYCLE is as follows:

The MCS-80 first presents the address①, then enables the data bus driver②, and later presents the data③. Shortly thereafter, the MCS-80 drops the control signal④for an interval of time and then raises the signal⑤. The MCS-80 then changes the address⑥in preparation for the next data transfer. The advance write signal of the 8238 is also shown⑦.

The basic timing of the MCS-85 BUS for a WRITE CYCLE is as follows:

The timing of the WRITE CYCLE is identical to the MCS-85 READ CYCLE with the exception of the AD_0-AD_7 lines. At the beginning of the cycle①, the low order eight bits of address are on AD_0-AD_7. After ALE drops, the eight bits of data②are put on AD_0-AD_7. They are removed③at the end of the WRITE CYCLE, in anticipation of the next data transfer.

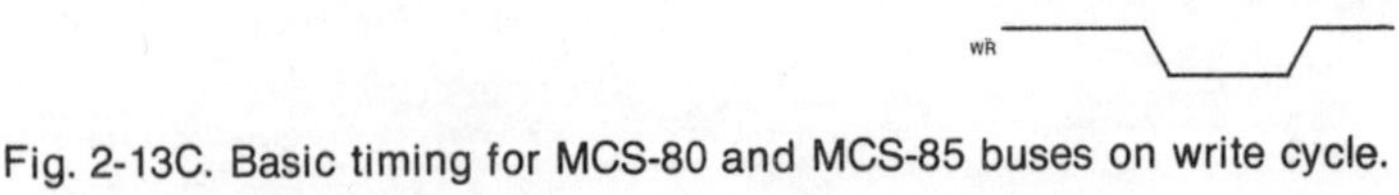

Fig. 2-13C. Basic timing for MCS-80 and MCS-85 buses on write cycle.

The following observations of the two buses can be made:

1. The access times from address leaving the processor to returning data are almost identical, even though the 8085A is operating 50% faster than the 8080.
2. With the addition of an 8212 latch to the 8085A, the basic timings of the two systems are very similar.
3. The 8085A has more time for address setup to RD than the 8080.

4. The MCS-80 has a wider $\overline{\text{RD}}$ signal, but a narrower WR signal than the 8085A.

5. The MCS-80 provides stable data setup to the leading and trailing edges of $\overline{\text{WR}}$, while the 8085 provides stable data setup to only the trailing edge of $\overline{\text{WR}}$.

6. The MCS-80 control signals have different widths and occur at different points in the machine cycle, while the 8085A control signals have identical timing.

7. While not shown on the chart, the MCS-80 data and address hold times are adversely affected by the processor preparing to

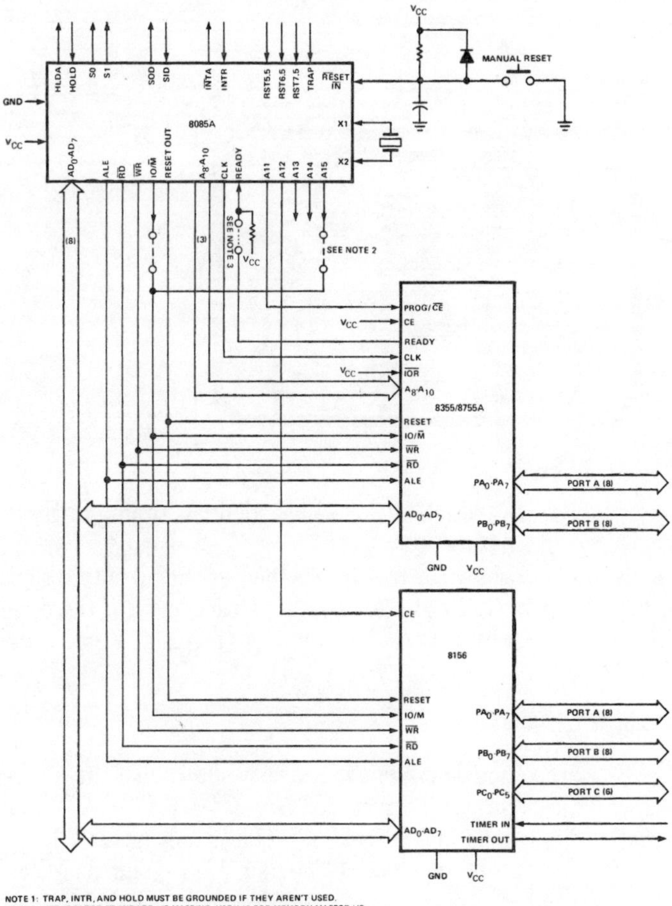

NOTE 1: TRAP, INTR, AND HOLD MUST BE GROUNDED IF THEY AREN'T USED.
NOTE 2: USE IO/M FOR STANDARD I/O MAPPING. USE A15 FOR MEMORY MAPPED I/O.
NOTE 3. CONNECTION IS NECESSARY ONLY IF ONE T_{WAIT} STATE IS DESIRED.

Fig. 2-14A. Minimum 8085 system.

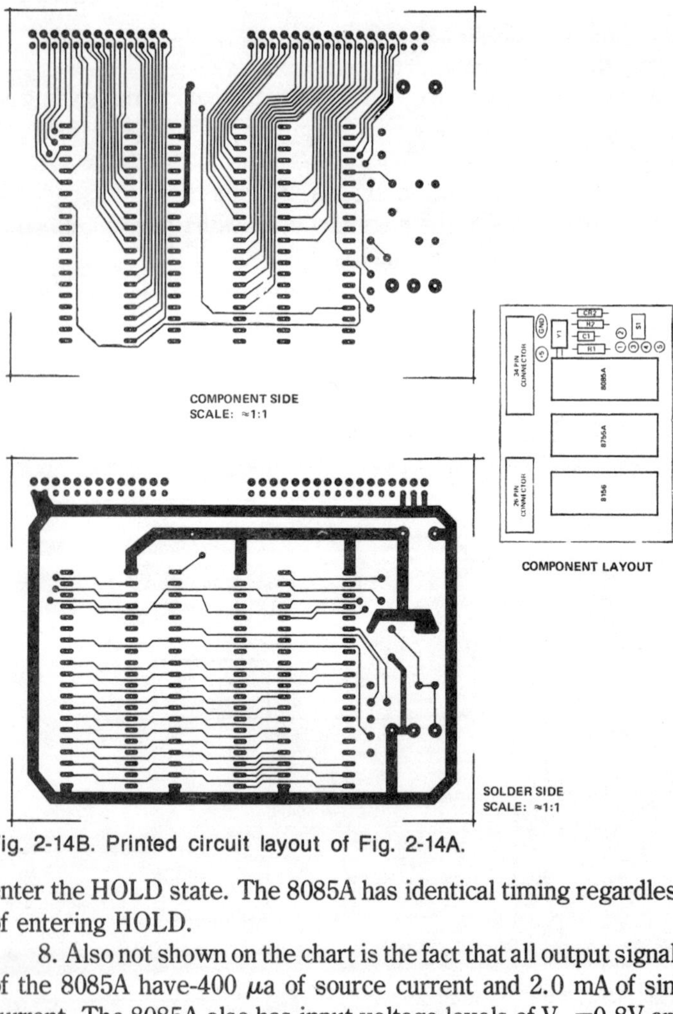

Fig. 2-14B. Printed circuit layout of Fig. 2-14A.

enter the HOLD state. The 8085A has identical timing regardless of entering HOLD.

8. Also not shown on the chart is the fact that all output signals of the 8085A have-400 μa of source current and 2.0 mA of sink current. The 8085A also has input voltage levels of V_{IL}=0.8V and V_{IH}=2.0V.

Conclusion:

The preceding discussion has clearly shown that the MCS-85 bus satisfies the two restrictions of COMPATIBILITY and SPEED. It is compatible because it requires only an 8212 latch to generate an MCS-80 type bus. If the four control signals $\overline{MEMR}$, $\overline{MENW}$, $\overline{IOR}$ and $\overline{IOW}$ are desired, they can be generated from $\overline{RD}$, $\overline{WR}$, and IO/$\overline{M}$ with a decoder or a few gates. The MCS-85 bus is also fast. While running at 3MHz, the 8085A generates better timing signals than the MCS-80 does at 2MHz. Furthermore, the multiplexed bus structure doesn't slow the 8085A down, because it is using the internal states to overlap the fetch and execution portions of different machine cycles. Finally, the MCS-85 can be slowed down or sped up considerably, while still providing reasonable timing.

TO USE. The $\overline{RD}$, $\overline{WR}$, and $\overline{INTA}$ control signals all have identical timing, which isn't affected by the CPU preparing to enter the HOLD state. Furthermore, the address and data bus have good setup and hold times relative to the control signals. The voltage and current levels for the interface signals will all drive buses of up to 40 MOS devices, or 1 schottky TTL device.

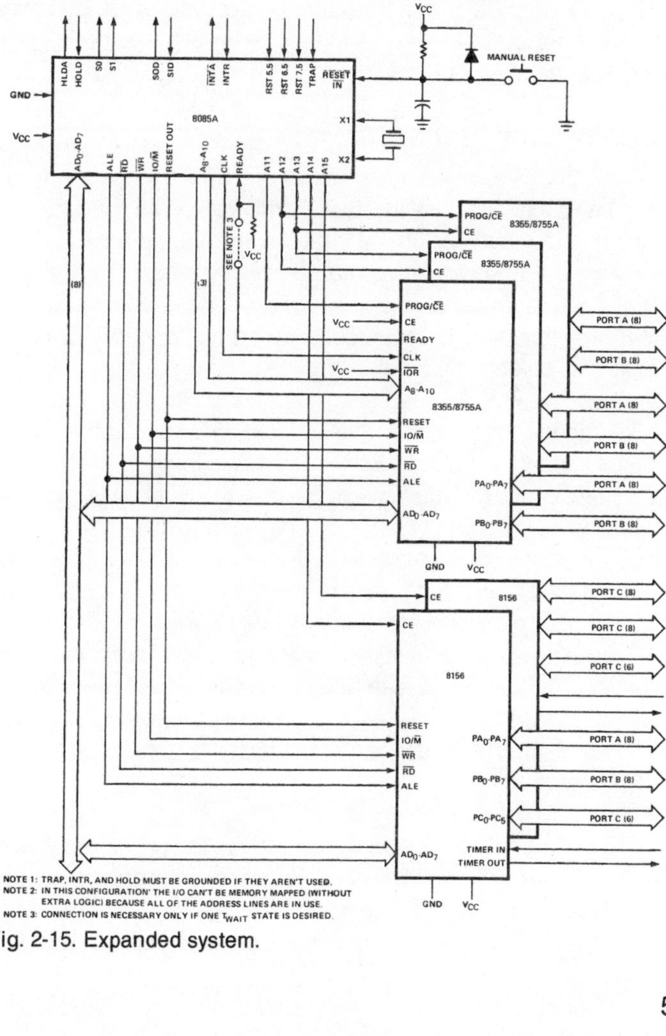

Fig. 2-15. Expanded system.

The MCS-85 system bus is also EFFICIENT. Efficiency is the reason that the lower eight address lines are multiplexed with the data bus. Every chip that needs to use both A_0-A_7 and D_0-D_7 saves 7 pins (the eighth pin is used for ALE) on the interface to the processor. That means that 7 more pins per part are available to either add features to the part or to use a smaller package in some cases. In the three chip system shown in Fig. 2-14, the use of the MCS-85 bus saves 3 × 7 = 21 pins, which are used for extra I/O and interrupt lines. A further advantage of the MCS-85 bus is apparent in Fig. 2-15, which shows a printed circuit layout of the circuit in Fig. 2-14. The reduced number of pins and the fact that compatible pinouts were used, provides for an extremely compact, simple, and efficient printed circuit. Notice that great care was taken when the pinouts were assigned to ensure that the signals would flow easily from chip to chip to chip.

2.12 INTERFACING TO THE 8085

Now that we understand how the MCS-85 system bus works, let us explore the ways that the 8085A can be connected to various memory and peripheral circuits. For the purposes of this discussion, it will be assumed that the reader is familiar with the functions and timing of the 8085A, 8155/56, 8355, 8755A, and all MCS-80 components. If a particular part is mentioned with which the reader is unfamiliar, he may wish to review the data sheet for that part.

Notice that the 8155/56, 8355, and 8755A have both memory elements and I/O elements. As we know, the 8085A interfaces to both memory and I/O devices by means of READ and WRITE machine cycles, the timing of which are practically identical. During each machine cycle the 8085A issues an address, a control signal, and then either sends data out on the bus or reads data from the bus. While the 8085A may actually be performing a MEMORY READ machine cycle, for instance, it neither knows nor cares what is actually providing the data byte that it reads. It could be a ROM, RAM, I/O device, a bank of switches, or even a floating bus; the 8085A will assume that there is something there to read and will go ahead and read it.

The only real difference between a variable read from memory, an input port, or an instruction opcode is the manner in which the CPU interprets what it has read. If it is expecting an opcode, it will treat it as an opcode. If it is expecting an I/O port it will treat it as an I/O port. The same thing is true for a MEMORY WRITE machine cycle. The 8085A issues an address, data, and a control signal. Unless it is requested to WAIT (by use of the READY line) it will complete the cycle and proceed on to the next machine cycle. Regardless of whether or not there was anything there to accept the data, and regardless of whether or not the device was the type it expected, it will go on.

The CPU executes one machine cycle at a time, one instruction at a time, in sequence until told to do otherwise. The program (which is merely a sequence of instructions) totally controls the sequence and nature of all machine cycles.

Once the system designer fully understands the implications of the above paragraph, he will be well on his way to making full and efficient use of the microcomputer. By rearranging the normal structure of the system, the designer can assign his hardware to the address space that best suits his purpose.

Memory Mapped I/O

For instance, while the 8085A has separate instructions (INPUT and OUTPUT) to communicate to I/O devices, many designers connect their I/O devices to the memory control lines, which is referred to as MEMORY-MAPPED I/O. Remember that as long as the I/O device responds like a memory device, the processor can't tell the difference. By using memory mapped I/O, the designer can take advantage of the larger instruction set that references the memory address space. Instead of simply being able to transfer a byte of data between the accumulator and the I/O port, the program can now perform arithmetic and logical operations on the port data as well as move the data between any of the internal registers and the I/O port. Consider the new meaning of the following instructions:

Examples:

MOVr,M	(Input Port to any Register)
MOV M,r	(Output any Register to Port)
MVI M	(Output immediate data to Port)
LDA	(Input Port to ACC)
STA	(Output from ACC to Port)
LHLD	(16-Bit Input)
SHLD	(16-Bit Output)
ADD M	(Add Port to ACC)
ANA M	("AND" Port with ACC)

Disadvantages of Memory Mapped I/O

While the new instructions may increase the flexibility of the I/O system, there are some drawbacks. Since the I/O devices will now be addressed as memory, there will be fewer addresses available for memory. A common practice is to use address bit 15 (A_{15}) to distinguish memory from I/O. If A_{15}=0 then memory is being addressed, while if A_{15}=1, I/O is being addressed. This particular scheme limits the maximum amount of memory that can be used to 32K bytes. A further disadvantage of memory mapped I/O is that it takes 3 bytes of instruction and 13 clock cycles using the LDA or STA instructions to specify moving a byte of data between the accumulator and an I/O device, while the INPUT and OUTPUT instructions require only two bytes and 10 clock cycles. This is because the I/O address space is smaller (only 256 bytes) and therefore requires fewer bits to completely specify an address. A further advantage of using the INPUT and OUTPUT instructions is that it allows the easy connection of the MCS-80 peripherals to the MCS-85 multiplexed bus. If the designer were to memory map the MCS-80 peripherals to the MCS-85 bus, it would be necessary to either latch the lower address bits with an 8212 or else use a tremendous portion of the memory address space by connecting the chip selects and address lines of the ports to the unmultiplexed upper eight lines of the address bus.

Address Assignment

Besides memory mapped I/O, another common trick is to not fully decode the address bus when generating chip selects. Every device has a given number of unique addresses associated with it. The 8355, for instance, has 2K bytes of ROM and therefore has 2K addresses associated with the ROM. Any one of these 2K addresses can be uniquely specified by a pattern on the 11 (2^{11}=2K) address lines. However, since the 8355 must work with other devices in a system, it isn't enough to simply specify the 11 bits further bits of information must be used to locate the 2K bytes within the 65K address space. The 2K bytes are located by the use of chip enable lines. If the 8355 was to occupy the first 2K bytes of the memory address space, it would, strictly speaking, be necessary to decode the fact that A_{15}-A_{11} were all zeroes, and use that condition as a chip enable. Then the 8355 would be selected only when the address bus was less than 2K.

However, if we know that there are other blocks of 2K bytes of addresses that aren't being used, we could combine those addresses and not decode all of the upper five address lines for the chip enable. In fact, in a small system we may need to decode only one bit of address, which is to say we connect that bit of the address bus to the chip enable line of the 8355. If we were to connect A11 to the CE line of the 8355 and tie CE to VCC, then the 8355 would be selected whenever the memory address was 0-2K. However, it would also be selected whenever the memory locations 4K-6K, 8K-10K, 61K-63K (i.e., whenever bit A11=0) were addressed. If the programmer is aware of this, and if there are no other devices assigned to the other address spaces, then it may be an acceptable condition. Care must be taken, however, to ensure that at no time will two different devices be selected simultaneously. Whenever one device is selected, that memory address must deselect all other devices, because if two devices are selected simultaneously for a READ operation, it may blow out one or both parts. Remember that the address bus may reflect an undesired address during T5, T6 of an OPCODE FETCH machine cycle and during address bus transitional periods in T1. Therefore, all memory and I/O devices must qualify their selection with RD or WR, so as to ignore all spurious addresses.

By paying careful attention to the above paragraph, we can see how the use of an address bit as a chip select can save decoding logic. This technique is referred to as LINEAR SELECTION. The direct consequence of linear selection is that you have the available address space for each single address bit used as a chip enable. If this penalty is too high, you can always use an 8205 one-of-eight decoder. Also, some chips have multiple chip enables which allows for some automatic decoding of the address.

One last drawback to linear selection is that the memory addresses of the different parts won't be contiguous. For example, if three 8355's are addressed using linear selection, one might be located at 0-2K, the next at 6K-8K, and the next at 10K-12K. The program would have to recognize these page boundaries and jump over them.

2.13 INTERFACING TO THE 8155/8156, 8355/8755A I/O MAPPED I/O:

Recall that the 8085A has the capability to address I/O devices in two ways. If the chips are connected as memory devices, they can be addressed using any of the memory reference instructions. If, however, they are connected as I/O devices (this is referred to as I/O MAPPED I/O OR AS STANDARD I/O) then they can be accessed only by use of the INPUT and OUTPUT instructions. Let us examine some of the techniques involved in connecting the MCS-85 COMBINATION MEMORY AND I/O chips to the 8085A as I/O devices.

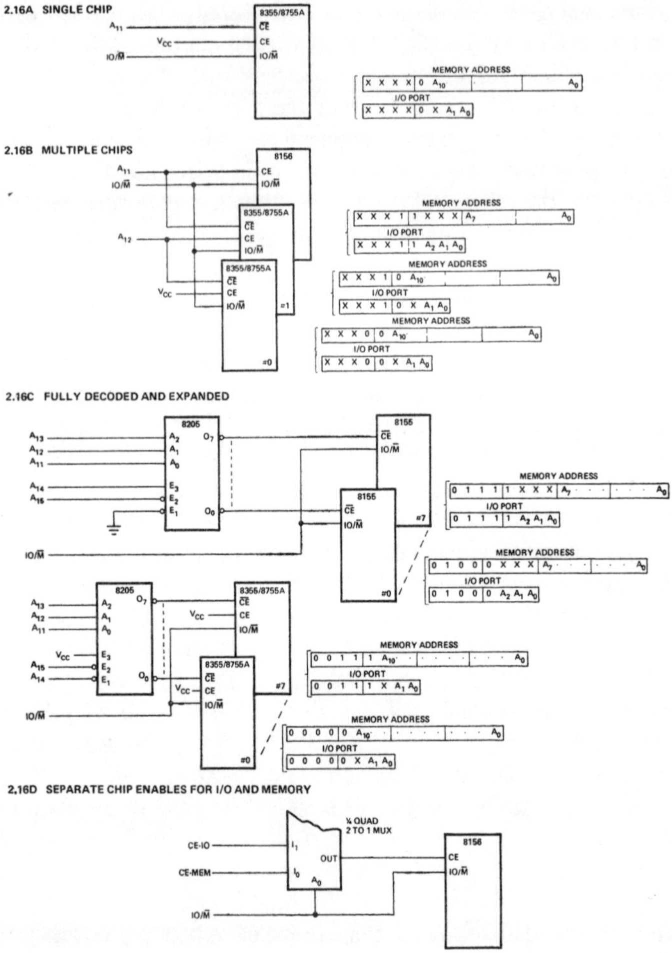

Fig. 2-16. MCS-85™ peripherals with I/O-mapped I/O.

Figure 2-16A shows a solitary 8355 connected to the 8085A bus. (In the interest of simplicity, only the chip enable and IO/$\overline{M}$ lines are shown; the other lines can be assumed to be connected as shown in Figs. 2-14 or 2-15.) The first thing we notice is that CE is tied to V_{CC} and $\overline{CE}$ is connected to A_{11}. This would be a fairly normal way to connect an 8355 in a system that had only one ROM/PROM circuit; this is because after RESET the processor always starts executing at location 0. Since the ROM normally contains the program, it must be selected when the address is all zeros.

One consequence of the ROM being selected by an all zero address is that the I/O ports on the chip will be selected only when $A_{11} = 0$. This is because the I/O ports and the memory have common chip enables, therefore forcing the selection conditions of one onto the other. Furthermore, since the $IO/\overline{M}$ line of the chip is connected to the $IO/\overline{M}$ line of the 8085A bus, the port has I/O MAPPED I/O. The I/O ports can be accessed only by use of the INPUT and OUTPUT instructions; since these are the only instructions that cause $IO/\overline{M}$ to go high.

The boxes to the right of the chip in Fig. 2-16A indicate the memory addresses and I/O Port No.'s required to access the chip. As a result of the LINEAR SELECTION technique used, there are many "DON'T-CARE" bits (marked by an "X") in the address. While they don't affect the addressing of this device, they may affect other devices in the system, which would force them to be either one or zero. Remember that two devices may not be selected simultaneously; thus each device must have an address that not only selects itself, but also deselects all other devices. If there are any bits which are truly "DON'T-CARES", they are customarily assigned to be zero. If all the "X" bits in Fig. 2-16A were DON'T-CARES, then the chip could be addressed as memory locations 0-2K, and I/O Ports 0-3.

Figure 2-16B shows a slightly larger system of two 8355's and one 8156. Notice that 8355 No. 1 uses its two chip enable lines to decode $A_{12} = 1$, $A_{11} = 0$. Also observe that it is possible to address each of the chips without selecting any of the others. Also notice that there are some illegal addresses (e.g., $A_{12} = 0$, $A_{11} = 1$) that would cause two of the devices to turn on simultaneously. The programmer must avoid using these addresses.

Figure 2-16C shows a very large MCS-85 system. While few actual systems would even approach this size, it is useful as an example. Two 8205's are used to completely decode the addresses. There are some interesting points to observe here. First, while some of the devices have multiple possible addresses (i.e., they have some DON'T-CARE bits), there aren't any addresses which can cause simultaneous selection of two or more parts. Second, since the I/O and memory portions share the chip enables, they are forced to live with each other's constraints. Third, only one 8205 per eight chips is required for the decoding; that's an overhead of only ⅛ of a chip per part.

Figure 2-16D shows a remedy to the problem illustrated in 2-16C, namely that I/O and memory portions of the chip are forced to live with each other's chip enable constraints. By using a quad 2 to 1 multiplexer, the chip enables of the I/O and memory portions of four chips can be independently assigned. This circuit can also be handy for interfacing the 8257 DMA circuit to a chip that doesn't have a $\overline{DACK}$ pin.

Memory Mapped I/O:

If the I/O ports of any device are connected to the 8085 as memory devices, they can then be accessed as memory locations, using the processor's memory reference instructions. This is referred to as MEMORY MAPPED I/O. Figure 2-17A shows an 8355 connected to the 8085A BUS. Since the IO/$\overline{M}$ pin of the 8355 is connected to A_{15}, whenever A_{15} = 1 the I/O Ports will be accessed. While A_{15} could be set to 1 by either a memory or I/O instruction, in this situation the port is usually accessed only by the memory instructions. The programmer could have the best of both worlds by accessing the ports as either memory locations (where A_{15} = 1, + 32K) or as I/O Ports (A_{15} =, + 128). Assuming that MEMORY MAPPED I/O is used, the addresses are shown in the boxes to the right in Fig. 2-17A. If one wanted to ensure that neither the I/O nor the memory was ever selected by any INPUT or OUTPUT

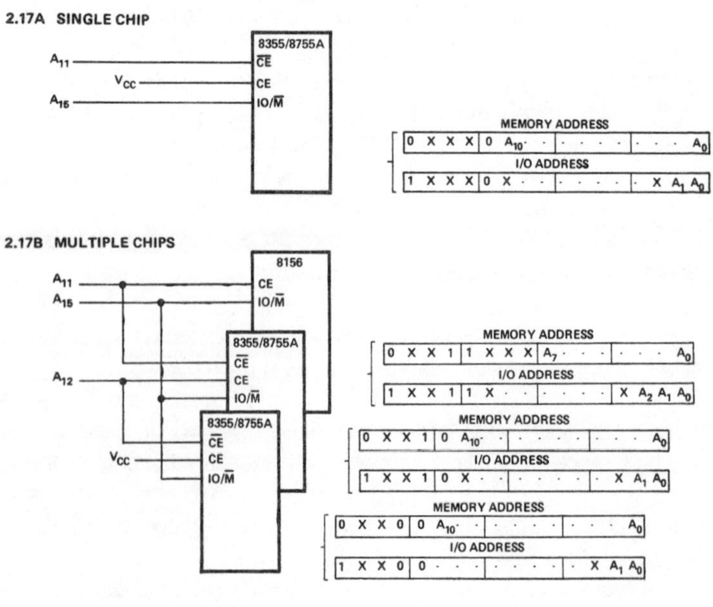

Fig. 2-17. MCS-85 peripherals with memory-mapped I/O.

instruction, then the chip enable would have to be conditioned by IO/$\overline{M}$ = 0.

Figure 2-17B shows a somewhat larger system also using MEMORY MAPPED I/O. As in Fig. 2-16B, we see that care must be exercised to ensure that no two devices are simultaneously accessed. We can also see that the memory address space is being used up even quicker as a result of using MEMORY MAPPED I/O.

2.14 INTERFACING TO MCS-80™ PERIPHERALS I/O MAPPED I/O:

There are two main differences between the MCS-80 peripherals and the MCS-85 I/O Ports. The first is that the MCS-85 devices use a multiplexed address/data bus to save pins while the MCS-80 components use unmultiplexed signals. The second difference is that the MCS-85 I/O Ports share their chip enables with memory circuits, while the MCS-80 peripherals have unique chip selects.

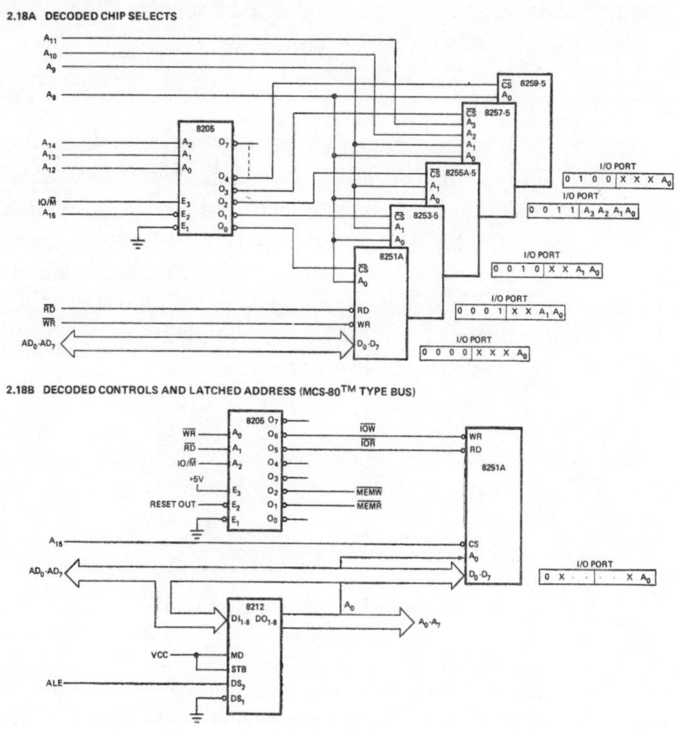

Fig. 2-18. MCS-80™ peripherals with I/O-mapped I/O.

To interface to an MCS-80 peripheral, we need only provide a constant address, a chip select, and $\overline{RD}$ or $\overline{WR}$. Since the upper address lines (A_8-A_{15}) of the 8085 are non-multiplexed, they can be tied directly to the peripherals, as shown in Fig. 2-16A. To provide I/O MAPPED I/O, we must either use linear selection (keeping the I/O and memory addresses non-coincidental), or else condition the chip selects of $\overline{RD}$ and $\overline{WR}$ with IO/$\overline{M}$ = 1. Figure 2-18A shows a technique of gating the chip selects with IO/$\overline{M}$ = 1, using an 8205. This technique is also nice in that it allows more I/O devices to be used than linear selection would allow. Note that this technique relies on the fact that the I/O Port number is copied onto A_8 - A_{15} as well as A_0 - A_7 during an INPUT or OUTPUT instruction.

Figure 2-18B shows an alternative approach to interfacing to MCS-80 components. By latching the lower 8-bits of address with an 8212, and decoding the control signals with an 8205, we have created an exact copy of the MCS-80 (8080A, 8224, 8228) bus. We can then use whatever circuits that have been previously developed for the 8080. The total cost is one 8212 and one 8205. Since the same signals might have needed buffering anyway, the overhead ranged from little to nothing.

Memory Mapped I/O:

Exactly the same techniques to memory map the I/O used for the MCS-85 apply to the MCS-80 I/O devices. Figure 2-19 shows an 8205 being used to qualify the chip select of the I/O device with IO/$\overline{M}$ = 0. Since the MCS-80 peripherals require non multiplexed address lines, linear select is not too useful unless the address lines are latched. This is because connecting both the chip selects and the address lines of the MCS-80 peripherals to A_8 - A_{15} would deplete all the useful address very quickly.

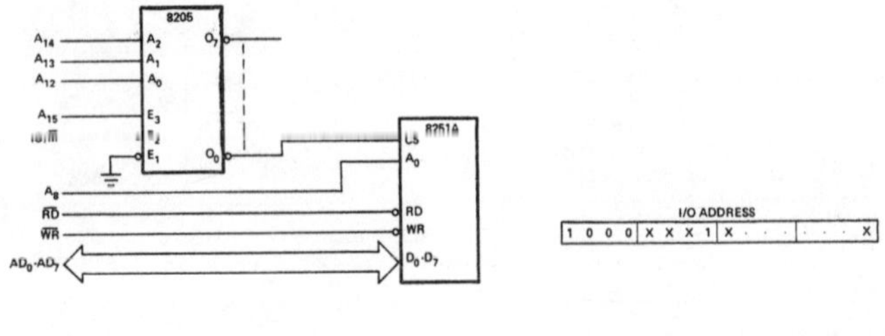

Fig. 2-19. MCS-80™ peripherals with memory-mapped I/O and decoded chip selects.

Interfacing to MCS-80™ Memories

Interfacing to MCS-80 memories is very similar to interfacing to MCS-85 memories with the exception that A_0-A_7 must be latched. Once this requirement is met, all the tricks discussed earlier can be used. Since the address lines would eventually require buffering as the system size grew, the overhead of the 8212 latch becomes negligible.

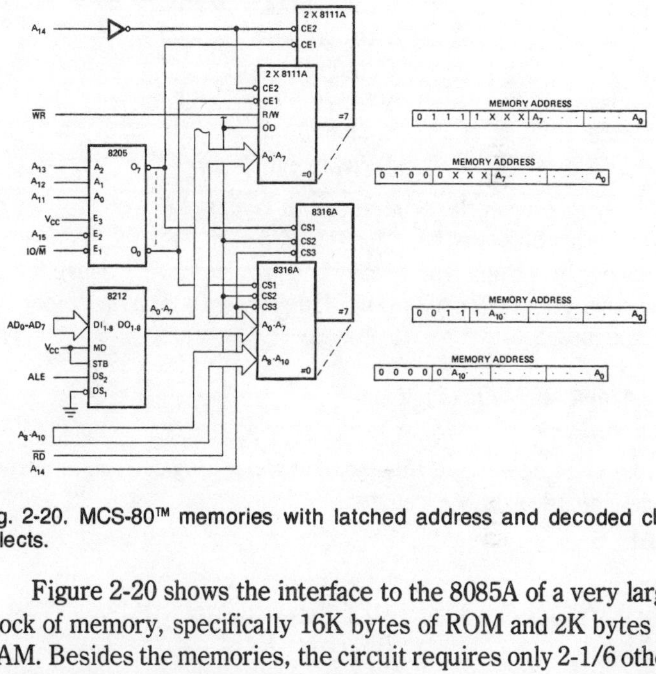

Fig. 2-20. MCS-80™ memories with latched address and decoded chip selects.

Figure 2-20 shows the interface to the 8085A of a very large block of memory, specifically 16K bytes of ROM and 2K bytes of RAM. Besides the memories, the circuit requires only 2-1/6 other parts for logical gating. If MCS-80 I/O parts were used, the 8212 latch could be shared between the two groups, further reducing the gating overhead per IC.

Minimum MCS-85 System™

We shall finish our discussion by examining the schematics of Fig. 2-14A (p. 55) and Fig. 2-15 (p. 57). These schematics depict a minimum system core. In actual size use, some of the processor control signals (TRAP, INTR, and HOLD) would have to be terminated. Also, interface logic to external devices as well as more memory and I/O devices may be desirable. The first thing one notices about the system in Fig. 2-14A is the scarcity of parts required to build this system. With a minimum of parts, we have constructed a microcomputer system that has the following functions:

PARTS	FUNCTION
1 8085A	1 CPU (Clock cycle ≤320 ns)
1 8355/8755A	2048 Bytes of either PROM or ROM
1 8156	256 Bytes of RAM
1 Crystal	5 Interrupts
2 Resistors	1 Programmable Timer/ Counter
1 Capacitor	1 Crystal and Oscillator
1 Diode	1 Clock
1 +5V Power Supply	1 Power-on Reset

By looking at the printed circuit layout of Fig. 2-14B, we can see that not only are there just 3 IC's, but that the interconnection of these parts is extremely easy and provides a very dense layout. Especially notice the easy flow of the system bus on the solder side of the board.

Expanded MCS-85™ System

Figure 2-15 shows the circuit of Fig. 2-14A expanded to its maximum size without the use of any extra logic. In an extremely small board area we can fit:

PARTS	FUNCTION
1 8085A	1 CPU (Clock cycle ≤320 ns);)
3 8355/8755A	6144 Bytes ROM/PROM
2 8156	768 Bytes RAM
1 Crystal	5 Interrupts
2 Resistors	2 Programmable Timer/ Counters
1 Capacitor	1 Crystal and Oscillator
1 Diode	1 Clock
	1 Power-on Reset

Chapter 3
8085A Single-Chip 8-Bit N-Channel Microprocessor

3.1 8085A REQUIREMENTS AND CHARACTERISTICS

- Single +5V Power Supply
- 100% Software Compatible with 8080A
- 1.3 μs Instruction Cycle
- On-Chip Clock Generator (with External Crystal or RC Network
- On-Chip System Controller; Advanced Cycle Status Information Available for Large System Control
- Four Vectored Interrupts (One is non-Maskable)
- Serial In/Serial Out Port
- Decimal, Binary and Double Precision Arithmetic
- Direct Addressing Capability to 64K Bytes of Memory

The Intel 8085A is a new generation, complete 8 bit parallel central processing unit (CPU). Its instruction set is 100% software compatible with the 8080A microprocessor, and it is designed to improve the present 8080's performance by higher system speed. Its high level of system integration allows a minimum system of three IC's: 8085A (CPU), 8156 (RAM) and 8355/8755A (ROM/PROM).

The 8085A incorporates all of the features that the 8224 (clock generator) and 8228 (system controller) provided for the 8080, thereby offering a high level of system integration.

The 8085A uses a multiplexed Data Bus. The address is split between the 8 bit address bus and the 8 bit data bus. The on-chip address latches of 8155/8156/8355/8755A memory products allows a direct interface with 8085A.

3.2 8085A FUNCTIONAL PIN DEFINITION

The following describes the function of each pin shown in Fig. 3-1.

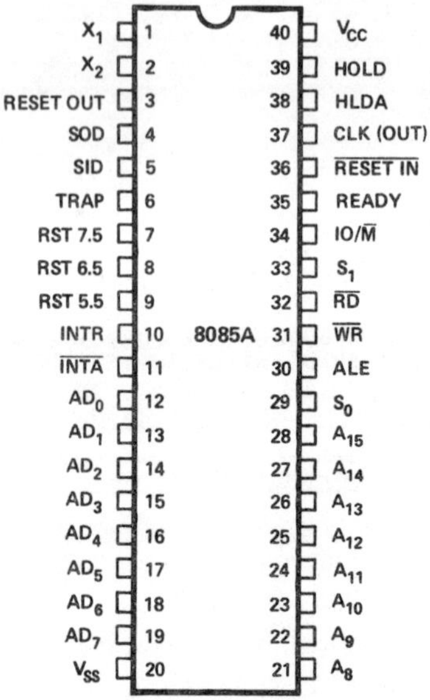

Fig. 3-1. 8085A pinout diagram.

A_8-A_{15} (Output 3-State)

Address Bus; The most significant 8-bits of the memory address or the 8-bits of the I/O address, 3-stated during Hold and Halt modes.

AD_{0-7}(Input/Output 3-state)

Multiplexed Address/Data Bus; Lower 8-bits of the memory address (or I/O address) appear on the bus during the first clock cycle of a machine state. It then becomes the data bus during the second and third clock cycles.

3-stated during Hold and Halt modes.

ALE (Output)

Address Latch Enable: It occurs during the first clock cycle of a machine state and enables the address to get latched into the on-chip latch of peripherals. The falling edge of ALE is set to guarantee setup and hold times for the address information. ALE can also be used to strobe the status information. ALE is never 3-stated.

SO, S1 (Output)

Data Bus Status. Encoded status of the bus cycle:

$\underline{S_1}$	$\underline{S_0}$	
0	0	HALT
0	1	WRITE
1	0	READ
1	1	FETCH

S_1 can be used as an advanced $R/\overline{W}$ status.

$\overline{RD}$ (Output 3-state)

READ; indicates the selected memory or I/O device is to be read and that the Data Bus is available for the data transfer. 3-stated during Hold and Halt.

$\overline{WR}$ (Output 3-state)

WRITE; indicates the data on the Data Bus is to be written into the selected memory or I/O location. Data is set up at the trailing edge of $\overline{WR}$. 3-stated during Hold and Halt modes.

READY (Input)

If READY is high during a read or write cycle, it indicates that the memory or peripheral is ready to send or receive data. If Ready is low, the CPU will wait for Ready to go high before completing the read or write cycle.

HOLD (Input)

HOLD; indicates that another Master is requesting the use of the Address and Data Buses. The CPU, upon receiving the Hold request, will relinquish the use of buses as soon as the completion of the current machine cycle. Internal processing can continue. The processor can regain the buses only after the Hold is removed. When the Hold is acknowledged, the Address, Data, $\overline{RD}$, $\overline{WR}$, and $IO/\overline{M}$ lines are 3-stated.

HLDA (Output)

HOLD ACKNOWLEDGE; indicates that the CPU has received the Hold request and that it will relinquish the buses in the next clock cycle. HLDA goes low after the Hold request is removed. The CPU takes the buses one half clock cycle after HLDA goes low.

INTR (Input)

INTERRUPT REQUEST; is used as a general purpose interrupt. It is sampled only during the next to the last clock cycle of the instruction. If it is active, the Program Counter (PC) will be inhibited from incrementing and an $\overline{\text{INTA}}$ will be issued. During this cycle a RESTART or CALL instruction can be inserted to jump to the interrupt service routine. The INTR is enabled and disabled by software. It is disabled by Reset and immediately after an interrupt is accepted.

$\overline{\text{INTA}}$ (Output)

INTERRUPT ACKNOWLEDGE; is used instead of (and has the same timing as) $\overline{\text{RD}}$ during the Instruction cycle after an INTR is accepted. It can be used to activate the 8259 Interrupt chip or some other interrupt port.

RST 5.5
RST 6.5 — **(Inputs)**
RST 7.5

RESTART INTERRUPTS; These three inputs have the same timing as INTR except they cause an internal RESTART to be automatically inserted.

RST 7.5 → Highest Priority
RST 6.5
RST 5.5 → Lowest Priority

The priority of these interrupts is ordered as shown above. These interrupts have a higher priority than the INTR.

TRAP (Input)

Trap interrupt is a nonmaskable restart interrupt. It is recognized at the same time as INTR. It is unaffected by any mask or Interrupt Enable. It has the highest priority of any interrupt.

$\overline{\text{RESET IN}}$ (Input)

Reset sets the Program Counter to zero and resets the Interrupt Enable and HLDA flip-flops. None of the other flags or registers (except the instruction register) are affected. The CPU is held in the reset condition as long as Reset is applied.

RESET OUT (Output)

Indicates CPU is being reset. Can be used as a system RESET. The signal is synchronized to the processor clock.

X_1, X_2 (Input)

Crystal or R/C network connections to set the internal clock generator. X_1 can also be an external clock input instead of a crystal. The input frequency is divided by 2 to give the internal operating frequency.

CLK (Output)

Clock Output for use as a system clock when a crystal or R/C network is used as an input to the CPU. The period of CLK is twice the X_1, X_2 input period.

$IO/\overline{M}$ (Output)

$IO/\overline{M}$ indicates whether the Read/Write is to memory or I/O. Tri-stated during Hold and Halt modes.

SID (Input)

Serial input data line. The data on this line is loaded into accumulator bit 7 whenever a RIM instruction is executed.

SOD (Output)

Serial output data line. The output SOD is set or reset as specified by the SIM instruction.

V_{CC}

+5 volt supply.

V_{SS}

Ground Reference.

3.3 FUNCTIONAL DESCRIPTION

The 8085A is a complete 8-bit parallel central processor. It is designed with N-channel depletion loads and requires a single +5 volt supply. Its basic clock speed is 3 MHz thus improving on the present 8080's performance with higher system speed. Also it is designed to fit into a minimum system of three IC's: The CPU, a RAM/IO, and a ROM or PROM/IO chip.

The 8085A uses a multiplexed Data Bus. The address is split between the higher 8-bit Address Bus and the lower 8-bit Address/Data Bus. During the first cycle the address is sent out. The lower 8-bits are latched into the peripherals by the Address Latch Enable (ALE). During the rest of the machine cycle the Data Bus is used for memory or I/O data.

The 8085A provides $\overline{RD}$, $\overline{WR}$, and $IO/\overline{Memory}$ signals for bus control. An Interrupt Acknowledge signal ($\overline{INTA}$) is also provided.

Hold, Ready, and all Interrupts are synchronized. The 8085A also provides serial input data (SID) and serial output data (SOD) lines for simple serial interface.

In addition to these features, the 8085A has three maskable, restart interrupts and one nonmaskable trap interrupt.

3.4 8085A VS. 8080A

The 8085A includes the following features on-chip in addition to all of the 8080A functions.

a. Internal clock generator
b. Clock output
c. Fully synchronized Ready
d. Schmitt action on $\overline{\text{RESET IN}}$
e. RESET OUT pin
f. $\overline{\text{RD}}$, $\overline{\text{WR}}$, and IO/$\overline{\text{M}}$ Bus Control Signals
g. Encoded Status information
h. Multiplexed Address and Data
i. Direct Restarts and nonmaskable Interrupt
j. Serial Input/Output lines.

The internal clock generator requires an external crystal or R-C network. It will oscillate at twice the basic CPU operating frequency. A 50% duty cycle, two phase, nonoverlapping clock is generated from this oscillator internally and one phase of the clock ($\phi 2$) is available as an external clock. The 8085A directly provides the external RDY synchronization previously provided by the 8224. The $\overline{\text{RESET IN}}$ input is provided with a Schmitt action input so that power-on reset only requires a resistor and capacitor. RESET OUT is provided for System RESET.

The 8085A provides $\overline{\text{RD}}$, $\overline{\text{WR}}$ and IO/$\overline{\text{M}}$ signals for Bus control. An $\overline{\text{INTA}}$ which was previously provided by the 8228 in 8080 system is also included in 8085A.

3.5 STATUS INFORMATION

Status information is directly available from the 8085A. ALE serves as a status strobe. The status is partially encoded, and provides the user with advanced timing of the type of bus transfer being done. IO/$\overline{\text{M}}$ cycle status signal is provided directly also. Decoded S_0. S_1 carries the following status information:

	S_1	S_0
HALT	0	0
WRITE	0	1
READ	1	0
FETCH	1	1

S1 can be interpreted as $R/\overline{W}$ in all bus transfers.

In the 8085A the 8LSB of address are multiplexed with the data instead of status. The ALE line is used as a strobe to enter the lower half of the address into the memory or peripheral address latch. This also frees extra pins for expanded interrupt capability.

3.6 INTERRUPT AND SERIAL I/O

The 8085A has 5 interrupt inputs: INTR, RST 5.5, RST 6.5, RST 7.5, and TRAP. INTR is identical in function to the 8080 INT. Each of three RESTART inputs, 5.5, 6.5, 7.5, has a programmable mask. TRAP is also a RESTART interrupt except it is nonmaskable.

The three RESTART interrupts cause the internal execution of RST (saving the program counter in the stack and branching to the RESTART address) if the interrupts are enabled and if the interrupt mask is not set. The nonmaskable TRAP causes the internal execution of a RST independent of the state of the interrupt enable or masks.

Name	RESTART Address (Hex)
TRAP	24_{16}
RST 5.5	$2C_{16}$
RST 6.5	34_{16}
RST 7.5	$3C_{16}$

There are two different types of inputs in the restart interrupts. RST 5.5 and RST 6.5 are *high level-sensitive* like INTR (and INT on the 8080) and are recognized with the same timing as INTR. RST 7.5 is *rising edge-sensitive*. For RST 7.5, only a pulse is required to set an internal flip flop which generates the internal interrupt request. The RST 7.5 request flip flop remains set until the request is serviced. Then it is reset automatically. This flip-flop may also be reset by using the SIM instruction or by issuing a RESET IN to the 8085A. The RST 7.5 internal flip flop will be set by a pulse on the RST 7.5 pin even when the RST 7.5 interrupt is masked out.

The status of the three RST interrupt masks can only be affected by the SIM instruction and RESET IN.

The interrupts are arranged in a fixed priority that determines which interrupt is to be recognized if more than one is pending as follows: TRAP-highest priority, RST 7.5, RST 6.5, RST 5.5, INTR-lowest priority. This priority scheme does not take into account for priority of a routine that was started by a higher priority interrupt. RST 5.5 can interrupt a RST 7.5 routine if the interrupts were reenabled before the end of the RST 7.5 routine.

The TRAP interrupt is useful for catastrophic errors such as power failure or bus error. The TRAP input is recognized just as any other interrupt but has the highest priority. It is not affected by any flag or mask. The TRAP input is both *edge and level sensitive*. The TRAP input must go high and remain high to be acknowledged, but will not be recognized again until it goes low, then high again. This avoids any false triggering due to noise or logic glitches. The following diagram illustrates the TRAP interrupt request circuitry within the 8085A.

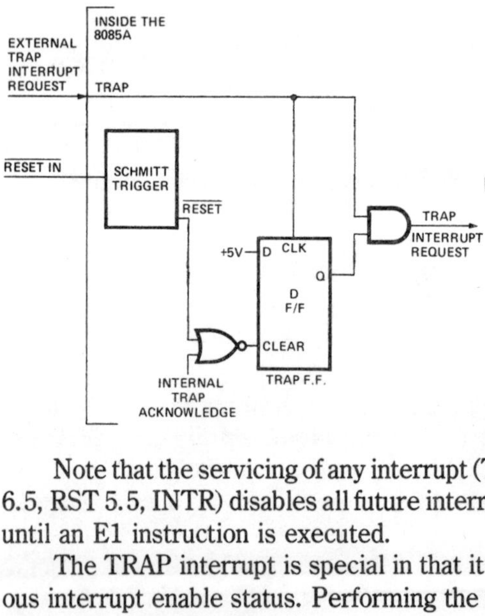

Fig. 3-2. Trap interrupt.

Note that the servicing of any interrupt (TRAP, RST 7.5, RST 6.5, RST 5.5, INTR) disables all future interrupts (except TRAPs) until an E1 instruction is executed.

The TRAP interrupt is special in that it preserves the previous interrupt enable status. Performing the first RIM instruction following a TRAP interrupt allows you to determine whether interrupts were enabled or disabled prior to the TRAP. All subsequent RIM instructions provide current interrupt enable status.

The serial I/O system is also controlled by the RIM and SIM instructions. SID is read by RIM, and SIM sets the SOD data.

3.7 BASIC SYSTEM TIMING

The 8085A has a multiplexed Data Bus. ALE is used as a strobe to sample the lower 8-bits of address on the Data Bus. Figure 3-2 shows an instruction fetch, memory read and I/O write cycle (OUT). Note that during the I/O write and read cycle that the

I/O port address is copied on both the upper and lower half of the address.

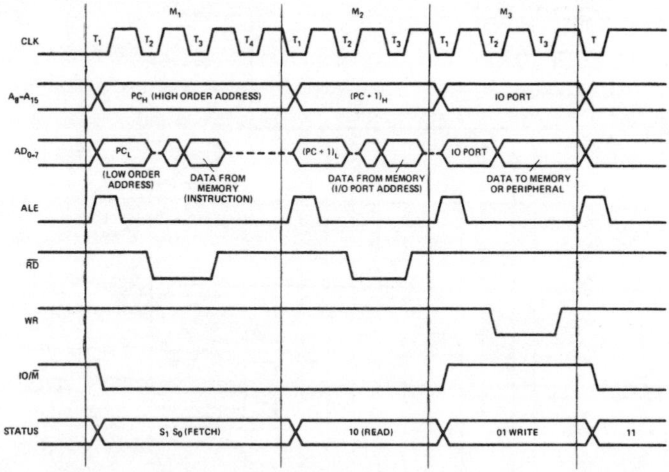

Fig. 3-3. 8085A basic system timing.

As in the 8080, the READY line is used to extend the read and write pulse lengths so that the 8085A can be used with slow memory. Hold causes the CPU to relinquish the bus when it is through with it by floating the Address and Data Buses.

3.8 SYSTEM INTERFACE

8085A family includes memory components, which are directly compatible to the 8085A CPU. For example, a system consisting of the three chips, 8085A, 8156, and 8355 will have the following features:

- 2K Bytes ROM
- 256 Bytes RAM
- 1 Timer/Counter
- 4 8-bit I/O Ports
- 1 6-bit I/O Port
- 4 Interrupt Levels
- Serial In/Serial Out Ports

This minimum system, using the standard I/O technique is as shown in Figure 3-4.

In addition to standard I/O, the memory mapped I/O offers an efficient I/O addressing technique. With this technique, an area of memory address space is assigned for I/O address, thereby, using

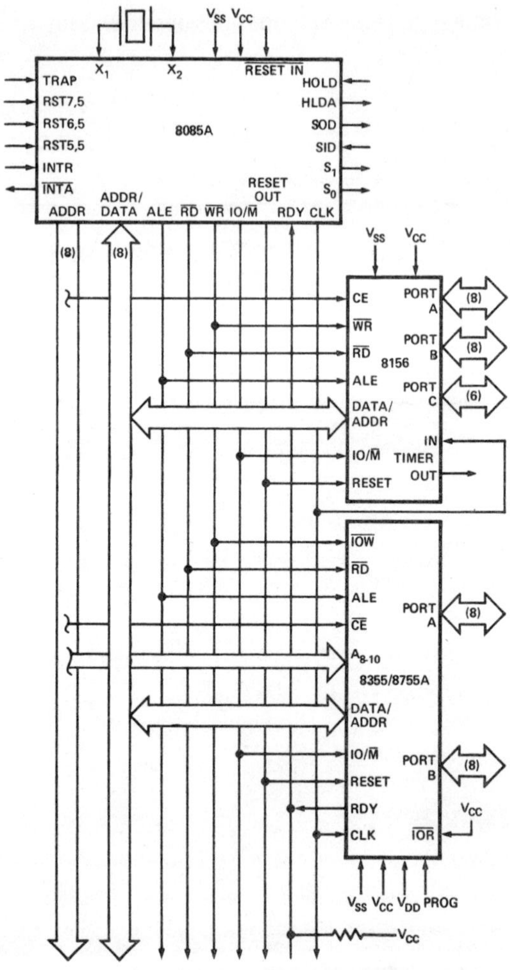

Fig. 3-4. 8085A minimum system (standard I/O technique).

the memory address for I/O manipulation. Figure 3-5A shows the system configuration of Memory Mapped I/O using 8085A.

The 8085A CPU can also interface with the standard memory that does *not* have the multiplexed address/data bus. It will require a simple 8212 (8-bit latch) as shown in Figure 3-5B.

3.9 DRIVING THE X_1 AND X_2 INPUTS

The user may drive the X_1 and X_2 inputs of the 8085A with a crystal, an external clock source or an RC network as shown below. The driving frequency must be twice the desired internal operating frequency (the 8085A would require a 6MHz crystal for 3MHz internal operation).

The 20pF capacitors are required to guarantee oscillation at the proper frequency during system startup.

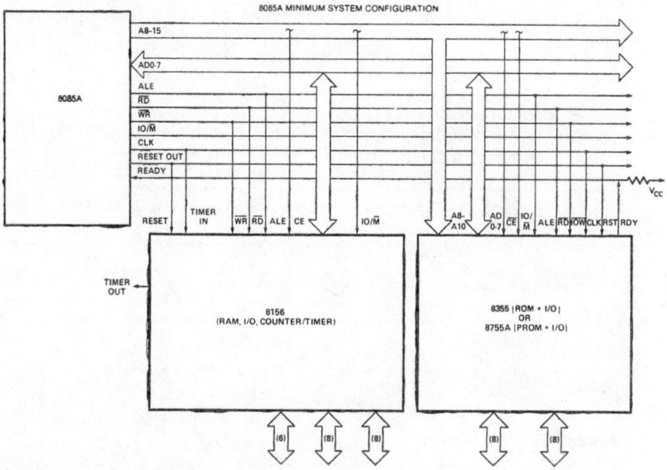

Fig. 3-5A: MCS-85 minimum system (memory-mapped I/O).

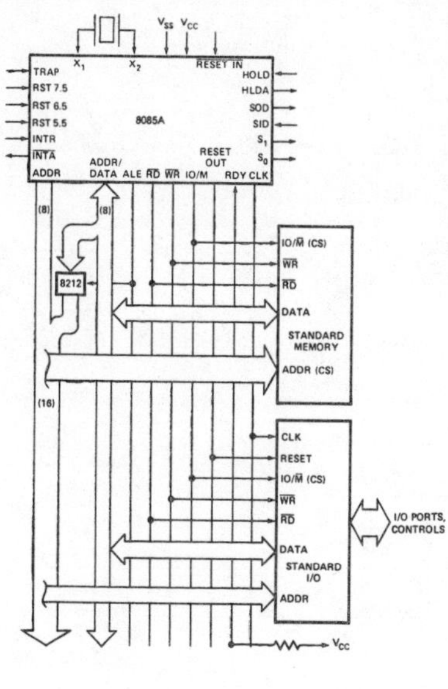

Fig. 3-5B: MCS-85 system (using standard memories).

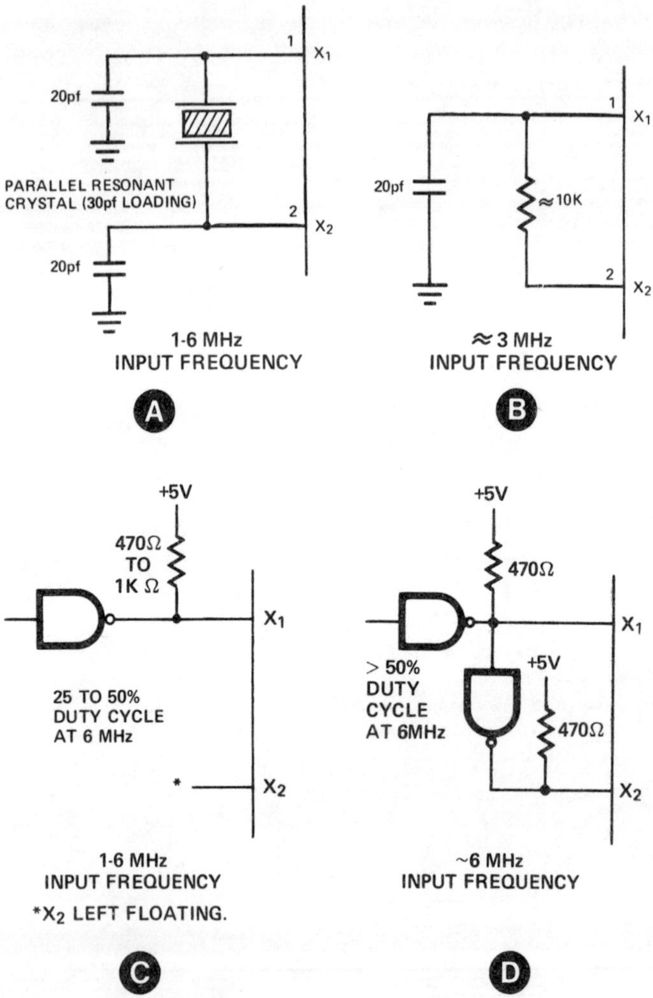

Fig. 3-6. Driving the clock inputs (X_1 and X_2) of 8085A.

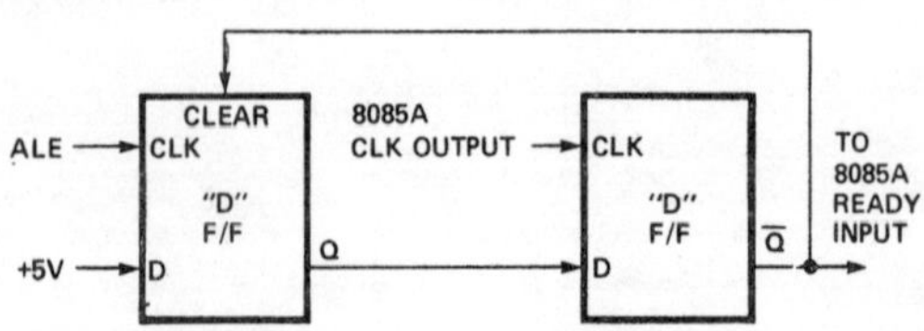

Fig. 3-7. Generation of a wait state for 8085A CPU.

Table 3-1. Characteristics of 8085A Microprocessor.

D.C. CHARACTERISTICS

(T_A = 0°C to 70°C; V_{CC} = 5V ±5%; V_{SS} = 0V; unless otherwise specified)

Symbol	Parameter	Min.	Max.	Units	Test Conditions
V_{IL}	Input Low Voltage	-0.5	+0.8	V	
V_{IH}	Input High Voltage	2.0	V_{CC} +0.5	V	
V_{OL}	Output Low Voltage		0.45	V	I_{OL} = 2mA
V_{OH}	Output High Voltage	2.4		V	I_{OH} = -400μA
I_{CC}	Power Supply Current		170	mA	
I_{IL}	Input Leakage		±10	μA	$V_{in} = V_{CC}$
I_{LO}	Output Leakage		±10	μA	$0.45V \leq V_{out} \leq V_{CC}$
V_{ILR}	Input Low Level, RESET	-0.5	+0.8	V	
V_{IHR}	Input High Level, RESET	2.4	V_{CC} +0.5	V	
V_{HY}	Hysteresis, RESET	0.25		V	

Bus Timing Specification as a T_{CYC} Dependent

t_{AL}	–	(1/2) T - 50	MIN
t_{LA}	–	(1/2) T - 60	MIN
t_{LL}	–	(1/2) T - 20	MIN
t_{LCK}	–	(1/2) T - 60	MIN
t_{LC}	–	(1/2) T - 30	MIN
t_{AD}	–	(5/2 + N) T - 225	MAX
t_{RD}	–	(3/2 + N) T - 180	MAX
t_{RAE}	–	(1/2) T - 10	MIN
t_{CA}	–	(1/2) T - 40	MIN
t_{DW}	–	(3/2 + N) T – 60	MIN
t_{WD}	–	(1/2) T - 60	MIN
t_{CC}	–	(3/2 + N) T – 80	MIN
t_{CL}	–	(1/2) T - 110	MIN
t_{ARY}	–	(3/2) T - 260	MAX
t_{HACK}	–	(1/2) T - 50	MIN
t_{HABF}	–	(1/2) T + 50	MAX
t_{HABE}	–	(1/2) T + 50	MAX
t_{AC}	–	(2/2) T - 50	MIN
t_1	–	(1/2) T - 80	MIN
t_2	–	(1/2) T - 40	MIN
t_{RV}	–	(3/2) T - 80	MIN

NOTE: N is equal to the total WAIT states.
T = t_{CYC}.

A.C. CHARACTERISTICS (T_A = 0°C to 70°C; V_{CC} = 5V ±5%; V_{SS} = 0V)

Symbol	Parameter	Min.	Max.	Units	Test Conditions
T_{CYC}	CLK Cycle Period	320	2000	ns	See notes 1, 2, 3, 4, 5
t_1	CLK Low Time	80		ns	
t_2	CLK High Time	120		ns	
t_r, t_f	CLK Rise and Fall Time		30	ns	
t_{AL}	Address Valid Before Trailing Edge of ALE	110		ns	
t_{LA}	Address Hold Time After ALE	100		ns	
t_{LL}	ALE Width	140		ns	
t_{LCK}	ALE Low During CLK High	100		ns	
t_{LC}	Trailing Edge of ALE to Leading Edge of Control	130		ns	
t_{AFR}	Address Float After Leading Edge of $\overline{READ}$ ($\overline{INTA}$)		0	ns	
t_{AD}	Valid Address to Valid Data In		575	ns	
t_{RD}	$\overline{READ}$ (or $\overline{INTA}$) to Valid Data		300	ns	
t_{RDH}	Data Hold Time After $\overline{READ}$ ($\overline{INTA}$)	0		ns	
t_{RAE}	Trailing Edge of $\overline{READ}$ to Re-Enabling of Address	150		ns	T_{CYC} = 320ns;
t_{CA}	Address (A8–A15) Valid After Control	120		ns	C_L = 150 pF

Table 3-1. Characteristics of 8085A Microprocessor (continued from page 81).

t_{DW}	Data Valid to Trailing Edge of $\overline{WRITE}$	420		ns
t_{WD}	Data Valid After Trailing Edge of $\overline{WRITE}$	100		ns
t_{CC}	Width of Control Low ($\overline{RD}$, $\overline{WR}$, $\overline{INTA}$)	400		ns
t_{CL}	Trailing Edge of Control to Leading Edge of ALE	50		ns
t_{ARY}	READY Valid From Address Valid		220	ns
t_{RYS}	READY Setup Time to Leading Edge of CLK	110		ns
t_{RYH}	READY Hold Time	0		ns
t_{HACK}	HLDA Valid to Trailing Edge of CLK	110		ns
t_{HABF}	Bus Float After HLDA		210	ns
t_{HABE}	HLDA to Bus Enable		210	ns
t_{LDR}	ALE to Valid Data In		460	ns
t_{RV}	Control Trailing Edge to Leading Edge of Next Control	400		ns
t_{AC}	Address Valid to Leading Edge of Control	270		ns
t_{HDS}	HOLD Setup Time to Trailing Edge of CLK	170		ns
t_{HDH}	HOLD Hold Time	0		ns
t_{INS}	INTR Setup Time to Falling Edge of CLK Also RST and TRAP	160		ns
t_{INH}	INTR Hold Time	0		ns

NOTES:
1. A8-15 Address Specs apply to IO/$\overline{M}$, S0 and S1.
2. For all output timing where $C_L \neq 150pf$ use the following correction factors:
   $25pf \leq C_L < 150pf$: -.10 ns/pf
   $150pf < C_L \leq 300pf$: +.30 ns/pf
3. Output timings are measured with purely capacitive load.
4. All timings are measured at output voltage V_L = .8V, V_H = 2.0V, and 1.5V with 20ns rise and fall time on inputs.
5. To calculate timing specifications at other values of T_{CYC} use the table in Table 2.

RC Mode causes a large drift in clock frequency because of the variation in on-chip timing generation parameters. Use of RC Mode should be limited to an application, which can tolerate a wide frequency variation.

3.10 ABSOLUTE MAXIMUM RATINGS*

Ambient Temperature Under Bias..............0°C to 70°C
Storage Temperature.......................−65°C to +150°C
Voltage on Any Pin
With Respect to Ground......................−0.3 to +7V
Power Dissipation..1.5 Watt

*COMMENT: Stresses above those listed under "Absolute Maximum Ratings" may cause permanent damage to the device. This is a stress rating only and functional operation of the device at these or any other conditions above those indicated in the operational sections of this specification is not implied. Exposure to absolute maximum rating conditions for extended periods may affect device reliability.

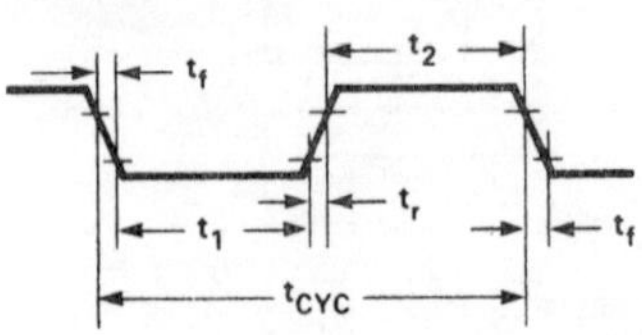

Fig. 3-8. Clock timing waveform.

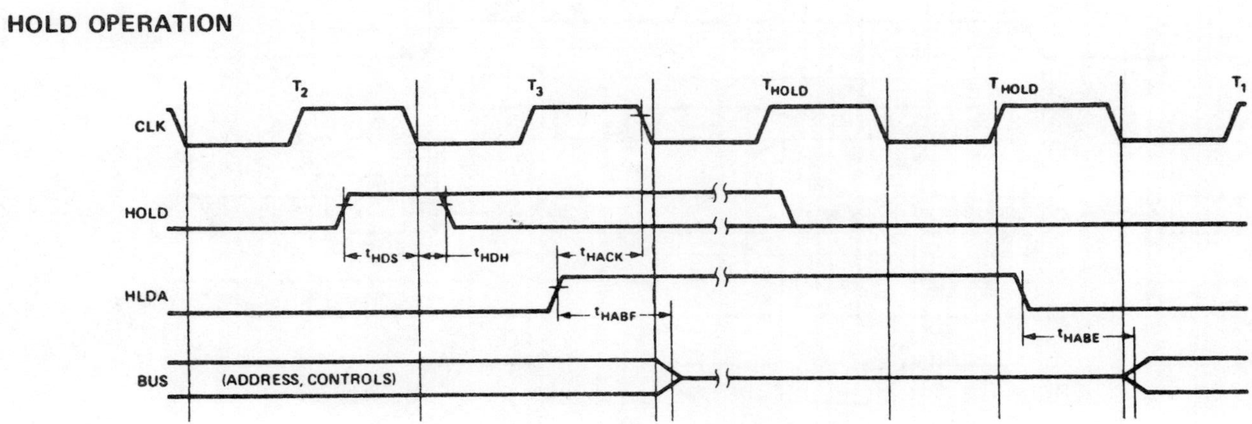

Fig. 3-9. 8085A hold timing.

READ OPERATION

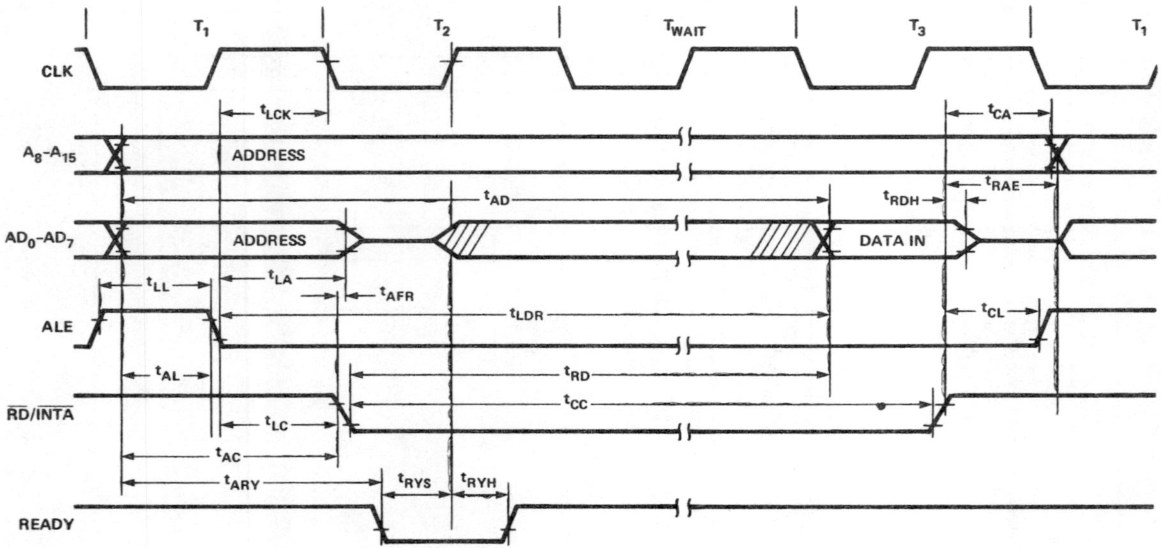

WRITE OPERATION

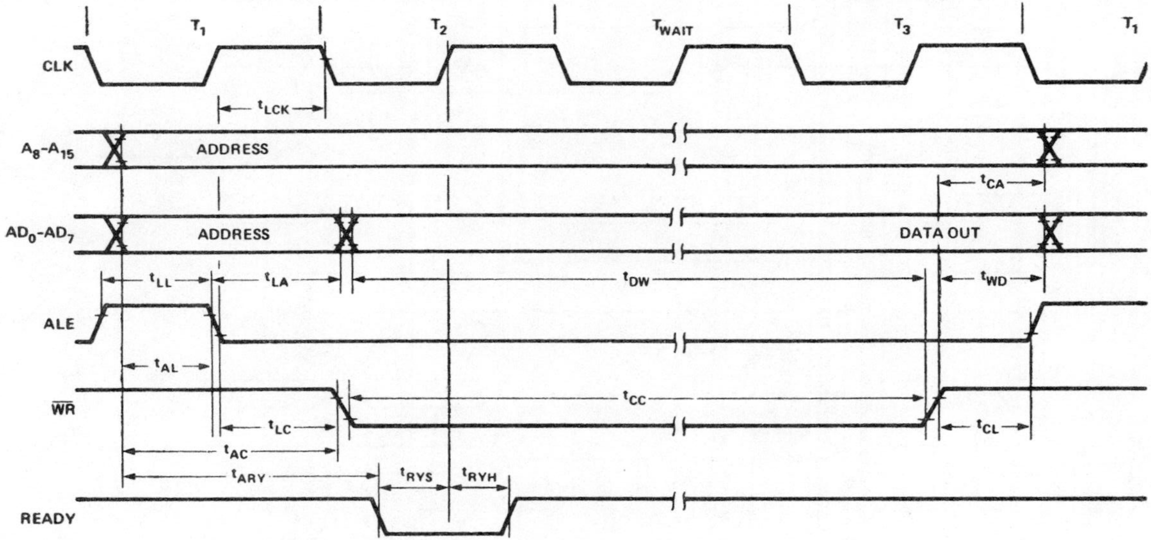

Fig. 3-10. 8085A bus timing.

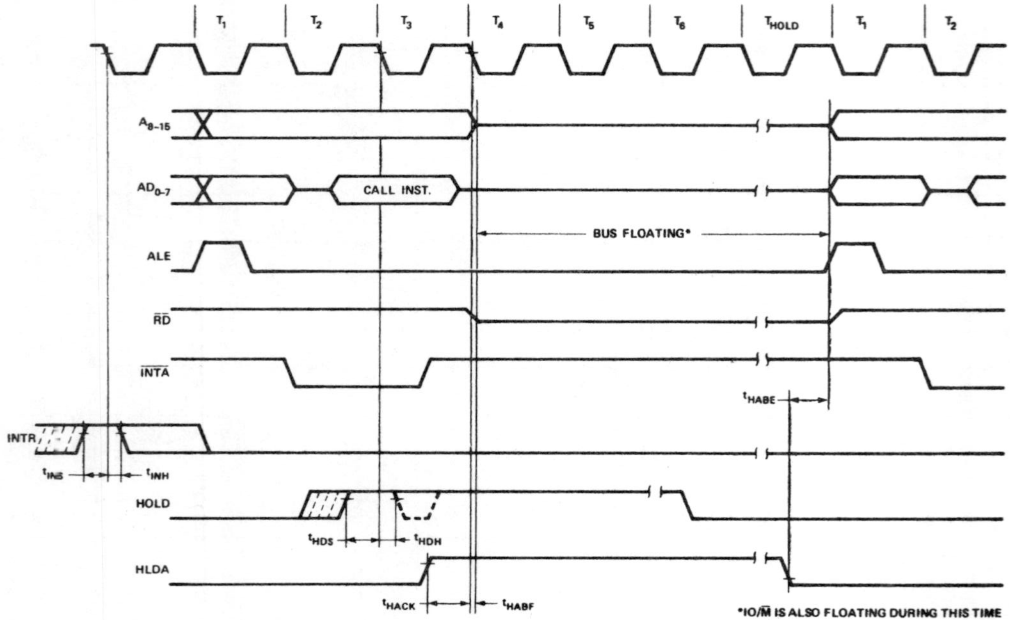

Fig. 3-11. 8085A interrupt and hold timing.

Chapter 4

8085A Instruction Set

4.1 INTRODUCTION

A computer, no matter how sophisticated, can only do what it is "told" to do. One "tells" the computer what to do via a series of coded instructions referred to as a *program*. The realm of the programmer is referred to as *software*, in contrast to the *hardware* that comprises the actual computer equipment. A computer's software refers to all of the programs that have been written for that computer.

When a computer is designed, the engineers provide the *central processing unit* (CPU) with the ability to perform a particular set of operations. The CPU is designed such that a specific operation is performed when the CPU control logic decodes a particular instruction. Consequently, the operations that can be performed by a CPU define the computer's Instruction Set.

Each computer instruction allows the programmer to initiate the performance of a specific operation. All computers implement certain arithmetic operations in their instruction set, such as an instruction to add the contents of two registers. Often logical operations (e.g., OR the contents of two registers) and register operate instructions (e.g., increment a register) are included in the instruction set. A computer's instruction set will also have instructions that move data between registers, between a register and memory, and between a register and an I/O device. Most instruction sets also provide *conditional instructions*. A conditional instruction specifies an operation to be performed only if certain conditions have been met; for example, jump to a particular instruction if the result of the last operation was zero. Conditional instructions provide a program with a decision-making capability.

By logically organizing a sequence of instructions into a coherent program, the programmer can "tell" the computer to perform a very specific and useful function.

The computer, however, can only execute programs whose instructions are in a binary coded form (i.e., a series of 1's and 0's), that is called ***machine code***. Because it would be extremely cumbersome to program in machine code, programming languages have been developed. There are programs available which convert the programming language instructions into machine code that can be interpreted by the processor.

One type of programming language is Assembly Language. A unique assembly language mnemonic is assigned to each of the computer's instructions. The programmer can write a program (called the *source program*) using these mnemonics and certain operands; the source program is then converted into machine instructions (called the *object code*). Each assembly language instruction is converted into one machine code instruction (1 or more bytes) by an *assembler* program. Assembly languages are usually machine dependent (i.e., they are usually able to run on only one type of computer).

4.2 THE 8085A INSTRUCTION SET

The 8085A instruction set includes five different types of instructions:

- Data Transfer Group—move data between registers or between memory and registers
- Arithmetic Group—add, subtract, increment or decrement data in registers or in memory
- Logical Group—AND, OR, EXCLUSIVE-OR, compare, rotate or complement data in registers or in memory
- Branch Group—conditional and unconditional jump instructions, subroutine call instructions and return instructions
- Stack, I/O and Machine Control Group—includes I/O instructions, as well as instructions for maintaining the stack and internal control flags.

Instruction and Data Formats:

Memory for the 8085A is organized into 8-bit quantities, called *bytes*. Each byte has a unique 16-bit binary address corresponding to its sequential position in memory.

The 8085A can directly address up to 65,536 bytes of memory, which may consist of both read-only memory (ROM) elements and random-access memory (RAM) elements (read/write memory).

Data in the 8085A is stored in the form of 8-bit binary integers:

DATA WORD

D_7	D_6	D_5	D_4	D_3	D_2	D_1	D_0
MSB							LSB

When a register or data word contains a binary number, it is necessary to establish the order in which the bits of the number are written. In the Intel 8085A, BIT 0 is referred to as the *least significant bit* (LSB), and BIT 7 (of an 8 bit number) is referred to as the *most significant bit* (MSB).

The 8085A program instructions may be one, two or three bytes in length. Multiple byte instructions must be stored in successive memory locations; the address of the first byte is always used as the address of the instructions. The exact instruction format will depend on the particular operation to be executed.

Single Byte Instructions

	D_7 … D_0	Op Code

Two-Byte Instructions

Byte One	D_7 … D_0	Op Code
Byte Two	D_7 … D_0	Data or Address

Three-Byte Instructions

Byte One	D_7 … D_0	Op Code
Byte Two	D_7 … D_0	Data or
Byte Three	D_7 … D_0	Address

Addressing Modes:

Often the data that is to be operated on is stored in memory. When multi-byte numeric data is used, the data, like instructions, is stored in successive memory locations, with the least significant byte first, followed by increasingly significant bytes. The 8085A has four different modes for addressing data stored in memory or in registers:

- Direct—Bytes 2 and 3 of the instruction contain the exact memory address of the data item (the low-order bits of the address are in byte 2, the high-order bits in byte 3).

- Register—The instruction specifies the register or register-pair in which the data is located.
- Register Indirect—The instruction specifies a register-pair which contains the memory address where the data is located (the high-order bits of the address are in the first register of the pair, the low-order bits in the second).
- Immediate—The instruction contains the data itself. This is either an 8-bit quantity or a 16-bit quantity (least significant byte first, most significant byte second).

Unless directed by an interrupt or branch instruction, the execution of instructions proceeds through consecutively increasing memory locations. A branch instruction can specify the address of the next instruction to be executed in one of two ways:

- Direct—The branch instruction contains the address of the next instruction to be executed. (Except for the 'RST' instruction, byte 2 contains the low-order address and byte 3 the high-order address.)
- Register indirect—The branch instruction indicates a register-pair which contains the address of the next instruction to be executed. (The high-order bits of the address are in the first register of the pair, the low-order bits in the second.)

The RST instruction is a special one-byte call instruction (usually used during interrupt sequences). RST includes a three-bit field; program control is transferred to the instruction whose address is eight times the contents of this three-bit field.

Condition Flags:

There are five condition flags associated with the execution of instructions on the 8085A. They are Zero, Sign, Parity, Carry, and Auxiliary Carry, and are each represented by a 1-bit register in the CPU. A flag is "set" by forcing the bit to 1; "reset" by forcing the bit to 0.

Unless indicated otherwise, when an instruction affects a flag, it affects it in the following manner:

Zero: If the result of an instruction has the value 0, this flag is set; otherwise it is reset.

Sign: If the most significant bit of the result of the operation has the value 1, this flag is set; otherwise it is reset.

Parity:	If the modulo 2 sum of the bits of the result of the operation is 0, (i.e., if the result has even parity), this flag is set; otherwise it is reset (i.e., if the result has odd parity).
Carry:	If the instruction resulted in a carry (from addition), or a borrow (from subtraction or a comparison) out of the high-order bit, this flag is set; otherwise it is reset.
Auxiliary Carry:	If the instruction caused a carry out of bit 3 and into bit 4 of the resulting value, the auxiliary carry is set; otherwise it is reset. This flag is affected by single precision additions, subtractions, increments, decrements, comparisons, and logical operations, but is principally used with additions and increments preceding a DAA (Decimal Adjust Accumulator) instruction.

Symbols and Abbreviations:

The following symbols and abbreviations are used in the subsequent description of the 8085A instructions:

SYMBOLS	MEANING
accumulator	Register A
addr	16-bit address quantity
data	8-bit data quantity
data 16	16-bit data quantity
byte 2	The second byte of the instruction
byte 3	The third byte of the instruction
port	8-bit address of an I/O device
r,r1,r2	One of the registers A,B,C,D,E,H,L
DDD,SSS	The bit pattern designating one of the registers A, B, C, D, E, H, L (DDD=destination, SSS= source):

DDD or SSS	REGISTER NAME
111	A
000	B
001	C
010	D
011	E
100	H
101	L

rp One of the register pairs:
B represents the B,C pair with B as the high-order register and C as the low-order register;
D represents the D, E pair with D as the high-order register and E as the low-order register;
H represents the H, L pair with H as the high-order register and L as the low-order register;
SP represents the 16-bit stack pointer register.

RP The bit pattern designating one of the register pairs B,D,H,SP:

RP	REGISTER PAIR
00	B-C
01	D-E
10	H-L
11	SP

rh The first (high-order) register of a designated register pair.

rl The second (low-order) register of a designated register pair.

PC 16-bit program counter register (PCH and PCL are used to refer to the high-order and low-order 8 bits respectively).

SP 16-bit stack pointer register (SPH and SPL are used to refer to the high-order and low-order 8 bits respectively).

rm Bit m of the register r (bits are number 7 through 0 from left to right).

Z,S,P,CY,AC The condition flags:
Zero,
Sign,
Parity,
Carry,
and Auxiliary Carry, respectively.

( ) The contents of the memory location or registers enclosed in the parentheses.

← "Is transferred to"

∧ Logical AND

$\veebar$	Exclusive OR
$\vee$	Inclusive OR
+	Addition
−	Two's complement subtraction
*	Multiplication
$\leftrightarrow$	"Is exchanged with"
—	The one's complement (e.g., (A))
n	The restart number 0 through 7
NNN	The binary representation 000 through 111 for restart number 0 through 7 respectively.

Description Format:

The following pages provide a detailed description of the instruction set of the 8085A. Each instruction is described in the following manner:

1. The MCS 85 macro assembler format, consisting of the instruction mnemonic and operand fields, is printed in BOLDFACE on the left side of the first line.
2. The name of the instruction is enclosed in parenthesis on the right side of the first line.
3. The next line(s) contain a symbolic description of the operation of the instruction.
4. This is followed by a narrative description of the operation of the instruction.
5. The following line(s) contain the binary fields and patterns that comprise the machine instruction.
6. The last four lines contain incidental information about the execution of the instruction. The number of machine cycles and states required to execute the instruction are listed first. If the instruction has two possible execution times, as in a Conditional Jump, both times will be listed, separated by a slash. Next, any significant data addressing modes are listed. The last line lists any of the five Flags that are affected by the execution of the instruction.

Data Transfer Group:

This group of instructions transfers data to and from registers and memory. Condition flags are not affected by any instruction in this group.

MOV r1, r2 (Move Register)

(r1) $\leftarrow$ (r2)

The content of register r2 is moved to register r1.

0	1	D	D	D	S	S	S

Cycles:1
States:4
Addressing:register
Flags:none

MOV r, M (Move from memory)

(r)←((H) (L))

The content of the memory location, whose address is in registers H and L, is moved to register r.

0	1	D	D	D	1	1	0

Cycles:2
States:7
Addressing:reg. indirect
Flags:none

MOV M, r (Move to memory)

((H) (L))←(r)

The content of register r is moved to the memory location whose address is in registers H and L.

0	1	1	1	0	S	S	S

Cycles:2
States:7
Addressing:reg. indirect
Flags:none

MVI r, data (Move Immediate)

(r)←(byte 2)

The content of byte 2 of the instruction is moved to register r.

0	0	D	D	D	1	1	0
data							

Cycles:2
States:7
Addressing:immediate
Flags:none

MVI M, data (Move to memory immediate)

((H) (L))←(byte 2)

The content of byte 2 of the instruction is moved to the memory location whose address is in registers H and L.

0	0	1	1	0	1	1	0
data							

Cycles:3
States:10
Addressing:immed./reg. indirect
Flags:none

LXI rp, data 16 (Load register pair immediate)

(rh)← (byte 3),
(rl) ←(byte 2)

Byte 3 of the instruction is moved into the high-order register (rh) of the register pair rp. Byte 2 of the instruction is moved into the low-order register (rl) of the register pair rp.

0	0	R	P	0	0	0	1
low-order data							
high-order data							

Cycles:3
States:10
Addressing:immediate
Flags:none

LDA addr (Load Accumulator direct)

(A)←((byte 3)(byte 2))

The content of the memory location, whose address is specified in byte 2 and byte 3 of the instruction, is moved to register A.

0	0	1	1	1	0	1	0
low-order addr							
high-order addr							

Cycles:4
States:13
Addressing:direct
Flags:none

STA addr (Store Accumulator direct)

((byte 3) (byte 2))←(A)

The content of the accumulator is moved to the memory location whose address is specified in byte 2 and byte 3 of the instruction.

0	0	1	1	0	0	1	0
low-order addr							
high-order addr							

Cycles:4
States:13
Addressing:direct
Flags:none

LHLD addr (Load H and L direct)
(L) ← ((byte 3)(byte 2))
(H) ← ((byte 3)(byte2) + 1)

The content of the memory location, whose address is specified in byte 2 and byte 3 of the instruction, is moved to register L. The content of the memory location at the succeeding address is moved to register H.

0	0	1	0	1	0	1	0
low-order addr							
high-order addr							

Cycles:5
States:16
Addressing:direct
Flags:none

SHLD addr (Store H and L direct)
((byte 3)(byte 2)) ← (L)
((byte 3)(byte 2) + 1) ← (H)
The content of register L is moved to the memory location whose address is specified in byte 2 and byte 3. The content of register H is moved to the succeeding memory location.

0	0	1	0	0	0	1	0
low-order addr							
high-order addr							

Cycles:5
States:16
Addressing:direct
Flags:none

LDAX rp (Load accumulator indirect)
(A) ← ((rp))

The content of the memory location, whose address is in the register pair rp, is moved to register A. Note: only register pairs rp=B (registers B and C) or rp=D (registers D and E) may be specified.

0	0	R	P	1	0	1	0

Cycles:2
States:7
Addressing:reg. indirect
Flags:none

STAX rp (Store accumulator indirect)

((rp)) ← (A)

The content of register A is moved to the memory location whose address is in the register pair rp. Note: only register pairs rp=B (registers B and C) or rp=D (registers D and E) may be specified.

0	0	R	P	0	0	1	0

Cycles:2
States:7
Addressing:reg. indirect
Flags:none

XCHG (Exchange H and L with D and E)

(H) ↔ (D)

(L) ↔ (E)

The contents of registers H and L are exchanged with the contents of registers D and E.

1	1	1	0	1	0	1	1

Cycles:1
States:4
Addressing:register
Flags:none

Arithmetic Group:

This group of instructions performs arithmetic operations on data in registers and memory.

Unless indicated otherwise, all instructions in this group affect the Zero, Sign, Parity, Carry, and Auxiliary Carry flags according to the standard rules.

All subtraction operations are performed via two's complement arithmetic and set the carry flag to one to indicate a borrow and clear it to indicate no borrow.

ADD r (Add Register)

$(A) \leftarrow (A) + (r)$

The content of register r is added to the content of the accumulator. The result is placed in the accumulator.

1	0	0	0	0	S	S	S

Cycles:1
States:4
Addressing:register
Flags:Z,S,P,CY,AC

ADD M (Add memory)

$(A) \leftarrow (A) + ((H)\ (L))$

The content of the memory location whose address is contained in the H and L registers is added to the content of the accumulator. The result is placed in the accumulator.

1	0	0	0	0	1	1	0

Cycles:2
States:7
Addressing:reg. indirect
Flags:Z,S,P,CY,AC

ADI data (Add immediate)

$(A) \leftarrow (A) + (\text{byte } 2)$

The content of the second byte of the instruction is added to the content of the accumulator. The result is placed in the accumulator.

1	1	0	0	0	1	1	0
data							

Cycles:2
States:7
Addressing:immediate
Flags:Z,S,P,CY,AC

ADC r (Add Register with carry)

$(A) \leftarrow (A) + (r) + (CY)$

The content of register r and the content of the carry bit are added to the content of the accumulator. The result is placed in the accumulator.

1	0	0	0	1	S	S	S

Cycles:1
States:4
Addressing:register
Flags:Z,S,P,CY,AC

ADC M (Add memory with carry)

(A)←(A) + ((H) (L)) + (CY)

The content of the memory location whose address is contained in the H and L registers and the content of the CY flag are added to the accumulator. The result is placed in the accumulator.

1	0	0	0	1	1	1	0

Cycles:2
States:7
Addressing:reg. indirect
Flags:Z,S,P,CY,AC

ACI data (Add immediate with carry)

(A)←(A) + (byte 2) + (CY)

The content of the second byte of the instruction and the content of the CY flag are added to the contents of the accumulator. The result is placed in the accumulator.

1	1	0	0	1	1	1	0
data							

Cycles:2
States:7
Addressing:immediate
Flags:Z,S,P,CY,AC

SUB r (Subtract Register)

(A)←(A) – (r)

The content of register r is subtracted from the content of the accumulator. The result is placed in the accumulator.

1	0	0	1	0	S	S	S

Cycles:1
States:4
Addressing:register
Flags:Z,S,P,CY,AC

SUB M (Subtract memory)

$(A) \leftarrow (A) - ((H)\ (L))$

The content of the memory location whose address is contained in the H and L registers is subtracted from the content of the accumulator. The result is placed in the accumulator.

1	0	0	1	0	1	1	0

Cycles:2
States:7
Addressing:reg. indirect
Flags:Z,S,P,CY,AC

SUI data (Subtract immediate)

$(A) \leftarrow (A) - (\text{byte } 2)$

The content of the second byte of the instruction is subtracted from the content of the accumulator. The result is placed in the accumulator.

1	1	0	1	0	1	1	0
data							

Cycles:2
States:7
Addressing:immediate
Flags:Z,S,P,CY,AC

SBB r (Subtract Register with borrow)

$(A) \leftarrow (A) - (r) - (CY)$

The content of register r and the content of the CY flag are both subtracted from the accumulator. The result is placed in the accumulator.

1	0	0	1	1	S	S	S

Cycles:1
States:4
Addressing:register
Flags:Z,S,P,CY,AC

SBB M (Subtract memory with borrow)

$(A) \leftarrow (A) - ((H)\ (L)) - (CY)$

The content of the memory location whose address is contained in the H and L registers and the content of the CY flag are both subtracted from the accumulator. The result is placed in the accumulator.

1	0	0	1	1	1	1	0

Cycles:2
States:7
Addressing:reg. indirect
Flags:Z,S,P,CY,AC

SBI data (Subtract immediate with borrow)

(A)←(A) – (byte 2) – (CY)

The contents of the second byte of the instruction and the contents of the CY flag are both subtracted from the accumulator. The result is placed in the accumulator.

1	1	0	1	1	1	1	0
data							

Cycles:2
States:7
Addressing:immediate
Flags:Z,S,P,CY,AC

INR r (Increment Register)

(r)←(r) + 1

The content of register r is incremented by one.
Note: All condition flags except CY are affected.

0	0	D	D	D	1	0	0

Cycles:1
States:4
Addressing:register
Flags:Z,S,P,AC

INR M (Increment memory)

((H) (L))←((H) (L)) + 1

The content of the memory location whose address is contained in the H and L registers is incremented by one.
Note: All condition flags except CY are affected.

0	0	1	1	0	1	0	0

Cycles:3
States:10
Addressing:reg. indirect
Flags:Z,S,P,AC

DCR r (Decrement Register)

(r)←(r) – 1

The content of register r is decremented by one.
Note: All condition flags except CY are affected.

0	0	D	D	D	1	0	1

Cycles:1
States:4
Addressing:register
Flags:Z,S,P,AC

DCR M (Decrement memory)

$((H)\ (L)) \leftarrow ((H)\ (L)) - 1$

The content of the memory location whose address is contained in the H and L registers is decremented by one.
Note: All condition flags except CY are affected.

0	0	1	1	0	1	0	1

Cycles:3
States:10
Addressing:reg. indirect
Flags:Z,S,P,AC

INX rp (increment register pair)

$(rh)\ (rl) \leftarrow (rh)\ (rl) + 1$

The content of the register pair rp is incremented by one.
Note: No condition flags are affected.

0	0	R	P	0	0	1	1

Cycles:1
States:6
Addressing:register
Flags:none

DCX rp (Decrement register pair)

$(rh)\ (rl) \leftarrow (rh)\ (rl) - 1$

The content of the register pair rp is decremented by one.
Note: No condition flags are affected.

0	0	R	P	1	0	1	1

Cycles:1
States:6
Addressing:register
Flags:none

DAD rp (Add register pair to H and L)

$(H)\ (L) \leftarrow (H)\ (L) + (rh)\ (rl)$

The content of the register pair rp is added to the content of the register pair H and L. The result is placed in the register pair H and L. Note: Only the CY flag is affected. It is set if there is a carry out of the double precision add; otherwise it is reset.

0	0	R	P	1	0	0	1

Cycles:3
States:10
Addressing:register
Flags:CY

DAA (Decimal Adjust Accumulator)

The eight-bit number in the accumulator is adjusted to form two four-bit Binary-Coded-Decimal digits by the following process:

1. If the value of the least significant 4 bits of the accumulator is greater than 9 or if the AC flag is set, 6 is added to the accumulator.
2. If the value of the most significant 4 bits of the accumulator is now greater than 9, or if the CY flag is set, 6 is added to the most significant 4 bits of the accumulator.

NOTE: All flags are affected.

0	0	1	0	0	1	1	1

Cycles:1
States:4
Flags:Z,S,P,CY,AC

Logical Group:

This group of instructions performs logical (Boolean) operations on data in registers and memory and on condition flags.

Unless indicated otherwise, all instructions in this group affect the Zero, Sign, Parity, Auxiliary Carry, and Carry flags according to the standard rules.

ANA r (AND Register)

$(A) \leftarrow (A) \wedge (r)$

The content of register r is logically anded with the content of the accumulator. The result is placed in the accumulator. The CY flag is cleared and AC is set.

1	0	1	0	0	S	S	S

Cycles: 1
States: 4
Addressing: register
Flags: Z, S, P, CY, AC

ANAM (AND memory)

(A)←(A) ∧((H) L))

The contents of the memory location whose address is contained in the H and L registers is logically anded with the content of the accumulator. The result is placed in the accumulator. The CY flag is cleared and AC is set.

1	0	1	0	0	1	1	0

Cycles: 2
States: 7
Addressing: reg. indirect
Flags: Z, S, P, CY, AC

ANI data (AND immediate)

(A)← (A) ∧ (byte 2)

The content of the second byte of the instruction is logically anded with the contents of the accumulator. The result is placed in the accumulator. The CY flag is cleared and AC is set.

1	1	1	0	0	1	1	0
data							

Cycles:2
States:7
Addressing:immediate
Flags:Z,S,P,CY,AC

XRA r (Exclusive OR Register)

(A) ← (A) ⊽ (r)

The content of register r is exclusive-or'd with the content of the accumulator. The result is placed in the accumulator. The CY and AC flags are cleared.

1	0	1	0	1	S	S	S

Cycles:1
States:4
Addressing:register
Flags:Z,S,P,CY,AC

XRA M (Exclusive OR Memory)

$(A) \leftarrow (A) \forall ((H)\ (L))$

The content of the memory location whose address is contained in the H and L registers is exclusive-OR'd with the content of the accumulator. The result is placed in the accumulator. The CY and AC flags are cleared.

1	0	1	0	1	1	1	0

Cycles:2
States:7
Addressing:reg. indirect
Flags:Z,S,P,CY,AC

XRI data (Exclusive OR immediate)

$(A) \leftarrow (A) \forall (\text{byte } 2)$

The content of the second-byte of the instruction is exclusive-OR'd with the content of the accumulator. The result is placed in the accumulator. The CY and AC flags are cleared.

1	1	1	0	1	1	1	0
data							

Cycles:2
States:7
Addressing:immediate
Flags:Z,S,P,CY,AC

ORA r (OR Register)

$(A) \leftarrow (A) \vee (r)$

The content of register r is inclusive-OR'd with the content of the accumulator. The result is placed in the accumulator. The CY and AC flags are cleared.

1	0	1	1	0	S	S	S

Cycles:1
States:4
Addressing:register
Flags:Z,S,P,CY,AC

ORA M (OR memory)

$(A) \leftarrow (A) \vee ((H)\ (L))$

The content of the memory location whose address is contained in the H and L registers is inclusive-OR'd with the content of the accumulator. The result is placed in the accumulator. The CY and AC flags are cleared.

1	0	1	1	0	1	1	0

Cycles:2
States:7
Addressing:reg. indirect
Flags:Z,S,P,CY,AC

ORI data (OR Immediate)

$(A) \leftarrow (A) \vee (\text{byte } 2)$

The content of the second byte of the instruction is inclusive-OR'd with the content of the accumulator. The result is placed in the accumulator. The CY and AC flags are cleared.

1	1	1	1	0	1	1	0
data							

Cycles:2
States:7
Addressing:immediate
Flags:Z,S,P,CY,AC

CMP r (Compare Register)

$(A) - (r)$

The content of register r is subtracted from the accumulator. The accumulator remains unchanged. The condition flags are set as a result of the subtraction. The Z flag is set to 1 if $(A) = (r)$. The CY flag is set to 1 if $(A) < (r)$.

1	0	1	1	1	S	S	S

Cycles:1
States:4
Addressing:register
Flags:Z,S,P,CY,AC

CMP M (Compare memory)

$(A) - ((H)\ (L))$

The content of the memory location whose address is contained in the H and L registers is subtracted from the accumulator. The accumulator remains unchanged. The condition flags are set as a result of the subtraction. The Z flag is set to 1 if $(A) = ((H)\ (L))$. The CY flag is set to 1 if $(A) < ((H)\ (L))$.

1	0	1	1	1	1	1	0

Cycles:2
States:7
Addressing:reg. indirect
Flags:Z,S,P,CY,AC

CPI data (Compare immediate)

(A) – (byte 2)

The content of the second byte of the instruction is subtracted from the accumulator. The condition flags are set by the result of the subtraction. The Z flag is set to 1 if (A) = (byte 2). The CY flag is set to 1 if (A) < (byte 2).

1	1	1	1	1	1	1	0
data							

Cycles:2
States:7
Addressing:immediate
Flags:Z,S,P,CY,AC

RLC (Rotate left)

$(A_n+1) \leftarrow (A_n)$; $(A_0) \leftarrow (A_7)$
$(CY) \leftarrow (A_7)$

The content of the accumulator is rotated left one position. The low order bit and the CY flag are both set to the value shifted out of the high order bit position. Only the CY flag is affected.

0	0	0	0	0	1	1	1

Cycles:1
States:4
Flags:CY

RRC (Rotate right)

$(A_n) \leftarrow (A_{n+1})$; $(A_7) \leftarrow (A_0)$
$(CY) \leftarrow (A_0)$

The content of the accumulator is rotated right one position. The high order bit and the CY flag are both set to the value shifted out of the low order bit position. Only the CY flag is affected.

0	0	0	0	1	1	1	1

Cycles:1
States:4
Flags:CY

RAL (rotate left through carry)

$(A_{n+1}) \leftarrow (A_n)$; $(CY) \leftarrow (A_7)$

$(A_0) \leftarrow (CY)$

The content of the accumulator is rotated left one position through the CY flag. The low order bit is set equal to the CY flag and the CY flag is set to the value shifted out of the high order bit. Only the CY flag is affected.

0	0	0	1	0	1	1	1

Cycles:1
States:4
Flags:CY

RAR (Rotate right through carry)

$(A_n) \leftarrow (A_{n+1})$; $(CY) \leftarrow (A_0)$

$(A_7) \leftarrow (CY)$

The content of the accumulator is rotated right one position through the CY flag. The high order bit is set to the CY flag and the CY flag is set to the value shifted out of the low order bit. Only the CY flag is affected.

0	0	0	1	1	1	1	1

Cycles:1
States:4
Flags:CY

CMA (Complement accumulator)

$(A) \leftarrow (A)$

The contents of the accumulator are complemented (zero bits become 1, one bits become 0). No flags are affected.

0	0	1	0	1	1	1	1

Cycles:1
States:4
Flags:none

CMC (Complement carry)

$(CY) \leftarrow (\overline{CY})$

The CY flag is complemented. No other flags are affected.

0	0	1	1	1	1	1	1

Cycles:1
States:4
Flags:CY

STC (Set carry)

(CY)←1

The CY flag is set to 1. No other flags are affected.

0	0	1	1	0	1	1	1

Cycles:1
States:4
Flags:CY

Branch Group:

This group of instructions alter normal sequential program flow.

Condition flags are not affected by any instruction in this group.

The two types of branch instructions are unconditional and conditional. Unconditional transfers simply perform the specified operation on register PC (the program counter). Conditional transfers examine the status of one of the four processor flags to determine if the specified branch is to be executed. The conditions that may be specified are as follows:

CONDITION	CCC
NZ — not zero (Z = 0)	000
Z — zero (Z = 1)	001
NC — no carry (CY = 0)	010
C — carry (CY = 1)	011
PO — parity odd (P = 0)	100
PE — parity even (P = 1)	101
P — plus (S = 0)	110
M — minus (S = 1)	111

JMP addr (Jump)

(PC)← (byte 3) (byte 2)

Control is tranferred to the instruction whose address is specified in byte 3 and byte 2 of the current instruction.

1	1	0	0	0	0	1	1
low-order addr							
high-order addr							

Cycles:3
States:10
Addressing:immediate
Flags:none

Jcondition addr (Conditional jump)

If (CCC),

(PC) ← (byte 3) (byte 2)

If the specified condition is true, control is transferred to the instruction whose address is specified in byte 3 and byte 2 of the current instruction; otherwise, control continues sequentially.

1	1	C	C	C	0	1	0
low-order addr							
high-order addr							

Cycles:2/3
States:7/10
Addressing:immediate
Flags:none

CALL addr (Call)

((SP) – 1) ← (PCH)
((SP) – 2) ← (PCL)
(SP) ← (SP) – 2
(PC) ← (byte 3) (byte 2)

The high-order eight bits of the next instruction address are moved to the memory location whose address is one less than the content of register SP. The low-order eight bits of the next instruction address are moved to the memory location whose address is two less than the content of register SP. The content of register SP is decremented by 2. Control is transferred to the instruction whose address is specified in byte 3 and byte 2 of the current instruction.

1	1	0	0	1	1	0	1
low-order addr							
high-order addr							

Cycles:5
States:18
Addressing:immediate/reg. indirect
Flags:none

Ccondition addr (Condition call)

If (CCC),

((SP) – 1) ← (PCH)
((SP) – 2) ← (PCL)
(SP) ← (SP) – 2
(PC) ← (byte 3) (byte 2)

If the specified condition is true, the actions specified in the CALL instruction (see above) are performed; otherwise, control continues sequentially.

1 1	C C C	1 0 0
low-order addr		
high-order addr		

Cycles:2/5
States:9/18
Addressing:immediate/
reg. indirect
Flags:none

RET (Return)

(PCL) ← ((SP));
(PCH) ← ((SP) + 1);
(SP) ← (SP) + 2;

The content of the memory location whose address is specified in register SP is moved to the low-order eight bits of register PC. The content of the memory location whose address is one more than the content of register SP is moved to the high-order eight bits of register PC. The content of register SP is incremented by 2.

1 1 0 0 1 0 0 1

Cycles:3
States:10
Addressing:reg. indirect
Flags:none

Rcondition (Conditional return)

If (CCC),
(PCL) ← ((SP))
(PCH) ← ((SP) + 1)
(SP) ← (SP) + 2

If the specified condition is true, the actions specified in the RET instruction (see above) are performed; otherwise, control continues sequentially.

1 1	C C C	0 0 0

Cycles:1/3
States:6/12
Addressing:reg. indirect
Flags:none

RST n (Restart)

((SP) – 1)←(PCH)
((SP) – 2)←(PCL)
(SP)←(SP) – 2
(PC)←8*(NNN)

The high-order eight bits of the next instruction address are moved to the memory location whose address is one less than the content of register SP. The low-order eight bits of the next instruction address are moved to the memory location whose address is two less than the content of register SP. The content of register SP is decremented by two. Control is transferred to the instruction whose address is eight times the content of NNN.

1	1	N	N	N	1	1	1

Cycles:3
States:12
Addressing:reg. indirect
Flags:none

15	14	13	12	11	10	9	8	7	6	5	4	3	2	1	0
0	0	0	0	0	0	0	0	0	0	N	N	N	0	0	0

Program Counter After Restart

PCHL (Jump H and L indirect—move H and L to PC)

(PCH)←(H)
(PCL)←(L)

The content of register H is moved to the high-order eight bits of register PC. The content of register L is moved to the low-order eight bits of register PC.

1	1	1	0	1	0	0	1

Cycles:1
States:6
Addressing:register
Flags:none

Stack, I/O, and Machine Control Group:

This group of instructions performs, I/O, manipulates the Stack, and alters internal control flags.

Unless otherwise specified, condition flags are not affected by any instructions in this group.

PUSH rp (Push)

$((SP) - 1) \leftarrow (rh)$

$((SP) - 2) \leftarrow (rl)$

$(SP) \leftarrow (SP) - 2$

The content of the high-order register of register pair rp is moved to the memory location whose address is one less than the content of register SP. The content of low-order register of register pair rp is moved to the memory location whose address is two less than the content of register SP. The content of register SP is decremented by 2. Note: Register pair rp = SP may not be specified.

1	1	R	P	0	1	0	1

Cycles:3
States:12
Addressing:reg. indirect
Flags:none

PUSH PSW (Push processor status word)

$((SP) - 1) \leftarrow (A)$

$((SP) - 2)_0 \leftarrow (CY), \quad ((SP) - 2)_1 \leftarrow X$

$((SP) - 2)_2 \leftarrow (P), \quad ((SP) - 2)_3 \leftarrow X$

$((SP) - 2)_4 \leftarrow (AC), \quad ((SP) - 2)_5 \leftarrow X$

$((SP) - 2)_6 \leftarrow (Z), \quad ((SP) - 2)_7 \leftarrow (S)$

$(SP) \leftarrow (SP) - 2$ X: Undefined.

The content of register A is moved to the memory location whose address is one less than register SP. The contents of the condition flags are assembled into a processor status word and the word is moved to the memory location whose address is two less than the content of register SP. The content of register SP is decremented by two.

1	1	1	1	0	1	0	1

Cycles:3
States:12
Addressing:reg. indirect
Flags:none

FLAG WORD

D_7	D_6	D_5	D_4	D_3	D_2	D_1	D_0
S	Z	X	AC	X	P	X	CY

X: undefined

POP rp (Pop)

$(rl) \leftarrow ((SP))$

$(rh) \leftarrow ((SP) + 1)$

$(SP) \leftarrow (SP) + 2$

The content of the memory location, whose address is specified by the content of register SP, is moved to the low-order register of register pair rp. The content of the memory location, whose address is one more than the content of register SP, is moved to the high-order register of register pair rp. The content of register SP is incremented by 2. Note: Register pair rp = SP may not be specified.

1	1	R	P	0	0	0	1

Cycles:3
States:10
Addressing:reg. indirect
Flags:none

POP PSW (Pop processor status word)

$(CY) \leftarrow ((SP))_0$

$(P) \leftarrow ((SP))_2$

$(AC) \leftarrow ((SP))_4$

$(Z) \leftarrow ((SP))_6$

$(S) \leftarrow ((SP))_7$

$(A) \leftarrow ((SP) + 1)$

$(SP) \leftarrow (SP) + 2$

The content of the memory location whose address is specified by the content of register SP is used to restore the condition flags. The content of the memory location whose address is one more than the content of register SP is moved to register A. The content of register SP is incremented by 2.

1	1	1	1	0	0	0	1

Cycles:3
States:10
Addressing:reg. indirect
Flags:Z,S,P,CY,AC

XTHL (Exchange stack top with H and L)

$(L) \leftrightarrow ((SP))$

$(H) \leftrightarrow ((SP) + 1)$

The content of the L register is exchanged with the content of the memory location whose address is specified by the content of register SP. The content of the H register is exchanged with the content of the memory location whose address is one more than the content of register SP.

1	1	1	0	0	0	1	1

Cycles:5
States:16
Addressing:reg. indirect
Flags:none

SPHL (Move HL to SP)

(SP) ← (H) (L)

The contents of registers H and L (16 bits) are moved to register SP.

1	1	1	1	1	0	0	1

Cycles:1
States:6
Addressing:register
Flags:none

IN port (Input)

(A) ← (data)

The data placed on the eight bit bi-directional data bus by the specified port is moved to register A.

1	1	0	1	1	0	1	1
port							

Cycles:3
States:10
Addressing:direct
Flags:none

OUT port (Output)

(data) ← (A)

The content of register A is placed on the eight bit bi-directional data bus for transmission to the specified port.

1	1	0	1	0	0	1	1
port							

Cycles:3
States:10

Addressing:direct
Flags:none

EI (Enable interrupts)

The interrupt system is enabled following the execution of the next instruction.

1	1	1	1	1	0	1	1

Cycles:1
States:4
Flags:none

NOTE: Interrupts are not recognized during the EI instruction.

DI (Disable interrupts)

The interrupt system is disabled immediately following the execution of the DI instruction.

1	1	1	1	0	0	1	1

Cycles:1
States:4
Flags:none

NOTE: Interrupts are not recognized during the DI instruction.

HLT (Halt)

The processor is stopped. The registers and flags are unaffected.

0	0	1	1	0	1	1	0

Cycles:1
States:5
Flags:none

NOP (No op)

No operation is performed. The registers and flags are unaffected.

0	0	0	0	0	0	0	0

Cycles:1
States:4
Flags:none

RIM (Read Interrupt Mask)

After the execution of the RIM instruction, the accumulator is loaded with the restart interrupt masks, the Interrupt

Enable Flag, any pending interrupts, and the contents of the serial input data line (SID).

When the first RIM instruction is executed following a TRAP interrupt, the IE bit in the accumulator reflects the *previous* interrupt enable status before the TRAP occurred. The first RIM after a TRAP also has the action of releasing the IE status bit such that all subsequent RIM's provide current interrupt enable status.

IMPORTANT: The RIM instruction must be executed following a TRAP interrupt in order to restore the correct Interrupt Enable Status.

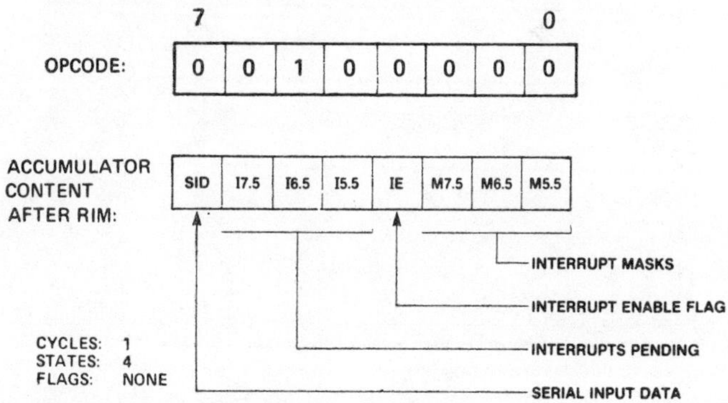

Fig. 4-1. RIM (read interrupt mask).

SIM (Set Interrupt Masks)

During execution of the SIM instruction, the contents of the accumulator will be used in programming the restart interrupt masks. Bits 0-2 will set/reset the mask bit for RST 5.5, 6.5, 7.5 of the interrupt mask register, if bit 3 is 1 ("set"). Bit 3 is a "Mask Set Enable" control.

Setting the mask (i.e. mask bit = 1) disables the corresponding interrupt.

	Set	Reset
RST 5.5 MASK	if bit 0 = 1	if bit 0 = 0
RST 6.5 MASK	bit 1 = 1	bit 1 = 0
RST 7.5 MASK	bit 2 = 1	bit 2 = 0

Fig. 4-2. SIM (set interrupt masks).

Table 4-1. Instruction Set Summary of 8085A.

Mnemonic	Description	D_7	D_6	D_5	D_4	D_3	D_2	D_1	D_0	Clock[2] Cycles
MOVE, LOAD, AND STORE										
MOVr1 r2	Move register to register	0	1	D	D	D	S	S	S	4
MOV M.r	Move register to memory	0	1	1	1	0	S	S	S	7
MOV r.M	Move memory to register	0	1	D	D	D	1	1	0	7
MVI r	Move immediate register	0	0	D	D	D	1	1	0	7
MVI M	Move immediate memory	0	0	1	1	0	1	1	0	10
LXI B	Load immediate register Pair B & C	0	0	0	0	0	0	0	1	10
LXI D	Load immediate register Pair D & E	0	0	0	1	0	0	0	1	10
LXI H	Load immediate register Pair H & L	0	0	1	0	0	0	0	1	10
LXI SP	Load immediate stack pointer	0	0	1	1	0	0	0	1	10
STAX B	Store A indirect	0	0	0	0	0	0	1	0	7
STAX D	Store A indirect	0	0	0	1	0	0	1	0	7
LDAX B	Load A indirect	0	0	0	0	1	0	1	0	7
LDAX D	Load A indirect	0	0	0	1	1	0	1	0	7
STA	Store A direct	0	0	1	1	0	0	1	0	13
LDA	Load A direct	0	0	1	1	1	0	1	0	13
SHLD	Store H & L direct	0	0	1	0	0	0	1	0	16
LHLD	Load H & L direct	0	0	1	0	1	0	1	0	16
XCHG	Exchange D & E H & L Registers	1	1	1	0	1	0	1	1	4
STACK OPS										
PUSH B	Push register Pair B & C on stack	1	1	0	0	0	1	0	1	12
PUSH D	Push register Pair D & E on stack	1	1	0	1	0	1	0	1	12
PUSH H	Push register Pair H & L on stack	1	1	1	0	0	1	0	1	12

Mnemonic	Description	D_7	D_6	D_5	D_4	D_3	D_2	D_1	D_0	Clock[2] Cycles
CPE	Call on parity even	1	1	1	0	1	1	0	0	9/18
CPO	Call on parity odd	1	1	1	0	0	1	0	0	9/18
RETURN										
RET	Return	1	1	0	0	1	0	0	1	10
RC	Return on carry	1	1	0	1	1	0	0	0	6/12
RNC	Return on no carry	1	1	0	1	0	0	0	0	6/12
RZ	Return on zero	1	1	0	0	1	0	0	0	6/12
RNZ	Return on no zero	1	1	0	0	0	0	0	0	6/12
RP	Return on positive	1	1	1	1	0	0	0	0	6/12
RM	Return on minus	1	1	1	1	1	0	0	0	6/12
RPE	Return on parity even	1	1	1	0	1	0	0	0	6/12
RPO	Return on parity odd	1	1	1	0	0	0	0	0	6/12
RESTART										
RST	Restart	1	1	A	A	A	1	1	1	12
INPUT/OUTPUT										
IN	Input	1	1	0	1	1	0	1	1	10
OUT	Output	1	1	0	1	0	0	1	1	10
INCREMENT AND DECREMENT										
INR r	Increment register	0	0	D	D	D	1	0	0	4
DCR r	Decrement register	0	0	D	D	D	1	0	1	4
INR M	Increment memory	0	0	1	1	0	1	0	0	10
DCR M	Decrement memory	0	0	1	1	0	1	0	1	10
INX B	Increment B & C registers	0	0	0	0	0	0	1	1	6
INX D	Increment D & E registers	0	0	0	1	0	0	1	1	6
INX H	Increment H & L registers	0	0	1	0	0	0	1	1	6
INX SP	Increment stack pointer	0	0	1	1	0	0	1	1	6
DCX B	Decrement B & C	0	0	0	0	1	0	1	1	6

PUSH PSW	Push A and Flags on stack	1	1	1	1	0	1	0	1	12
POP B	Pop register Pair B & C off stack	1	1	0	0	0	0	0	1	10
POP D	Pop register Pair D & E off stack	1	1	0	1	0	0	0	1	10
POP H	Pop register Pair H & L off stack	1	1	1	0	0	0	0	1	10
POP PSW	Pop A and Flags off stack	1	1	1	1	0	0	0	1	10
XTHL	Exchange top of stack. H & L	1	1	1	0	0	0	1	1	16
SPHL	H & L to stack pointer	1	1	1	1	1	0	0	1	6
JUMP										
JMP	Jump unconditional	1	1	0	0	0	0	1	1	10
JC	Jump on carry	1	1	0	1	1	0	1	0	7/10
JNC	Jump on no carry	1	1	0	1	0	0	1	0	7/10
JZ	Jump on zero	1	1	0	0	1	0	1	0	7/10
JNZ	Jump on no zero	1	1	0	0	0	0	1	0	7/10
JP	Jump on positive	1	1	1	1	0	0	1	0	7/10
JM	Jump on minus	1	1	1	1	1	0	1	0	7/10
JPE	Jump on parity even	1	1	1	0	1	0	1	0	7/10
JPO	Jump on parity odd	1	1	1	0	0	0	1	0	7/10
PCHL	H & L to program counter	1	1	1	0	1	0	0	1	6
CALL										
CALL	Call unconditional	1	1	0	0	1	1	0	1	18
CC	Call on carry	1	1	0	1	1	1	0	0	9/18
CNC	Call on no carry	1	1	0	1	0	1	0	0	9/18
CZ	Call on zero	1	1	0	0	1	1	0	0	9/18
CNZ	Call on no zero	1	1	0	0	0	1	0	0	9/18
CP	Call on positive	1	1	1	1	0	1	0	0	9/18
CM	Call on minus	1	1	1	1	1	1	0	0	9/18

DCX D	Decrement D & E	0	0	0	1	1	0	1	1	6
DCX H	Decrement H & L	0	0	1	0	1	0	1	1	6
DCX SP	Decrement stack pointer	0	0	1	1	1	0	1	1	6
ADD										
ADD r	Add register to A	1	0	0	0	0	S	S	S	4
ADC r	Add register to A with carry	1	0	0	0	1	S	S	S	4
ADD M	Add memory to A	1	0	0	0	0	1	1	0	7
ADC M	Add memory to A with carry	1	0	0	0	1	1	1	0	7
ADI	Add immediate to A	1	1	0	0	0	1	1	0	7
ACI	Add immediate to A with carry	1	1	0	0	1	1	1	0	7
DAD B	Add B & C to H & L	0	0	0	0	1	0	0	1	10
DAD D	Add D & E to H & L	0	0	0	1	1	0	0	1	10
DAD H	Add H & L to H & L	0	0	1	0	1	0	0	1	10
DAD SP	Add stack pointer to H & L	0	0	1	1	1	0	0	1	10
SUBTRACT										
SUB r	Subtract register from A	1	0	0	1	0	S	S	S	4
SBB r	Subtract register from A with borrow	1	0	0	1	1	S	S	S	4
SUB M	Subtract memory from A	1	0	0	1	0	1	1	0	7
SBB M	Subtract memory from A with borrow	1	0	0	1	1	1	1	0	7
SUI	Subtract immediate from A	1	1	0	1	0	1	1	0	7
SBI	Subtract immediate from A with borrow	1	1	0	1	1	1	1	0	7
LOGICAL										
ANA r	And register with A	1	0	1	0	0	S	S	S	4

Table 4-1. Instruction Set Summary of 8085A (continued from page 119).

8085A

8085A INSTRUCTION SET SUMMARY (Cont.)

Mnemonic	Description	Instruction Code[1] D_7	D_6	D_5	D_4	D_3	D_2	D_1	D_0	Clock[2] Cycles
XRA r	Exclusive Or register with A	1	0	1	0	1	S	S	S	4
ORA r	Or register with A	1	0	1	1	0	S	S	S	4
CMP r	Compare register with A	1	0	1	1	1	S	S	S	4
ANA M	And memory with A	1	0	1	0	0	1	1	0	7
XRA M	Exclusive Or memory with A	1	0	1	0	1	1	1	0	7
ORA M	Or memory with A	1	0	1	1	0	1	1	0	7
CMP M	Compare memory with A	1	0	1	1	1	1	1	0	7
ANI	And immediate with A	1	1	1	0	0	1	1	0	7
XRI	Exclusive Or immediate with A	1	1	1	0	1	1	1	0	7
ORI	Or immediate with A	1	1	1	1	0	1	1	0	7
CPI	Compare immediate with A	1	1	1	1	1	1	1	0	7
ROTATE										
RLC	Rotate A left	0	0	0	0	0	1	1	1	4
RRC	Rotate A right	0	0	0	0	1	1	1	1	4

Mnemonic	Description	Instruction Code[1] D_7	D_6	D_5	D_4	D_3	D_2	D_1	D_0	Clock[2] Cycles
RAL	Rotate A left through carry	0	0	0	1	0	1	1	1	4
RAR	Rotate A right through carry	0	0	0	1	1	1	1	1	4
SPECIALS										
CMA	Complement A	0	0	1	0	1	1	1	1	4
STC	Set carry	0	0	1	1	0	1	1	1	4
CMC	Complement carry	0	0	1	1	1	1	1	1	4
DAA	Decimal adjust A	0	0	1	0	0	1	1	1	4
CONTROL										
EI	Enable Interrupts	1	1	1	1	1	0	1	1	4
DI	Disable Interrupt	1	1	1	1	0	0	1	1	4
NOP	No-operation	0	0	0	0	0	0	0	0	4
HLT	Halt	0	1	1	1	0	1	1	0	5
NEW 8085A INSTRUCTIONS										
RIM	Read Interrupt Mask	0	0	1	0	0	0	0	0	4
SIM	Set Interrupt Mask	0	0	1	1	0	0	0	0	4

NOTES: 1. DDD or SSS: B 000. C 001. D 010. E 011 H 100 L 101 Memory 110 A 111
2. Two possible cycle times (6/12) indicate instruction cycles dependent on condition flags

Table 4-2. Summary of 8085A Instructions.

INSTR	STATES	CYCLES	NOTES
AR r	4	1	
AR I	7	2	
AR M	7	2	
CALL	18	5	2
CCN	9/18	2/5	2,4
CMC	4	1	
CMA	4	1	
DAA	4	1	
DAD	10	3	
DCR r	4	1	3
DCR M	10	3	
DCX	6	1	2
DI	4	1	
EI	4	1	
HLT	5	1	5
IN	10	3	
INR r	4	1	3
INR M	10	3	
INX	6	1	2
JMP	10	3	
JCN	7/10	2/3	4
LDS	13	4	
LDAX	7	2	
LHLD	16	5	
LXU	10	3	
MVI M	10	3	
MVI r	7	2	
MOV M,r	7	2	
MOV r,M	7	2	
MOV r,r	4	1	3
NOP	4	1	

INSTR	STATES	CYCLES	NOTES
OUT	10	3	
PCHL	6	1	2
POP	10	3	
PUSH	12	3	2
ROT	4	1	
RET	10	3	
RCN	6/12	1/3	2
RIM*	4	1	
RST	12	3	2
SHLD	16	5	
SIM*	4	1	
STA	13	4	
STAX	7	2	
STC	4	1	
XCHG	4	1	
XTHL	16	5	
SPHL	6	1	2

*New Instruction

NOTES:
1. Two possible state-cycle times indicates dependence on condition flag.
2. Increase in states over 8080 due to necessity of a T_6 during M_1.
3. Decreased from 5 to 4 states during M_1.
4. Instruction branches over last address fetch if condition false.
5. 5 cycles to get a HLT state. 1 cycle necessary to get out a HLT.

The RST 7.5 (edge triggered) internal request flip flop will be reset if bit 4 of the accumulator = 1; regardless of whether RST 7.5 is masked or not.

A hardware RESET of the 8085A will set all RST MASKs, and reset/disable all interrupts.

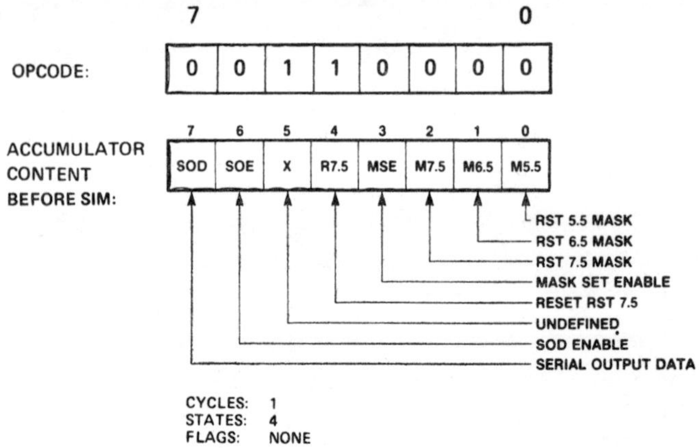

Fig. 4-3. SIM loaded with SOD output latch.

SIM can also load the SOD output latch. Accumulator bit 7 is loaded into the SOD latch if bit 6 is set. The latch is unaffected if bit 6 is a zero. RESET IN input sets the SOD latch to zero.

Chapter 5
MCS-85™ Applications

5.1 INTRODUCTION

When the first microprocessor was introduced about five years ago, it was largely ignored by the electronics industry. However, since that inauspicious beginning, this new device has become the hottest topic in current technology. As more and more product designers become familiar with the capabilities of microcomputers, the number of new applications increases geometrically. In most of these applications, the new technology has been used to replace designs which were formerly implemented with TTL logic and under-utilized microcomputers. However, an increasing number of products are surfacing which would have been impractical prior to the microcomputer era.

Microcomputers are being applied to a wide range of data communications tasks. The field of telephone equipment is being invaded by systems which control and monitor calls. Point of sale terminals are increasing daily with the addition of interface to coin changers, electronic scales and remote computers. Small stand-alone computers are relying heavily upon microcomputers in tele-processing, time-sharing, data base management and similar interactive applications. An increasing number of microcomputer based data terminals are providing local interactive intelligence with programmable character sets, vector generation and the pre-processing of data.

Instrumentation is widely utilizing the microprocessor for a variety of control and arithmetic processing functions. Microcomputers are controlling laboratory equipment such as oscilloscopes, DVM's, network analyzers and frequency synthesizers. Medical electronics are crediting microcomputers with tasks such as patient monitoring, blood analysis and X-ray scanning. Travel is becoming microcomputerized by automotive control, air and ocean navigation equipment and rapid transit systems.

5.2 MCS-85™ SYSTEM

Many possible microcomputer applications have been overlooked because of the design tasks required to build the microcomputer. These tasks include the system clock, read/write memory, I/O ports, serial communications interface and bus control logic. The MCS-85 system will enable the design engineer to concentrate on the application of the microcomputer, rather than on the implementation details.

The MCS-85 is yet another family of components which has the potential to provide a solution to the three problems which will always plague designers: coat, size and power. The reduced component count of an MCS-85 microcomputer, coupled with the increased integration of functions reduces both cost and size while increasing power.

Small System

The schematic on the following pages is of a complete microcomputer with only 6 IC's. The system contains its own serial I/O communication lines, multi-level interrupt, two programmable timers, and power-on reset. System capacity is 512 bytes of RAM, 4K bytes of PROM, and 76 lines of programmable I/O.

Baud Rate Generator

Shown in Fig. 5-2 is a minimum system configuration with the 8155 timer output connected to an 8085 interrupt input.

This configuration allows convenient use of the timer as a baud rate generator. A 6.144 MHz crystal is used as the frequency control element of the 8085, providing integral divisors for the standard baud rates (300, 600, 1200, 2400, 4800, 9600 baud). The timer is programmed with the appropriate divisor (Fig. 1) for the selected baud rate resulting in one pulse on the timer output for each bit cell time. The clock output (CLK) of the 8085 is used to clock the timer (TIMERIN). The frequency of this clock is one-half the crystal frequency or in this example 3.072 MHz. TIMEROUT now provides a crystal controlled pulse train at the baud rate selected.

Sample Applications

Calculating Oscilloscope	Intelligent Terminal	Navigation Equipment	Disk Controller
Blood Analyzer	N.C. Machine	Vending Machine	Patient Monitor
Programmable Video Game	Digital Multimeter	Spectrum Analyzer	Network Analyzer
Process Control System	Graphic Terminal	Front End Processor	Frequency Synthesizer
Line Printer	Automotive Control	Credit Verifier	

APPLICATION	PERIPHERAL DEVICES ENCOUNTERED	MCS-85™ COMPONENTS	
Intelligent Terminals	Cathode Ray Tube Display Printing Units Synchronous and Asynchronous data lines Cassette Tape Unit Keyboards	8275 8155 8251 8279	8085 8355
Gaming Machines	Keyboards, pushbuttons and switches Various display devices Coin acceptors Coin dispensers	8279 8155	8085 8355
Cash Registers	Keyboard or Input Switch Array Change Dispenser Digital Display Ticket Printer Magnetic Card reader Communication interface	8279 8155 8273	8085 8355
Accounting and Billing Machines	Keyboard Printer Unit Cassette or other magnetic tape unit "Floppy" disks	8279 8155 8257 8271	8085 8355
Telephone Switching Control	Telephone Line Scanner Analog Switching Network Dial Registers Class of Service Parcel	8253 8155	8085 8355
Numerically Controlled Machines	Magnetic or Paper Tape Reader Stepper Motors Optical Shaft Encoders	8155	8085 8355
Process Control	Analog-to-Digital Converters Digital-to-Analog Converters Control Switches Displays	8155 8279	8085 8355

Table 5-1. Sample Applications of the MCS-85.

BAUD RATE	COUNT (DECIMAL)
300	10,240
600	5,120
1200	2,560
2400	1,280
4800	640
9600	320

Fig. 5-1. Serial communications supported with minimum system.

Serial Communications

By feeding the $\overline{\text{TIMEROUT}}$ signal of the 8155 back to the edge triggered RST7.5 input of the 8085, the processor can be interrupt driven at the required baud rate. As shown in Fig. 5-1, the minimum system supports serial communications with only the addition of the send and receive interface circuits.

The SID (SERIAL INPUT DATA) line and the SOD (SERIAL OUTPUT DATA) line are connected directly to a TTY or RS232 interface circuit. Assuming inverted data at the SID input, a direct connection is made to the RST6.5 input for detection of the start bit.

Block Move, Block Search

In a large system application high speed block moves may be necessary. The addition of an 8257 Direct Memory Access (DMA) controller and an 8255 Programmable Peripheral Interface (PPI) device with some miscellaneous logic removes the task from the 8085 and results in a very high speed capability. The addition of an eight bit comparator also permits block searches. (See Fig. 5-4).

Basic operation, for a block move, is that the CPU loads the 8257 with the starting address of the source block and the length* of the block into Channel 0. Channel 1 is programmed with the starting location of the destination block and the length. A bit in Port C of the 8255 is set by the CPU which initiates a DMA request on Channels 0 and 1. Because the 8257 is initialized to the rotating priority mode, the first DMA cycle is from Channel 0 which latches the data from the first location of the source block into the 8212. The second cycle will be from Channel 1 which will store the latched data into the first location of the destination block. The next cycle will return to Channel 0 and the sequence will start over again until the length (terminal count) is reached. Programming the 8257

*(The value loaded into the low-order 14-bits of the terminal count register specifies the number of DMA cycles minus one before the Terminal Count (TC) output is activated. For instance, a terminal count of 0 would cause the TC output to be active in the first DMA cycle for that channel. In general, if Length = the number of desired DMA cycles, load the value Length-1 into the low-order 14-bits of the terminal count register.)

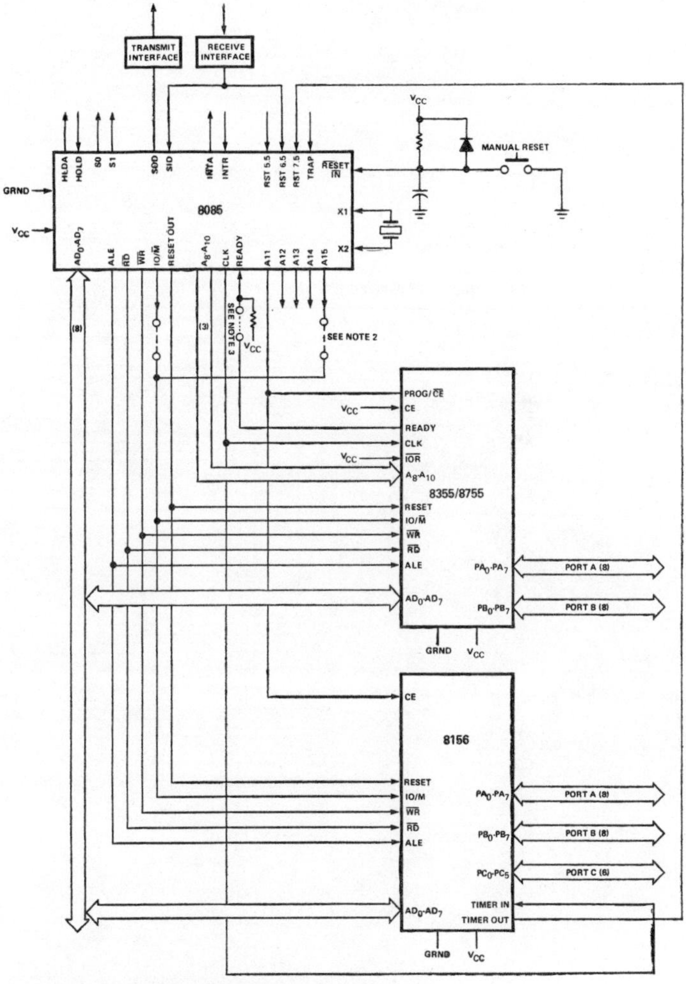

NOTE 1: TRAP, INTR, AND HOLD MUST BE GROUNDED IF THEY AREN'T USED.
NOTE 2: USE IO/M FOR STANDARD I/O MAPPING. USE A15 FOR MEMORY MAPPED I/O.
NOTE 3. CONNECTION IS NECESSARY ONLY IF ONE T_{WAIT} STATE IS DESIRED.

Fig. 5-2. Minimum system configuration.

stop bit insures that each channel will be disabled when its respective terminal count is reached.

This configuration also supports a block fill. DMA Channel 0 points to a location containing the fill value and has a length of one. Channel 1 points to the starting location of the destination block and contains the length. When the sequence is initiated the value will be loaded into the latch by Channel 0. Channel 0 reaches TC

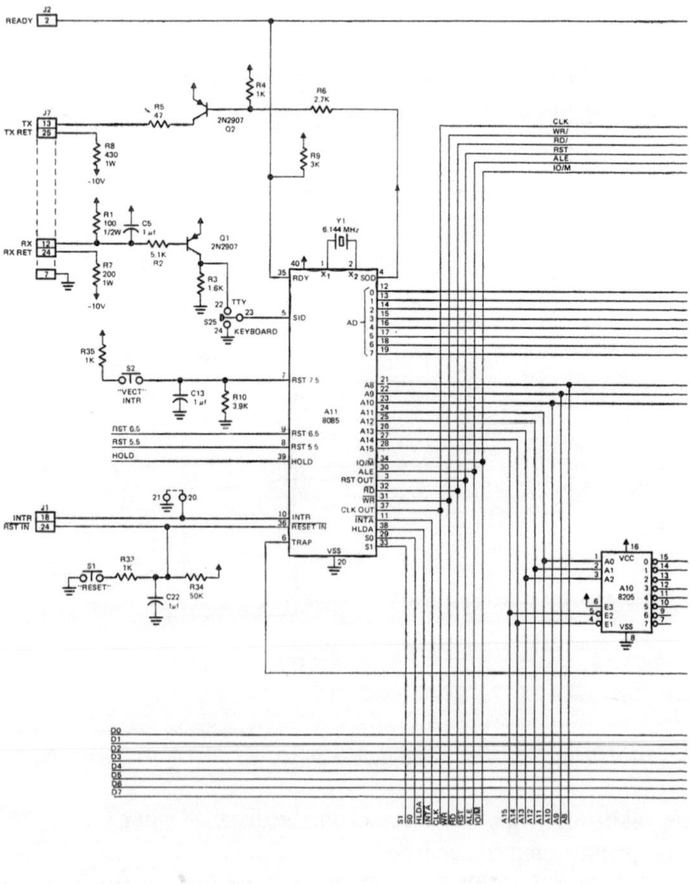

Fig. 5-3. Small system schematic.

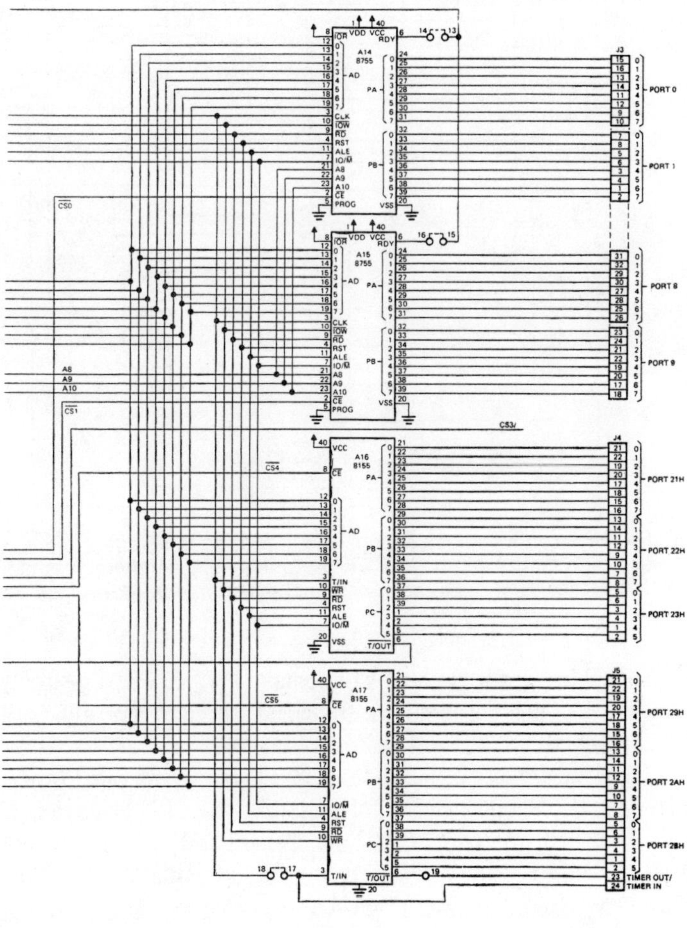
A14
8755
A15
8755
A16
8155
A17
8155
VDD
VCC
RDY
IOR
IOW
RD
WR
CLK
RST
ALE
IO/M
A8
A9
A10
CE
PROG
VSS
T/IN
T/OUT
AD
PA
PB
PC
CS0
CS1
CS3
CS4
CS5
J3
J4
J5
PORT 0
PORT 1
PORT 8
PORT 9
PORT 21H
PORT 22H
PORT 23H
PORT 29H
PORT 2AH
PORT 2BH
TIMER OUT/
TIMER IN

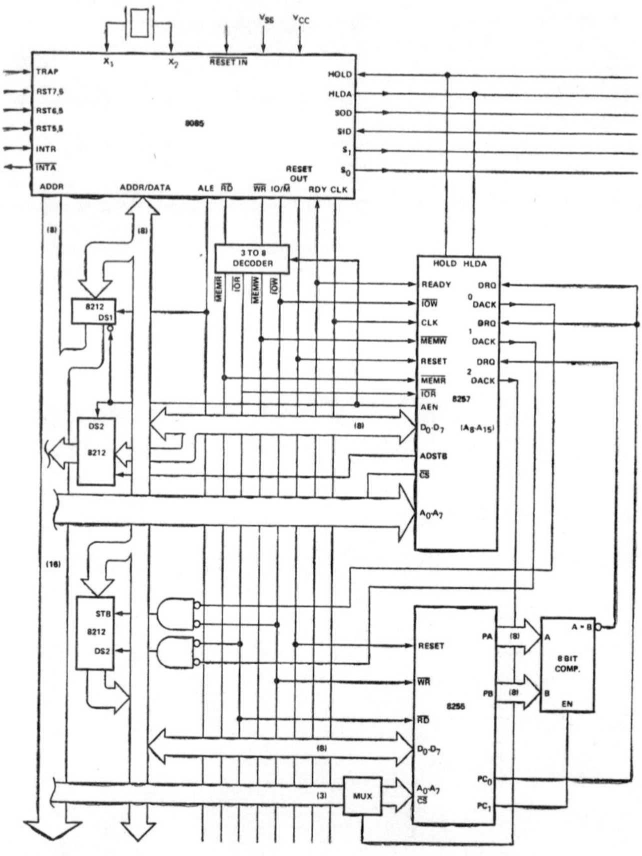

Fig. 5-4. Block move, block search addition of an 8257 direct memory access (DMA) controller and an 8255 programmable peripheral interface (PPI) device permits block searches, high-speed block moves (2.5 μs/word).

and is disabled. Priority rotates to Channel 1 which will repeatedly write into the destination block the value stored in the latch until TC is reached.

Block search operations use the 8-bit comparator and Ports A & B of the 8255 and Channel 2 of the 8257. The CPU loads Port B with the search value and the DMA channel with the search area (starting address and length). A Port C bit initiates the DMA READ request. Channel 2 DMA Acknowledge sets Port A of the 8255 up as the receiver for the DMA READ cycle by multiplexing A_0, A_1, and $\overline{CS}$. Each cycle of the DMA then loads Port A with the

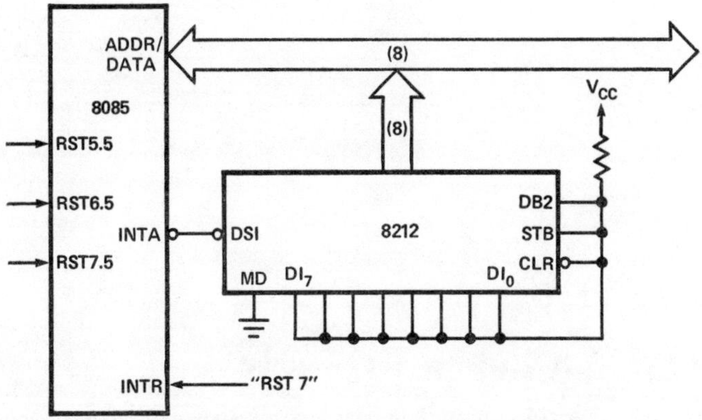

Fig. 5-5. Block search diagram.

value of the pointed-to location in the block. When Port A equals Port B, the output of the comparator will gate off the DMA request. The requesting program can now read the Channel 2 address which

RESTART	VECTOR LOCATION
RST 7	38_{16}
RST 5.5	$2C_{16}$
RST 6.5	34_{16}
RST 7.5	$3C_{16}$
TRAP	24_{16}

Fig. 5-6. Restart and vector locations.

is pointing to the search value plus one. However, if the statue register of the 8257 indicates that TC of Channel 2 has been reached, then no match was found.

Chapter 6
Basic Software Projects

6.1 INTRODUCTION

The projects in this chapter can be executed with the purchase of the BASIC SDK-85 trainer (see Sec 1.1), on which no modification need be made. The projects in this chapter usually have a description of the program objective. The programs are written in a form that has three main headings:

1. MEMORY INSTRUCTION
2. INSTRUCTION
3. COMMENT

The MEMORY INSTRUCTION has three subheadings:

1a. Address
1b. Data
1c. Label

The *Address* is the hexadecimal memory location of the *Data* or *program*. The *Label* is a one-word statement describing the Data, or what is being executed in the program. For example, the first or starting Address is labeled "START", and usually the last program Address is labeled "EXIT". If the word "RESULT" is listed in the Data memory Address, one of the results in the program is stored in that Data Address and is considered data. Most of the one-word statements are self-explanatory, but if an explanation is necessary the one-word statement will be defined under COMMENTS.

All the programs will begin with the word "START" in the Label column. Most START address locations are the hexadecimal number $(2010)_{16}$. All of the Address locations are hexadecimal numbers written in *sequence*. Next to the Address under the *Data* column is program information generalized to be called Data. In other words, we have machine language or object code in the Data column next to every Address location in the program.

The main heading INSTRUCTION includes the subheadings:

2a. Opcode
2b. Operand

The INSTRUCTION portion of the programming form is the assembly language statements or mnemonics of the program. The subheading *Opcode* defines the 8085A Instruction Set employed in the program. Remember: the 8085A Instruction Set is given in an earlier chapter of this book.

The *Operand* column is the register location or memory location or data required in the program. Also, any combination of the register, memory location or data required can be included in the Operand column.

The comment column includes statements to clarify the execution of the programs. The last Comment of each program for the SDK-85 trainer is the same statement "Back to Monitor Program". This comment will be used in the first few programs, but it will be eliminated in the remaining programs.

PROJECT 9: COMPLEMENT OF A NUMBER IN THE ACCUMULATOR

This program will take the contents of memory location 2000 and load it into the accumulator. It will then take that number and complement it, and then store the results in memory location 2001. The program will then go back to the monitor program where you can use the substitute memory key to examine memory locations one at a time.

MEMORY INFORMATION			INSTRUCTION		
ADDRESS	DATA	LABEL	OPCODE	OPERAND	COMMENT
2000	ANY				Location of Data to be
2001		RESULT			Complemented
2010	3A	START	LDA	2000	Get Data From 2000
2011	00				
2012	20				
2013	2F		CMA		Complement It
2014	32		STA	2001	
2015	01				Store it in 2001
2016	20				
2017	CF		RST	1	Back to Monitor Program

The reader should refer to the following example of how to load the data and program into the SDK-85, then check to see if the program has executed properly. Project 9 will be used as the example program, and each keystroke on the SDK-85 will be listed under the column headed KEY. The next two columns in the example ADDR and DATA will tell the reader what characters the reader will see on the LED display of the SDK-85. The ADDR characters will be seen in the Address Field of the LED display and the DATA characters will be seen in the Data Field of the LED display after the reader has pressed the proper KEY instruction. A column headed COMMENTS is furnished in order to make special remarks about the execution of the program.

The other programs in this book do not contain the step-by-step example provided for Project 9. Hence, the authors suggest that if the reader needs reinforcement in the proper keystrokes for future programs, he or she should refer to this example for the needed reinforcement. Another suggestion is to refer to the SDK-85 User's Manual where simpler keystroke examples are provided. Keystroke confidence will eventual be obtained by practice, practice, practice. If special keystroke requirements are needed in future programs presented in this book, they will be shown at the proper time.

Example:

This example will provide the reader with the proper Keystroke techniques to execute the programs presented in this book. Project 9 will be used as the example program. To execute Project 9 follow the keystrokes listed below, after the 5 Volt DC supply has been connected to the SDK-85 trainer.

KEY	ADDR	DATA	COMMENTS
RESET	–80	85	The monitor is ready to accept a command
SUBST MEM	x		The Address Field is ready
2	0002.		
0	0020.		
0	0200.		
0	2000.		
NEXT	2000	??.	The symbol ? means that any character on the keyboard could be displayed in the Data Field. Note the decimal moved to the Data Field
0	2000	?0.	
1	2000	01.	The hexadecimal number 01 is in address 2000.
NEXT	2001	??	Address Field advances one position, and displays whatever (??.) is contained in that location

KEY	ADDR	DATA	COMMENTS
0	2001	?0.	
0	2001	00.	
NEXT NEXT NEXT	2010	??.	Press NEXT fifteen times advancing the fields until address location 2010 appears in the Address Field as shown below.
3	2010	?3.	Data entered.
A	2010	3A.	The first data statement has been entered in address 2010, which is the starting location of this program.
NEXT	2011	??.	Address advanced
0	2011	?0.	Data entered
0	2011	00.	The second data statement has been entered
NEXT	2012	??.	Address advanced
2	2012	?2.	Data entered
0	2012	20.	The third data statement has been entered.
NEXT	2013	??.	Address advanced
2	2013	?2.	Data entered
F	2013	2F.	The fourth data statement has been entered
NEXT	2014	??.	Address advanced
3	2014	?3.	Data entered
2	2014	32.	The fifth data statement has been entered
NEXT	2015	??.	Address advanced
0	2015	?0.	Data entered
1	2015	01.	The sixth data statement has been entered
NEXT	2016	??.	Address advanced
2	2016	?2.	Data entered
0	2016	20.	The seventh data statement has been entered.
NEXT	2017	??.	Address advanced
C	2017	?C.	Data entered
F	2017	CF.	The eighth and final data statement has been entered
NEXT	2018	??.	The authors recommend that another NEXT keystroke be made before program execution takes place, although the entire program has been keystroked into the SDK-85
EXEC	-		The first keystroke has been made in order to execute the program. The program is now in the memory locations we have addressed.
SUBST MEM			This command will allow us to go back and check the address locations in order to see if we have loaded the correct data in the proper address locations
2	0002.		
0	0020.		
0	0200.		
0	2000.		

KEY	ADDR	DATA	COMMENTS
NEXT	2000	01.	The correct data is contained in this memory location. The reader should keep pressing NEXT to examine the other address locations in this program
NEXT	2001	00.	Press NEXT fifteen times advancing the fields until address location 2010 appears in the Address Field as shown below.
NEXT	2010	3A.	If any of the data statements in the
		DATA	column are not the same as the
NEXT	2011	00.	program data statements, you can correct the program in the SDK-85 by merely
NEXT	2012	20.	pressing the correct characters on the keyboard for that particular address before
NEXT	2013	2F.	pressing the NEXT key.
NEXT	2014	32.	
NEXT	2015	01.	
NEXT	2016	20.	
NEXT	2017	CF.	If the program is correct proceed as follows
EXEC	-		
GO	????.	??	Any characters could appear in both fields
2	0002.		
0	0020.		
1	0201.		
0	2010.		The first address of the program appears
EXEC	-80	85	If the 8085 message appears on the LED display, the program has been properly executed.
SUBST MEM	x		We are now going to check if the program has been properly executed by checking address 2000 and 2001. Address 2001 should contain the complement of address 2000. In other words 01 in 2000 should be stored as FE in 2001. If the reader proceeds with the following keystrokes the reader will observe that the program has been executed properly
2	0002.		
0	0020.		
0	0200.		
0	2000.		
NEXT	2000	01.	The original number to be complemented
NEXT	2001	FE.	The answer to the program. In other words the Hex. number stored in location 2000 (01) has been complemented by this program and then stored in location 2001 (FE)

In the table below we provide the reader with a few hexadecimal numbers, their complements, and their additive inverse. The reader can use the information in the table to check the programs in Projects 9 and 10.

NUMBER	COMPLEMENT	ADDITIVE INVERSE = COMPLEMENT + 1
00	FF	00 (FF + 1)
01	FE	FF (FE + 1)
02	FD	FE (FD +1)
03	FC	FD (FC + 1)

6.3 PROJECT 10: FINDING THE ADDITIVE INVERSE OF A NUMBER IN THE ACCUMULATOR

This program will take the contents of location 2000, find its additive inverse and store it in 2001. The program will then go back to the monitor program where you can use the substitute memory key to examine memory locations one at a time.

MEMORY INFORMATION			INSTRUCTION		COMMENT
ADDRESS	DATA	LABEL	OPCODE	OPERAND	
2000	Data				Test Number in Hexadecimal
2001		Result			Result or Stored Answer
2010	3A	START	LDA	2000	
2011	00				Get the Number
2012	20				
2013	2F		CMA		Complement the Number
2014	3C		INR	A	Generate the Inverse
2015	32		STA	2001	Store the Result
2016	01				
2017	20				
2018	CF		RST	1	Back to Monitor Program

6.4 PROJECT 11: THE ADDITIVE INVERSE TEST

This program will prove that the additive inverse was generated by adding it back to the original number and storing the result in 2001.

MEMORY INFORMATION			INSTRUCTION		COMMENT
ADDRESS	DATA	LABEL	OPCODE	OPERAND	
2000	DATA				Test Number in Hexadecimal
2001		RESULT			Result (should be Ø) or Stored Answer
2010	21	START	LXI	H,2000	
2011	00				
2012	20				
2013	7E		MOV	A,M	Get the Number
2014	2F		CMA		
2015	3C		INR	A	Generate the Inverse
2016	86		ADD	M	Add the Numbers
2017	23		IN X	H	Store Result
2018	77		MOV	M,A	
2019	CF	EXIT	RST	1	Back to Monitor Program

6.5 PROJECT 12: SUBTRACTION EMPLOYING ADDITIVE INVERSE

This program will subtract the number in address 2000 from the number in address 2001 by adding the complement of the number to be subtracted. The result will be stored in address 2002.

MEMORY INFORMATION			INSTRUCTION		
ADDRESS	DATA	LABEL	OPCODE	OPERAND	COMMENT
2000	DATA				
2001	DATA				Number to be Subtracted From.
2002		RESULT			Result
2010	21	START	LXI	H,2000	
2011	00				
2012	20				
2013	7E		MOV	A,M	Point to and Get First Number
2014	2F		CMA		Generate Inverse
2015	3C		INR	A	
2016	2C		INR	L	Point to Second Number
2017	86		ADD	M	Add the two Numbers
2018	2C		INR	L	Store the Result
2019	77		MOV	M,A	
201A	CF	EXIT	RST	1	

Example:

ADDR DATA

2000 02 Subtrahend
2001 05 Minuend
2002 03 Answer (5 - 2)

Example:

ADDR DATA

2000 05 Subtrahend
2001 02 Minuend
2002 FD Answer (2 - 5)

6.6 PROJECT 13: HEXADECIMAL ADDITION OF TWO NUMBERS

This program will take the contents of location 2000, add it to 2001, store the result in location 2002 and then return to the monitor program

MEMORY INFORMATION			INSTRUCTION		
ADDRESS	DATA	LABEL	OPCODE	OPERAND	COMMENT
2000	ANY				First Number to be Added
2001	ANY				Second Number to be Added
2002		RESULT			Result
2010	21	START	LXI	H,2000	Point to First Number in Memory
2011	00				
2012	20				
2013	7E		MOV	A,M	Load the Accumulator
2014	23		INX	H	Advance Pointer
2015	86		ADD	M	Add Second Number
2016	23		INX	H	Advance Pointer
2017	77		MOV	M,A	Store Result
2018	CF	EXIT	RST	1	Back to Monitor Program

Example:

ADDR	*DATA*
2000	08
2001	03
2002	OB Data in Hex Numbers

6.7 PROJECT 14: THE DECIMAL ADDITION OF TWO NUMBERS

This program will add the decimal numbers in 2000 and 2001, and then store the result in decimal in the address 2002.

MEMORY INFORMATION			INSTRUCTION		
ADDRESS	DATA	LABEL	OPCODE	OPERAND	COMMENT
2000	ANY				Two Decimal Number to be added
2001	ANY				
2002		RESULT			Result
2010	21	START	LXI	H,2000	Point to First Number
2011	00				
2012	20				
2013	7E		MOV	A,M	Load it Into Accumulator
2014	23		INX	H	Point to Second Number
2015	86		ADD	M	Add the Two Numbers
2016	27		DAA		Convert to Decimal
2017	23		INX	H	Point to Storage
2018	77		MOV	M,A	Store It
2019	CF		RST	1	

Example:

ADDR	*DATA*
2000	10 Data in decimal.
2001	20 Data in decimal.
2002	30 Answer in decimal.

6.8 PROJECT 15: ADD TWO NUMBERS IN HEXADECIMAL AND CONVERT THE ANSWER TO DECIMAL

This program adds two numbers which are stored in memory at address 2000 and 2001. The numbers are hexadecimal and the resulting addition is stored in address 2003 as a hexadecimal number. Also, the resulting addition is stored in address 2004 as a decimal number.

MEMORY INFORMATION			INSTRUCTION		
ADDRESS	DATA	LABEL	OPCODE	OPERAND	COMMENT
2010	3A	START	LDA	2000	Load No. to Accumulator
2011	00				
2012	20				
2013	47		MOV	B,A	Move Accumulator into B
2014	3A		LDA	2001	Loads 2001 into A

MEMORY INFORMATION			INSTRUCTION		COMMENT
ADDRESS	DATA	LABEL	OPCODE	OPERAND	
2015	01				
2016	20				
2017	80		ADD	B	Adds A and B together
2018	32		STA	2003	Stores Result in 2003
2019	03				
201A	20				
201B	27	DAA			Changes Answer to Decimal
201C	32		STA	2004	Stores Decimal Result in 2004
201D	04				
201E	20				
201F	CF	RST	1		

6.9 PROJECT 16: SIXTEEN BIT ADDITION

This program will add two sixteen-bit numbers and store the answer in address 2004. The program also sets the carry flag if the result is greater than the hexadecimal number FFFF.

MEMORY INFORMATION			INSTRUCTION		COMMENT
ADDRESS	DATA	LABEL	OPCODE	OPERAND	
2000	ANY	LSB			} First 16-bit Number
2001	ANY	MSB			
2002	ANY	LSB			} Second 16-bit Number
2003	ANY	MSB			
2004	LSB				Result of Addition
2005	MSB				
2010	2A	START	LHLD	2000	Load the HL Register With the
2011	00				First Number
2012	20				
2013	EB		XCHG		Exchange the HL and DE Registers
2014	2A		LHLD	2002	Load the HL Register With the
2015	02				Second Number
2016	20				
2017	19		DAD		ADD HL and DE Registers
2018	22		SHLD	2004	Store the Result in 2004
2019	04				
201A	20				
201B	CF		RST	1	

Example:

ADDR	*DATA*
2000	04 LSB1
2001	02 MSB1
2002	10 LSB2
2003	30 MSB2
2004	14 LSB1 + LSB2 (04 + 10)
2005	32 MSB1 + MSB2 (02 + 30)

6.10 PROJECT 17: COUNTING DECIMAL NUMBER DISPLAY (00 TO 99)

If the program has been properly executed, the character E will appear on the LED display and a two-digit decimal number will begin counting. The two-digit decimal number may be stopped by pressing the VECT INTR key. The two-digit decimal number can resume its count by pressing any key except VECT INTR or RESET.

MEMORY INFORMATION			INSTRUCTION		
ADDRESS	DATA	LABEL	OPCODE	OPERAND	COMMENT
2010	31		LXI	SP, 20C2	Initialize Stock Pointer
2011	C2				
2012	20				
2013	3E		MVI	A, 1A	} Enable Vect Intr. Button
2014	1A				
2015	30		SIM		
2016	AF		XRA	A	Zero Counter
2017	FB	LOOP	EI		
2018	78		MOV	A,B	
2019	3C		INR	A	} Increment Count and
201A	27		DAA		Adjust to Decimal
201B	47		MOV	B,A	
201C	C5		PUSH	B	
201D	CD		CALL	036E	Display Count
201E	6E				
201F	03				
2020	16		MVI	D, 18H	
2021	18				
2022	CD		CALL	05F1	Pause Before Continuing
2023	F1				
2024	05				
2025	C1		POP	B	
2026	C3		JMP	LOOP	Continue
2027	17				
2028	20				
20CE	FB		EI		
20CF	76		HLT		Wait for Interrupt
20DO	C9		RET		Back to Main Program

6.11 PROJECT 18: MULTI-BYTE ADDITION

This program will add two hexadecimal numbers that are N-Bytes long and store the result starting at address 2001. The lowest address location should contain the least significant byte.

MEMORY INFORMATION		INSTRUCTION			COMMENT
ADDRESS	DATA	LABEL	OPCODE	OPERAND	
2000	(1-7)				No. of Bytes to Add (7 places) maximum
2001		LSB1			Number 1, (3 Byte number) Example
2002					
2003		MSB1			
2004					
2008		LSB2			Number 2 (3 Byte number) Example
2009					
200A		MSB2			
2010	3A	START	LDA	2000	
2011	00				
2012	20				
2013	47		MOV	B,A	Get no. of Bytes to Add
2014	21		LXI	H,2001	Point HL to 2001 for First No.
2015	01				
2016	20				
2017	11		LXI	D,2008	Point DE to 2008 for Second No.
2018	08				
2019	20				
201A	AF		XRA		Clear A and Flag
201B	1A	LOOP	LDAX	D	Load Second Number into Accumulator
201C	8E		ADC	M	Add First Number to It
201D	77		MOV	M,A	Store Result
201E	13		INX	D	Point to Next Bytes
201F	23		INX	H	
2020	05		DCR	B	Check to See If Done
2021	C2		JNZ	LOOP	
2022	1B				
2023	20				
2024	CF		RST	1	

Example:

ADDR DATA

2000 07 Program adjusts for 7 places
2001 15 LSB1
2002 23
2003 46 MSB1
2008 4C LSB2
2009 2F
200A 1A MSB2

After the program executes the answer will be stored as follows.

2001 61 LSB of answer
2002 52
2003 60 MSB of answer

6.12 PROJECT 19: ADDITION OF 8-BIT NUMBER SERIES

This program adds a variable amount of hexadecimal numbers and places the result in address 2000. At the start of the program, address 2000 will hold the total amount of numbers to be added. Care should be taken that the sum does not exceed the hexadecimal number FF.

MEMORY INFORMATION		INSTRUCTION			
ADDRESS	DATA	LABEL	OPCODE	OPERAND	COMMENT
2000	ANY				The No. of Numbers to Be Added and Later the Result Equals Number
2001					of Data Address or Pieces of Data
2002					Numbers to Be Added
2003					
2004					
2010	21	START	LXI	H,2000	Point to First Number
2011	00				
2012	20				
2013	46		MOV	B,M	Load Count Into B Register
2014	AF		XRA	A	Clear A Register
2015	23	LOOP	INX	H	Point to First Number
2016	86		ADD	M	Add Memory to Total
2017	05		DCR	B	Subtract From Count
2018	C2		JNZ	Loop	Test to See If Done
2019	15				
201A	20				
201B	32		STA	2000	Store Result
201C	00				
201D	20				
201E	CF		RST	1	

Example:

ADDR DATA

2000 04 The number of hexadecimal numbers to be added.
2001 10 First Hex number
2002 02 Second Hex number.
2003 08 Third Hex number.
2004 04 Fourth Hex number.

After the program executes the answer will be stored in location 2000 as follows.

2000 1E Answer is in Hexadecimal.

6.13 PROJECT 20: FINDING THE LARGER OF TWO NUMBERS

This program will compare the contents of locations 2000 and 2001 and store the larger of the two numbers in address 2002.

MEMORY INFORMATION			INSTRUCTION		
ADDRESS	DATA	LABEL	OPCODE	OPERAND	COMMENT
2000	ANY				Any Two Nos. to Be Compared
2001	ANY				
2002		LARGER			Larger of the Two
2010	21	START	LXI	H,2000	Set Pointer to 2000
2011	00				
2012	20				
2013	7E		MOV	A,M	Get First Number
2014	23		INX	H	Point to Second Number
2015	BE		CMP	M	Compare the Two Numbers
2016	D2		JNC	EXIT	If Accumulator is Larger
2017	1A				Go To Exit
2018	20				
2019	7E		MOV	A,M	Load 2001 Into the Accumulator
201A	23	EXIT 1	INX	H	Point to 2002
201B	77		MOV	M,A	Store the Accumulator Into 2002
201C	CF	EXIT	RST	1	Back to Monitor Program

6.14 PROJECT 21: SEPARATION OF HEXADECIMAL NUMBERS INTO TWO DIGITS (HEX-ITS)

This program will take the contents in location 2000, separate the least and most significant four bits, and store them in locations 2001 and 2002 respectively.

MEMORY INFORMATION			INSTRUCTION		
ADDRESS	DATA	LABEL	OPCODE	OPERAND	COMMENT
2000	ANY				No. to Be Separated
2001		RESULT 1			LSB Storage
2002		RESULT 2			MSB Storage
2010	3A	START	LDA	2000	Get the Number
2011	00				
2012	20				
2013	E6		ANI	OF	Mask Off the First Four
2014	OF				Bits
2015	32		STA	2001	Store Result One
2016	01				
2017	20				
2018	3A		LDA	2000	Get the Number Again
2019	00				
201A	20				
201B	E6		ANI	FO	Mask Off the Last Four Bits
201C	FO				
201D	32		STA	2002	Store Result Two
201E	02				
201F	20				
2020	CF		RST	1	

Example:

ADDR DATA

2000 AF Number stored.

2001 00 Memory before program execution.

2002 00 Memory before program execution.

After the program executes, the memory locations will contain the following results.

2000 AF

2001 OF LSB separated from AF.

2002 AO MSB separated from AF.

6.15 PROJECT 22: COMBINING HEX-ITS INTO A HEXADECIMAL NUMBER (GAME PROGRAM PREREQUISITE)

This program will put two single-digit hexadecimal numbers together. The first single digit hexadecimal or hex-it would be the MSB, and the second hex-it would be the LSB.

MEMORY INFORMATION			INSTRUCTION		
ADDRESS	DATA	LABEL	OPCODE	OPERAND	COMMENT
2000					Data for MSB; Ø Ø Through 0F
2001					Data for LSB ; Ø Ø Through 0F
2002		Result			Result
2010	21	START	LXI	H,2000	Point to First Number
2011	00				
2012	20				
2013	7E		MOV	A,M	Get It
2014	07		RLC		
2015	07		RLC		Move It to MSB
2016	07		RLC		
2017	07		RLC		
2018	23		INX	H	Point to Next Number
2019	B6		ORA	M	Or the Two Numbers Together
201A	23		INX	H	
201B	77		MOV	M,A	Store the Result
201C	CF		RST	1	

Example:

ADDR DATA

2000 04 MSB

2001 05 LSB

2002 00

After the program executes, the memory locations will contain the following results.

2000 04

2001 05

2002 45

6.16 PROJECT 23: TESTING FOR THE CONDITION (HIGH OR LOW STATE) OF BIT THREE OF AN 8-BIT (HEX-IT) NUMBER

This program will test Bit-3 of a Hex-It number with the location of Bit-3 in 2000. If Bit-3 is High ("1") the number in 2000 will be stored in 2001. IF Bit-3 is Low ("0"), no action is taken and the data address locations will be in the null state.

MEMORY INFORMATION			INSTRUCTION		
ADDRESS	DATA	LABEL	OPCODE	OPERAND	COMMENT
2000	ANY				Data To Be Tested
2001		Results			Data copied if bit 3 set
2010	21	START	LXI	H,2000	
2011	00				
2012	20				Get No. to Be Tested
2013	7E		MOV	A,M	
2014	0F		RRC		
2015	0F		RRC		Rotate Bit 3 into the Carry
2016	0F		RRC		Flags for Test
2017	0F		RRC		
2018	D2		JNC	EXIT	Jump if Bit 3 is Not Set
2019	1E				
201A	20				
201B	7E		MOV	A,M	
201C	23		INX	H	Store No. in 2001
201D	77		MOV	M,A	
201E	CF	EXIT	RST	1	

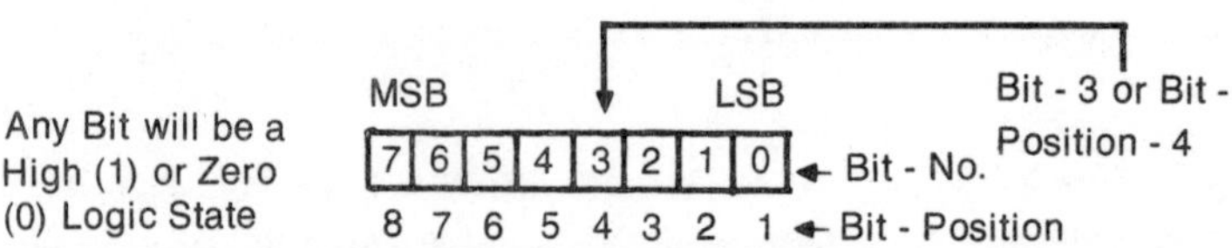

8 - Bit (Hex-It) Number Diagram

6.17 PROJECT 24: NEW AND IMPROVED BIT TESTING PROGRAM OF BIT THREE OF AN 8-BIT NUMBER

This program does exactly the same thing as Project 23, except that it does it faster and with less memory using the ANI instruction. Please refer to Project 23 for the details of the program objective.

MEMORY INFORMATION			INSTRUCTION		
ADDRESS	DATA	LABEL	OPCODE	OPERAND	COMMENT
2000	ANY				Data to Be Tested
2001		Results			Data to Be Copied if Bit 3 is High

MEMORY INFORMATION			INSTRUCTION		
ADDRESS	DATA	LABEL	OPCODE	OPERAND	COMMENT
2010	21	START	LXI	H,2000	Get No.
2011	00				
2012	20				
2013	7E		MOV	A,M	
2014	E6		ANI	08	Reset all Bits Except No. 3
2015	08				Jmp if Nothing Left
2016	CA		JZ	EXIT	
2017	IC				
2018	20				
2019	7E		MOV	A,M	Copy data from 2000 to 2001
201A	23		INX	H	
201B	77		MOV	M,A	
201C	CF	EXIT	RST	1	

6.18 PROJECT 25: TESTING FOR THE CONDITION (HIGH OR LOW STATE) OF BIT ZERO OF AN 8-BIT (HEX-IT) NUMBER

This program does exactly the same thing as Project 24, except that it tests the condition of the initial bit position of an 8-Bit number; that is Bit-Ø. In many microprocessor applications it is necessary to test bit conditions (High or Low) and store this information for reference. Hence, the authors believe it behooves the reader to know the exact bit testing programs for each bit of a Hex-It number, although only minor program changes occur in each of the bit testing programs. The reader is reminded to refer to Projects 23 and 24 for the details of the program objectives.

MEMORY INFORMATION			INSTRUCTION		
ADDRESS	DATA	LABEL	OPCODE	OPERAND	COMMENT
2000	ANY				Data to Be Tested
2001		RESULT			Data Copied if Bit 0 is High
2010	21	START	LXI	H,2000	Point to the Number
2011	00				
2012	20				
2013	7E		MOV	A,M	
2014	E6		ANI	01	Reset All the Bits Except 0
2015	01				
2016	CA		JZ	EXIT	Jump if Nothing Left
2017	1C				
2018	20				
2019	7E		MOV	A,M	Get the No. Again and Copy it
201A	23		INX	H	to 2001
201B	77		MOV	M,A	
201C	CF	EXIT	RST	1	

6.19 PROJECT 26: TESTING FOR THE CONDITION (HIGH OR LOW STATE) OF BIT ONE OF AN 8-BIT (HEX-IT) NUMBER

This program does exactly the same thing as Project 24, except that it tests the condition of the second bit position of an 8-Bit number; that is Bit-1. In many microprocessor applications it is necessary to test bit conditions (High or Low) and store this information for reference. Hence, the authors believe it behooves the reader to know the exact bit testing programs for each bit of a Hex-It number, although only minor program changes occur in each of the bit testing programs. The reader is reminded to refer to Projects 23 and 24 for the details of the program objectives.

MEMORY INFORMATION			INSTRUCTION		
ADDRESS	DATA	LABEL	OPCODE	OPERAND	COMMENT
2000	ANY				Data to Be Tested
2001		RESULT			Data Copied if Bit 1 is High
2010	21	START	LXI	H,2000	Point to the Number
2011	00				
2012	20				
2013	7E		MOV	A,M	
2014	E6		ANI	01	Reset All the Bits Except 1
2015	02				
2016	CA		JZ	EXIT	Jump if Nothing Left
2017	1C				
2018	20				
2019	7E		MOV	A,M	Get the No. Again and Copy it
201A	23		INX	H	to 2001
201B	77		MOV	M,A	
201C	CF	EXIT	RST	1	

6.20 PROJECT 27: TESTING FOR THE CONDITION (HIGH OR LOW STATE) OF BIT TWO OF AN 8-BIT (HEX-IT) NUMBER

This program does exactly the same thing as Project 24, except that it tests the condition of the third bit position of an 8-Bit number; that is Bit-2. In many microprocessor applications it is necessary to test bit conditions (High or Low) and store this information for reference. Hence, the authors believe it behooves the reader to know the exact bit testing programs for each bit of a Hex-It number, although only minor program changes occur in each of the bit testing programs. The reader is reminded to refer to Projects 23 and 24 for the details of the program objectives.

MEMORY INFORMATION			INSTRUCTION		
ADDRESS	DATA	LABEL	OPCODE	OPERAND	COMMENT
2000	ANY				Data to Be Tested
2001		RESULT			Data Copied if Bit 2 is High
2010	21	START	LXI	H,2000	Point to the Number
2011	00				
2012	20				
2013	7E		MOV	A,M	
2014	E6		ANI	04	Reset All the Bits except 2
2015	04				
2016	CA		JZ	EXIT	Jump if Nothing Left
2017	1C				
2018	20				
2019	7E		MOV	A,M	Get the No. again and
201A	23		INX	H	copy it to 2001
201B	77		MOV	M,A	
201C	CF	EXIT	RST	1	

6.21 PROJECT 28: TESTING FOR THE CONDITION (HIGH OR LOW STATE) OF BIT FOUR OF AN 8-BIT (HEX-IT) NUMBER

This program does exactly the same thing as Project 24, except that it tests the condition of the fifth bit position of an 8-Bit number; that is Bit-4. In many microprocessor applications it is necessary to test bit conditions (High or Low) and store this information for reference. Hence, the authors believe it behooves the reader to know the exact bit testing programs for each bit of a Hex-It number, although only minor program changes occur in each of the bit testing programs. The reader is reminded to refer to Projects 23 and 24 for the details of the program objectives.

MEMORY INFORMATION			INSTRUCTION		
ADDRESS	DATA	LABEL	OPCODE	OPERAND	COMMENT
2000	ANY				Data to Be Tested
2001		RESULT			Data Copied if Bit 4 is High
2010	21	START	LXI	H,2000	Point to The Number
2011	00				
2012	20				
2013	7E		MOV	A,M	
2014	E6		ANI	10	Reset All the Bits Except 4
2015	10				
2016	CA		JZ	EXIT	Jump if Nothing Left
2017	1C				
2018	20				
2019	7E		MOV	A,M	Get the No. Again and Copy it
201A	23		INX	H	to 2001
201B	77		MOV	M,A	
201C	CF	EXIT	RST	1	

6.22 PROJECT 29: TESTING FOR THE CONDITION (HIGH OR LOW STATE) OF BIT FIVE OF AN 8-BIT (HEX-IT) NUMBER

This program does exactly the same thing as Project 24, except that it tests the condition of the sixth bit position of an 8-Bit number; that is Bit-5. In many microprocessor applications it is necessary to test bit conditions (High or Low) and store this information for reference. Hence, the authors believe it behooves the reader to know the exact bit testing programs for each bit of a Hex-It number, although only minor programs changes occur in each of the bit testing programs. The reader is reminded to refer to Projects 23 and 24 for the details of the program objectives.

MEMORY INFORMATION			INSTRUCTION		
ADDRESS	DATA	LABEL	OPCODE	OPERAND	COMMENT
2000	ANY				Data to Be Tested
		RESULT			Data Copied if Bit 5 is High
2010	21	START	LXI	H,2000	Point to the Number
2011	00				
2012	20				
2013	7E		MOV	A,M	
2014	E6		ANI	IO	Reset All the Bits Except 5
2015	20				
2016	CA		JZ	EXIT	Jump if Nothing Left
2017	1C				
2018	20				
2019	7E		MOV	A,M	Get the No. Again and Copy It
201A	23		INX	H	to 2001
201B	77		MOV	M,A	
201C	CF	EXIT	RST	1	

6.23 PROJECT 30: TESTING FOR THE CONDITION (HIGH OR LOW STATE) OF BIT SIX OF AN 8-BIT (HEX-IT) NUMBER

This program does exactly the same thing as Project 24, except that it tests the condition of the seventh bit position of an 8-Bit number; that is Bit-6. In many microprocessor applications it is necessary to test bit conditions (High or Low) and store this information for reference. Hence, the authors believe it behooves the reader to know the exact bit testing programs for each bit of a Hex-It number, although only minor program changes occur in each of the bit testing programs. The reader is reminded to refer to Projects 23 and 24 for the details of the program objectives.

MEMORY INFORMATION			INSTRUCTION		
ADDRESS	DATA	LABEL	OPCODE	OPERAND	COMMENT
2000	ANY				Data to Be TESTED
2001		RESULT			Data Copied if Bit 6 is High
2010	21	START	LXI	H,2000	Point to the Number
2011	00				
2012	20				
2013	7E		MOV	A,M	
2014	E6		ANI	40	Reset All the Bits Except 6
2015	40				
2016	CA		JZ	EXIT	Jump if Nothing Left
2017	1C				
2018	20				
2019	7E		MOV	A,M	Get the No. Again and Copy it
201A	23		INX	H	to 2001
201B	77		MOV	M,A	
201C	CF	EXIT	RST	1	

6.24 PROJECT 31: TESTING FOR THE CONDITION (HIGH OR LOW STATE) OF BIT SEVEN OF AN 8-BIT (HEX-IT) NUMBER

This program does exactly the same thing as Project 24, except that it tests the condition of the eighth bit position of an 8-Bit number; that is Bit-7. In many microprocessor applications it is necessary to test bit conditions (High or Low) and store this information for reference. Hence, the authors believe it behooves the reader to know the exact bit testing programs for each bit of a Hex-it number, although only minor program changes occur in each of the bit testing programs. The reader is reminded to refer to Projects 23 and 24 for the details of the program objectives.

MEMORY INFORMATION			INSTRUCTION		
ADDRESS	DATA	LABEL	OPCODE	OPERAND	COMMENT
2000	ANY				Data to Be Tested
		RESULT			Data Copied if Bit 7 is High
2010	21	START	LXI	H,2000	Point to the Number
2011	00				
2012	20				
2013	7E		MOV	A,M	
2014	E6		ANI	80	Reset All the Bits Except 7
2015	80				
2016	CA		JZ	EXIT	Jump if Nothing Left
2017	1C				
2018	20				
2019	7E		MOV	A,M	Get the No. Again and Copy It
201A	23		INX	H	to 2001
201B	77		MOV	M,A	
201C	CF	EXIT	RST	1	

6.25 PROJECT 32: COMPARISON OF TWO NUMBERS TO TEST FOR EQUALITY

This program will compare the contents of data location 2000 and 2001 to test the numbers in these locations to see if they are equal. If the numbers are equal they will be put into memory location 2002, and if they are not equal the number 00 will be stored in location 2002.

MEMORY INFORMATION			INSTRUCTION		COMMENT
ADDRESS	DATA	LABEL	OPCODE	OPERAND	
2000		DATA			First Number
2001		DATA			Second Number
2002		RESULT			Equal Numbers Put Into This Location; if Not 00 Will Appear.
2010	21		LXI	H,2000	
2011	00				
2012	20				
2013	7E		MOV	A,M	Get the 1st Number
2014	2C		INR	L	
2015	BE		CMP	M	Compare the Two Numbers
2016	CA		JZ	EQUAL	Jump to Equal If They are Equal
2017	1D				
2018	20				
2019	2C		INR	L	
201A	36		MVI	A,00	Store 00 Because They are Not Equal
201B	00				
201C	CF		RST	1	
201D	2C	EQUAL	INR	L	
201E	77		MOV	M,A	Store the No. Because They are Equal
201F	CF		RST	1	

6.26 PROJECT 33: ODD OR EVEN PARITY CHECK

This program will determine if the parity of the number in memory location 2000 is odd or even. If the number is odd a 00 will be stored in 2001 and if the number is even an EE will be stored in 2001.

MEMORY INFORMATION			INSTRUCTION		COMMENT
ADDRESS	DATA	LABEL	OPCODE	OPERAND	
2000		DATA			Data
2001		RESULT			Data Even Number EE Appears Data Odd Number 00 Appears
2010	21		LXI	H,2000	
2011	00				

MEMORY INFORMATION		INSTRUCTION			
ADDRESS	DATA	LABEL	OPCODE	OPERAND	COMMENT
2012	20				
2013	7E		MOV	A,M	Get the No.
2014	B7		ORA	A	Set the Flag
2015	E2		JPO	ODD	If its Odd Go to the Odd Routine
2016	1C				
2017	20				
2018	2C		INR	L	Point to Result
2019	36		MVI	M,EE	Store EE for Even
201A	EE				
201B	CF		RST	1	
201C	2C	ODD	INR	L	Point to Result
201D	36		MVI	M,00	Store 00 for Odd
201E	00				
201F	CF	EXIT	RST	1	

6.27 PROJECT 34: MULTIPLICATION BY TWO, EMPLOYING BIT ROTATION

This program will take the contents of location 2000 and shift it to the left, which is the same as multiplying the number by 2. The results will be stored in address 2001 and if the number is greater than hexadecimal FF the carry flag will be set.

MEMORY INFORMATION		INSTRUCTION			
ADDRESS	DATA	LABEL	OPCODE	OPERAND	COMMENT
2000	ANY				Number to Be Multiplied By 2
2001		RESULT			Storage for the Result
2010	3A	START	LDA	2000	Load No, to Be Multiplied
2011	00				
2012	20				
2013	37		STC		Set the Carry Flag } Clear Carry
2014	3F		CMC		Reset the Carry Flag } Clear Carry
2015	17		RAL		Shift (Multiply by 2)
2016	32		STA	2001	Store the Results
2017	01				
2018	20				
2019	CF		RST	1	

Chapter 7
Intermediate Software Projects

7.1 INTRODUCTION

Some of the projects in this chapter can be executed with the purchase of the BASIC SDK-85 trainer. However, the authors suggest that, at this time, the reader make the necessary modifications to expand the BASIC SDK-85 trainer so all of the projects in this chapter can be executed.

Refer to Chapter one and perform all of the hardware projects in order to expand the trainer. The expansion of the trainer requires the purchase of additional IC chips from INTEL and Texas Instrument Corp. Also, LEDs and switches must be purchased. Details of purchase are given in Chapter one.

The program format for the projects in this chapter correspond to the format of the previous chapter. Sometimes obvious data statements are eliminated where appropriate.

7.2 PROJECT 35: MULTIPLICATION OF TWO EIGHT BIT NUMBERS BY REPETITIVE ADDITION

This program will multiply two numbers together from the contents of data location 2000 and 2001, and then determine the quickest method of multiplication and store the result in address 2002 and 2003.

MEMORY INFORMATION			INSTRUCTION		
ADDRESS	DATA	LABEL	OPCODE	OPERAND	COMMENT
2000	ANY				Two Numbers That Are To Be
2001	ANY				Multiplied Together
2002		RESULT			MSB Of Answer
2003		RESULT			LSB Of Answer
2010	06	START	MVI	B,00	Set B Of BC To Ø
2011	00				
2012	21		LXI	H,0000	Clear HL For Addition
2013	00				
2014	00				
2015	3A		LDA	2000	Get First Number
2016	00				And Put In C
2017	20				
2018	4F		MOV	C,A	
2019	3A		LDA	2001	Get Second Number
201A	01				
201B	20				
201C	B9		CMP	C	Compare The Lowest Of Two No.
201D	DA		JC	LOOP	Jump If Set For
201E	24				Quickest Multiplication
201F	20				
2020	4F		MOV	C,A	
2021	3A		LDA	2000	Reverse If Not
2022	00				
2023	20				
2024	3D	LOOP	DCR	A	
2025	09		DAD	B	Loop For Multiplication
2026	C2		JNZ	LOOP	C Repetitive Addition
2027	24				
2028	20				
2029	22		SHLD	2002H	Store Result In 2002
202A	02				And 2003
202B	20				
202C	CF		RST	1	

7.3 PROJECT 36: THE DIVISION OF TWO EIGHT BIT NUMBERS BY REPETITIVE SUBTRACTION

This program will divide the number in data location 2000 by the number in data location 2001. The result will be rounded off and stored in location 2002.

MEMORY INFORMATION			INSTRUCTION		
ADDRESS	DATA	LABEL	OPCODE	OPERAND	COMMENT
2000	ANY				Number To Be Divided
2001	ANY	EXCEPTØ			Divisor
2002		RESULT			Answer
2010	21	START	LXI	H,2000	
2011	00				Point To First Number
2012	20				And Load It
2013	7E		MOV	A,M	
2014	23		INX	H	Point To Second Number
2015	46		MOV	B,M	And Load It
2016	0E		MVI	C,00	Clear Counter
2017	00				
2018	B8	CONT	CMP	B	Test If A>C And Jump If Not
2019	DA		JC	ROUND	
201A	21				
201B	20				
201C	90		SUB	B	Subtract And Increase Counter
201D	0C		INC	C	
201E	C3		JMP	CONT	Loop Back
201F	18				
2020	20				
2021	07	ROUND	RLC		Multiply Remainder By Two (2)
2022	B8		CMP	B	Test If A>B At This Time
2023	DA		JC	DONE	If Not Jump
2024	27				
2025	20				
2026	0C		INR	C	Round Up
2027	23	DONE	INX	H	Store Result
2028	71		MOV	M,C	
2029	CF		RST	1	

7.4 PROJECT 37: MEMORY COPY

This program will move a block of data from one place in memory to another. The source will be pointed to by HL registers; the destination will be the DE registers; and the BC registers will contain the number of bytes. (See EXAMPLE before loading program).

MEMORY INFORMATION			INSTRUCTION		
ADDRESS	DATA	LABEL	OPCODE	OPERAND	COMMENT
2010	21	START	LXI	H,2010	Get START Address
2011	10				
2012	20				

MEMORY INFORMATION			INSTRUCTION		
ADDRESS	DATA	LABEL	OPCODE	OPERAND	COMMENT
2013	11		LXI	D,2030	Get Destination Address
2014	30				
2015	20				
2016	01		LXI	B,0020	Number Of Bytes To Move
2017	20				
2018	00				
2019	7E	LOOP	MOV	A,M	Get a Byte
201A	12		STAX	D	Store It
201B	23		INX	H	Increment Pointers
201C	13		INX	D	
201D	0B		DCX	B	Decrement Count And Test To See If Done
201E	78		MOV	A,B	
201F	B1		ORA	C	
2020	C2		JNZ	LOOP	If Not Go Back
2021	19				
2022	20				
2023	CF		RST	1	

7.5 PROJECT 38: FINDING THE SQUARE OF A NUMBER EMPLOYING A LOOK-UP TABLE

This program will look-up a value in a table and return the value in location 2000. Values should be between the decimal numbers 1 and 9 because of the length of words for this trainer.

Example:

Copy this program between memory locations 2030 and 2043. In other words, the destination address of this program is 2030, hence the ending address of the copied program must be 2043.

1. Before loading the program into memory, make all memory locations between 2030 and 2043 have 00 for data.
2. Load the program in Project 37 and execute.
3. If the program has executed properly, it will be copied in locations 2030 and 2043.

The memory copy doesn't have to be this program; it can be from any start address to any destination address.

MEMORY INFORMATION			INSTRUCTION		
ADDRESS	DATA	LABEL	OPCODE	OPERAND	COMMENT
2000	ANY				Number To Be Squared Between 1 And 9
2001	01				Decimal values for squares
2002	04				
2003	09				
2004	16				

MEMORY INFORMATION			INSTRUCTION		
ADDRESS	DATA	LABEL	OPCODE	OPERAND	COMMENT
2005	25				Decimal Values For Squares
2006	36				
2007	49				
2008	64				
2009	81				
2010	26	START	MVI	H,0	
2011	00				
2012	3A		LDA	2000	Get Value Of Number
2013	00				To Look Up (Offset)
2014	20				
2015	6F		MOV	L,A	Store Offset As 16-Bit No. In HL
2016	11		LXI	D,2000	Load Start Of Table
2017	00				
2018	20				
2019	19		DAD	D	Add To Get New Address
201A	7E		MOV	A,M	Get Answer
201B	32		STA	2000	Store Answer
201C	00				
201D	20				
201E	CF		RST	1	

7.6 PROJECT 39: ECHO KEYBOARD TO DISPLAY

This program will accept an input from the keyboard and display it on the LEDs. When the program has been executed properly an E will appear in the Address Field.

MEMORY INFORMATION			INSTRUCTION		
ADDRESS	DATA	LABEL	OPCODE	OPERAND	COMMENT
2010	31	START	LXI	SP,20C2	Set The Stack Pointer
2011	C2				
2012	20				
2013	3E		MVI	A,0E	Set Interrupt Mask
2014	0E				
2015	30		SIM		
2016	FB	LOOP	EI		Enable Interrupt
2017	CD		CALL	02E7	Call Keyboard Routine And Return
2018	E7				With Character In A Register
2019	02				
201A	CD		CALL	036E	Call Display Routine With
201B	6E				Character In A Register
201C	03				
201D	C3		JMP	LOOP	Do It All Over Again
201E	16				
201F	20				E Will Appear On The LED Display
					The Program Is Executing

Example: (E must appear in the Address Field)

You may press any key except RESET, VECT INTR, NEXT, and EXEC and display character(s) and the LEDs. Pressing the following keys will display the character(s) shown below.

KEY	DISPLAY	KEY	DISPLAY
0	00	GO	12
1	01	SUBST	13
2	02	MEM	
3	03	EXAM	14
4	04	REG	
5	05	SINGLE	15
6	06	STEP	
7	07		
8	08		
9	09		
A	0A		
B	0B		
C	0C		
D	0D		
E	0E		
F	0F		

7.7 PROJECT 40: TWO CHARACTER KEYBOARD DISPLAY

This program is similar to the previous project, except that it takes two characters from the keyboard and displays them on the LEDs.

MEMORY INFORMATION			INSTRUCTION		
ADDRESS	DATA	LABEL	OPCODE	OPERAND	COMMENT
2010	31	START	LXI	SP,20C2	Load Stack Pointer
2011	C2				
2012	20				
2013	3E		MVI	0E	Set Interrupt Mask
2014	0E				
2015	30		SIM		
2016	FB		EI		
2017	CD		CALL	02E7	Get First Character
2018	E7				
2019	02				
201A	F5		PUSH	PSW	Save It Display It
201B	CD		CALL	036E	
201C	6E				
201D	03				

MEMORY INFORMATION			INSTRUCTION		
ADDRESS	DATA	LABEL	OPCODE	OPERAND	COMMENT
201E	F1		POP	PSW	Shift It Into The MSB
201F	07		RLC		
2020	07		RLC		
2021	07		RLC		
2022	07		RLC		
2023	47		MOV	B,A	Put It In B And Save It
2024	C5		PUSH	B	
2025	CD		CALL	02E7	Get Next Character
2026	E7				
2027	02				
2028	C1		POP	B	Put Them Together
2029	B0		ORA	B	
202A	CD		CALL	036E	Display The Result
202B	6E				
202C	03				
202D	C3		JMP	START	START OVER
202E	10				
202F	20				

7.8 PROJECT 41: ADD TWO HEXADECIMAL NUMBERS FROM THE KEYBOARD EMPLOYING CALCULATOR STYLE

This program should function as a simple Hex calculator by adding only 1-byte with no overflow error message.

MEMORY INFORMATION			INSTRUCTION		
ADDRESS	DATA	LABEL	OPCODE	OPERAND	COMMENT
2010	AF	NEW NO.	XRA	A	
2011	32		STA	2000	Clear No. Storage
2012	00				
2013	20				
2014	31	AGAIN	LXI	SP,20C2	Load Stack Pointer
2015	C2				
2016	20				
2017	3E		MVI	A,0E	
2018	0E				
2019	30		SIM		Set Interrupt Mask
201A	FB		EI		
201B	CD		CALL	02E7	Get First Number
201C	E7				
201D	02				
201E	F5		PUSH	PSW	
201F	CD		CALL	036E	Save And Display It
2020	6E				
2021	03				

MEMORY ADDRESS	INFORMATION DATA	LABEL	INSTRUCTION OPCODE	OPERAND	COMMENT
2022	F1		POP	PSW	Restore No.
2023	07		RLC		
2024	07		RLC		Shift It Into The MSB
2025	07		RLC		
2026	07		RLC		
2027	47		MOV	B,A	Put No. In B And Save
2028	C5		PUSH	B	
2029	CD		CALL	02E7	
202A	E7				Get Next Number
202B	02				
202C	C1		POP	B	Combine Numbers
202D	B0		ORA	B	
202E	F5		PUSH	PSW	Store And Display
202F	CD		CALL	036E	
2030	6E				
2031	03				
2032	21		LXI	H,2000	Point To Storage
2033	00				
2034	20				
2035	AF		XRA	A	
2036	BE		CMP	M	
2037	C2		JNZ	ADD	Test To See If Storage Contains
2038	3F				A Number
2039	20				
203A	F1		POP	PSW	If Not Put No. There
203B	77		MOV	M,A	
203C	C3		JMP	AGAIN	Go Get Second No.
203D	14				
203E	20				
203F	F1	ADD	POP	PSW	Add The Two Numbers
2040	86		ADD	M	
2041	00		NOP		
2042	CD		CALL	036E	Display Answer
2043	6E				
2044	03				
2045	C3		JMP	NEW NO.	Start Over
2046	10				
2047	20				

After the program is executed, the character E will appear in the Address Field. The following examples will illustrate how this project can be used as a Hex calculator by adding two 1-byte numbers but with NO overflow message.

EXAMPLE 1: Adding 01 + 02 = 03

KEY	ADDR	DATA	COMMENTS
0	E	00	First keystroke.
1	E	01	Second keystroke.
0	E	00	Third keystroke.
2	E	03	Fourth keystroke yields answer in Data Field.

To clear the Data Field the following keystrokes must be made:
RESET, SUBST, 2010, EXEC, GO, 2010, EXEC
MEM

When the preceding keystrokes are made, the character E will appear in the Address Field. Before going on to the next example make sure E appears in the Address Field; if not repeat the keystrokes after EXAMPLE 1.

EXAMPLE 2: Adding 1F + 01 = 20.

KEY	ADDR	DATA	COMMENTS
1	E	01	
F	E	1F	
0	E	00	
1	E	20	Fourth Keystroke yields answer.

7.9 PROJECT 42: ADD TWO DECIMAL NUMBERS FROM THE KEYBOARD EMPLOYING CALCULATOR STYLE

This program should function as a simple decimal calculator by adding only 1-byte with another byte. No overflow error message is given.

MEMORY INFORMATION			INSTRUCTION		
ADDRESS	DATA	LABEL	OPCODE	OPERAND	COMMENT
2010	AF	NEW NO.	XRA	A	
2011	32		STA	2000	Clear No. Storage
2012	00				
2013	20				
2014	31	AGAIN	LXI	SP,20C2	Load Stack Pointer
2015	C2				
2016	20				
2017	3E		MVI	A,0E	
2018	0E				
2019	30		SIM		Set Interrupt Mask
201A	FB		EI		

MEMORY INFORMATION			INSTRUCTION		
ADDRESS	DATA	LABEL	OPCODE	OPERAND	COMMENT
201B	CD		CALL	02E7	Get First No.
201C	E7				
201D	02				
201E	F5		PUSH	PSW	
201F	CD		CALL	036E	Save And Display It
2020	6E				
2021	03				
2022	F1		POP	PSW	Restore No.
2023	07		RLC		
2024	07		RLC		Shift It Into The MSB
2025	07		RLC		
2026	07		RLC		
2027	47		MOV	B,A	Put No. In B And Save
2028	C5		PUSH	B	
2029	CD		CALL	02E7	Get Next No.
202A	E7				
202B	02				
202C	C1		POP	B	} Combine Numbers
202D	B0		ORA	B	
202E	F5		PUSH	PSW	} Store And Display
202F	CD		CALL	036E	
2030	6E				
2031	03				
2032	21		LXI	H,2000	Point To Storage
2033	00				
2034	20				
2035	AF		XRA	A	
2036	BE		CMP	M	
2037	C2		JNZ	ADD	Test To See If Storage Contains A Number
2038	3F				
2039	20				
203A	F1		POP	PSW	} If Not Put No. There
203B	77		MOV	M,A	
203C	C3		JMP	AGAIN	Go Get Second No.
203D	14				
203E	20				
203F	F1	ADD	POP	PSW	Add The Two Numbers
2040	86		ADD	M	
2041	27			DAA	
2042	CD		CALL	036E	Display Answer
2043	6E				
2044	03				
2045	C3		JMP	NEW NO.	Start Over
2046	10				
2047	20				

KEY	ADDR	DATA	COMMENTS
1	E	01	First keystroke
0	E	10	Second keystroke.
2	E	02	Third keystroke.
0	E	30	Fourth keystroke yields answer.

7.10 PROJECT 43: COMBINATION LOCK

This program will turn the SDK-85 trainer into a combination lock. The 6 digit combination is stored in location 2050 through 2055, the error check storage is in location 2057, and location 2058 contains the open message with location 2060 containing the locked message.

After the program is executed properly, the letter E will appear in the Address Field. The reader can now press any 6 digit combination. If the wrong six digits are pressed the message LOCH will appear on the LED display. If the 6 digit combination is pressed as appears in memory locations 2052 through 205B the message OPEr will appear on the LED display. In both of the examples the character E will not appear when LOCH or OPEr is displayed on the LEDs. If the reader OPENs the lock and then presses another 6 digit combination which is not the correct combination, the message LOCH should appear again.

MEMORY INFORMATION			INSTRUCTION		COMMENT
ADDRESS	DATA	LABEL	OPCODE	OPERAND	
200F	FB		EI		
2010	31	START	LXI	SP,20C2H	
2011	C2				
2012	20				
2013	AF		XRA	A	
2014	32		STA	2057H	Clear Error Flag
2015	57				
2016	20				
2017	3E		MVI	A,0EH	
2018	0E				
2019	30		SIM		Set Mask For Keyboard
201A	21		LXI	H,2050	Interrupt
201B	50				
201C	20				
201D	E5	GET CHAR	PUSH	H	Point To Combination And Store It
201E	CD		CALL	RDKBD	Get Character
201F	E7				
2020	02				
2021	E1		POP	H	
2022	BE		CMP	M	Compare With Correct Combination

MEMORY INFORMATION		INSTRUCTION			COMMENT
ADDRESS	DATA	LABEL	OPCODE	OPERAND	
2023	CA		JZ	GO	Jump If Correct
2024	2B				
2025	20				
2026	3E		MVI	A,08H	
2027	08				
2028	32		STA	2057H	Set Error Flag
2029	57				
202A	20				
202B	2C	GO	INR	L	Point To Next Digit
202C	3E		MVI	A,56H	
202D	56				
202E	BD		CMP	L	Check If End Of Combination
202F	CA		JZ	MSG	Go If End
2030	35				
2031	20				
2032	C3		JMP	GET CHAR	If Not Get Next
2033	1D				
2034	20				
2035	21	MSG	LXI	H,2057	
2036	57				
2037	20				
2038	7E		MOV	A,M	Get Error Offset
2039	2C		INR	L	Point To First Message
203A	8D		ADC	L	Add Error Offset (If Any)
203B	6F		MOV	L,A	Point HL To Correct Message
203C	AF		XRA	A	} Set Conditions For Display
203D	47		MOV	B,A	
203E	CD		CALL	OPPT	Display Message
203F	B7				
2040	02				
2041	C3		JMP	START	Do It All Again
2042	10				
2043	20				
2050	00				} Combination
2051	01				
2052	02				
2053	03				
2054	04				
2055	05				
2058	00		O		} Oper Message "OPEN"
2059	12		P		
205A	0E		E		
205B	14		r		

MEMORY INFORMATION		INSTRUCTION			
ADDRESS	DATA	LABEL	OPCODE	OPERAND	COMMENT
2060	11		L		LOCH Message "LOCKED"
2061	00		O		
2062	0C		C		
2063	10		H		

7.11 PROJECT 44: RANDOM NUMBER GENERATOR NO.1

This program is executed by going to location 2010 and pressing the vector interrupt button which will cause a random number to appear between the hexadecimal numbers 00 and FF.

MEMORY INFORMATION		INSTRUCTION			
ADDRESS	DATA	LABEL	OPCODE	OPERAND	COMMENT
2010	31	START	LXI	SP,20CEH	
2011	C2				
2012	20				
2013	3E		MVI	A,1A	Enable And Clear 7.5 Interrupt
2014	1A				
2015	30		SIM		
2016	FB		EI		
2017	21		LXI	H,2000H	Point To Random No. Storage
2018	00				
2019	20				
201A	3C	GEN	INR	A	Count
201B	C3		JMP	GEN	
201C	1A				
201D	20				
201E	77	NUM	MOV	M,A	Store Random Number
201F	D1		POP	DE	Remove Return Address From Stack
2020	CD		CALL	036EH	Display Random Number
2021	6E				
2022	03				
2023	C3		JMP	2010H	Do It Again
2024	10				
2025	20				
20CE	C3		JMP	NUM	Go To Rest Of Program
20CF	1E				
20DO	20				

7.12 PROJECT 45: NUMBER GUESS GAME

This program is a game between you and the computer. To start the game you must go to location 2010, then press the vector interrupt button and enter your guess of a hexadecimal number between 00 and FF.

MEMORY INFORMATION			INSTRUCTION		
ADDRESS	DATA	LABEL	OPCODE	OPERAND	COMMENT
2010	31	BEGIN	LXI	SP,20C2	
2011	C2				
2012	20				
2013	3E		MVI	A,1A	Reset Unmask And Enable 7.5 Interrupt
2014	1A				
2015	30		SIM		
2016	FB		EI		
2017	21		LXI	H,2000	Point To Mystery Storage
2018	00				
2019	20				
201A	3C	START	INR	A	Count Until Interrupted
201B	C3		JMP	START	
201C	1A				
201D	20				
201E	77	GAME	MOV	M,A	Store Number
201F	21	RUN	LXI	H,2000	Point Again
2020	00				
2021	20				
2022	E5		PUSH	H	
2023	3E		MVI	A,1E	Get First Digit From Keyboard
2024	1E				
2025	30		SIM		
2026	FB		EI		
2027	CD		CALL	02E7	
2028	E7				
2029	02				
202A	F5		PUSH	PSW	
202B	CD		CALL	036E	Display Digit
202C	6E				
202D	03				
202E	F1		POP	PSW	
202F	07		RLC		
2030	07		RLC		Shift Character Into The MSB
2031	07		RLC		
2032	07		RLC		
2033	47		MOV	B,A	Put It Into B And Safe it
2034	C5		PUSH	B	
2035	CD		CALL	02E7	
2036	E7				Get Next Character
2037	02				
2038	C1		POP	B	
2039	B0		ORA	B	Or The Two Characters Together
203A	F5		PUSH	PSW	
203B	CD		CALL	036E	Display The Guess

MEMORY INFORMATION		INSTRUCTION			
ADDRESS	DATA	LABEL	OPCODE	OPERAND	COMMENT
203C	6E				
203D	03				
203E	F1		POP	PSW	
203F	E1		POP	H	
2040	BE		CMP	M	Test If Guess Is Correct
2041	CA		JZ	RIGHT	
2042	59				
2043	20				
2044	DA		JC	LO	
2045	4F				
2046	20				
2047	2C		INR	L	Guess Is Too High
2048	AF		XRA	A	
2049	CD		CALL	02B7	
204A	B7				
204B	02				
204C	C3		JMP	RUN	
204D	1F				
204E	20				
204F	21	LO	LXI	H,2005	Guess Is Too Low
2050	05				
2051	20				
2052	AF		XRA	A	
2053	CD		CALL	02B7	
2054	B7				
2055	02				
2056	C3		JMP	RUN	
2057	1F				
2058	20				
2059	21	RIGHT	LXI	H,2009	Show That Guess Is Correct
205A	09				
205B	20				
205C	AF	XRA	A		
205D	CD		CALL	02B7	
205E	B7			START	
205F	02				
2060	C3		JMP		Begin Over Again At 2010
2061	10				
2062	20				
20CE	C3		JMP	GAME	Vector For 7.5 Interrupt
20CF	1E				
20DO	20				

MEMORY INFORMATION		INSTRUCTION			
ADDRESS	DATA	LABEL	OPCODE	OPERAND	COMMENT
2000	00				Data For Words
2001	15				
2002	10				Hi-Lo And Correct
2003	13				
2004	15				
2005	15				
2006	11				
2007	00				
2008	15				
2009	0C				
200A	00				
200B	00				
200C	14				

After the program is loaded into memory, the character E will appear in the Address Field. The game is ready to play. The following example will illustrate a few keystrokes to help the reader play the game.

EXAMPLE:

KEY	ADDR	DATA	COMMENTS
VECT INTR	E		The first keystroke to play the game will not change the display.
00	L0	00	The first guess we put in is purposely low in order to illustrate the display of a low guess. We know we have guessed low; therefore, our next guess must be higher than our low guess.
FF	HI	FF	The second guess is purposely high to illustrate the display of a high guess. As indicated in the first two guesses, the Address Field shows whether you are lower (LO) or higher (HI) than the random number stored in location 2000 for this game. The Data Field shows your guess.
XX	C00r	XX	Keep entering a guess until the correct number (XX) is entered and matches the random stored in location 2000. The Address Field will display C00r when the guess is correct.

To start another game press RESET and VECT INTR and begin another game.

7.13 PROJECT 46: A GAME CALLED TWENTY-ONE (21) MATCHES

This program is a game which you can play against the computer. The computer has twenty-one decimal (15 hexadecimal) matches. You and the computer will take away 1, 2, or 3 matches per turn, until there are NO matches remaining. The player who takes away the last match wins.

MEMORY INFORMATION			INSTRUCTION		
ADDRESS	DATA	LABEL	OPCODE	OPERAND	COMMENT
2010	31	START	LXI	SP,20C2	
2011	C2				
2012	20				
2013	06		MVI	B, 15H	Store Number Of Matches
2014	15				
2015	3E		MVI	A,0E	
2016	0E				Set Interrupt For Keyboard
2017	30		SIM		
2018	C5	LOOP 1	PUSH	B	
2019	78		MOV	A,B	
201A	CD		CALL	036E	Display Number of Matches
201B	6E				
201C	03				
201D	CD	GET	CALL	02E7	Get Character
201E	E7				
201F	02				
2020	E6		ANI	03	Make It A Legal Number If It Isn't
2021	03				
2022	CA		JZ	GET	
2023	1D				
2024	20				
2025	F5		PUSH	PSW	
2026	CD		CALL	036E	Display The Number
2027	6E				
2028	03				
2029	11		LXI	D,FFFF	Pause For ≅ 1 = Second
202A	FF				
202B	FF				
202C	CD		CALL	05F1	
202D	F1				
202E	05				
202F	C1		POP	B	
2030	F1		POP	PSW	
2031	90		SUB	B	Take Matches Away And Put
2032	47		MOV	B,A	Number Back In B
2033	AF		XRA	A	
2034	C6	GEN	ADI	A,04	Generates The Computers
2035	04				Number Of Matches

MEMORY INFORMATION			INSTRUCTION		
ADDRESS	DATA	LABEL	OPCODE	OPERAND	COMMENT
2036	B8		CMP	B	
2037	DA		JC	GEN	
2038	34				
2039	20				
203A	D6		SUI	04	
203B	04				
203C	4F		MOV	C,A	
203D	78		MOV	A,B	
203E	91		SUB	C	
203F	E6		ANI	03	
2040	03				
2041	C2		JNZ	CONT	Jump If The Computer Will Win
2042	46		r		
2043	20				
2044	3E		MVI	A,01	
2045	01				
2046	4F	CONT	MOV	C,A	
2047	78		MOV	A,B	
2048	91		SUB	C	Subtract Computers Number
2049	47		MOV	B,A	And Store Number Back In B
204A	FA		JM	WIN	
204B	5D				
204C	20				
204D	CA		JZ	LOST	Test For Win, Lost
204E	53				Or Not Done
204F	20				
2050	C3		JMP	LOOP 1	
2051	18				
2052	20				
2053	AF	LOST	XRA	A	
2054	21		LXI	H,2000	
2055	00				Point To And Display
2056	20				Lose Message
2057	CD		CALL	02B7	
2058	B7				
2059	02				
205A	C3		JMP	START	
205B	10				
205C	20				
205D	AF	WIN	XRA	A	
205E	21		LXI	H,2004	
205F	04				Point To And Display
2060	20				0000 For Win
2061	CD		CALL	02B7	

MEMORY INFORMATION			INSTRUCTION		
ADDRESS	DATA	LABEL	OPCODE	OPERAND	COMMENT
2062	B7				
2063	02				
2064	C3		JMP	START	
2065	10				
2066	20				
2000	11	L			Indication Of Game Winner
2001	00	O			
2002	05	S			
2003	0E	E			
2004	0B	G			
2005	00	O			
2006	00	O			
2007	0D	D			

After the program is executed, the character E will appear in the Address Field and the hexadecimal number 15 (equivalent to decimal 21) will appear in the Data Field. The game is ready to be played. The reader can now pick one of three numbers—1, 2, or 3—by pressing one of those keys. Your number pick will appear for one second in the Data Field. Then your pick will be subtracted from 15, along with the computer's selection. In other words, two numbers will be subtracted from 15, yours and the computer's. At this point another selection must be made by the reader, and the above procedure will be repeated by the program. The selection process continues until there are NO matches remaining. The player or computer taking away the last match wins. The word GOOD is displayed if the reader wins, and the word LOSE is displayed if the computer wins. When the game is over 15 will appear in the Data Field with either the word LOSE or GOOD appearing in the Address Field. At this point a new game can be played.

7.14 PROJECT 47: ROTATING ONE BLANK LIGHT WITH CONTROLLING SPEED

The remainder of the projects in this book require the reader to employ all of the hardware projects in Chapter one. This program rotates one blank (OFF) LED back and forth on output Port 22. The switches on input Port 21 are employed to control the speed of the rotating lights.

After the program has been properly executed, the character E will appear in the Address Field. Also, the LEDs connected to OUT PORT 22 will begin rotating. The reader can vary the speed of the rotating blank LED by moving the switches on the DIP package.

MEMORY INFORMATION			INSTRUCTION		
ADDRESS	DATA	LABEL	OPCODE	OPERAND	COMMENT
2011	31		LXI	SP,20C2	
2012	C2				
2013	20				
2014	3E		MVI	A,02	Define Port 22 As Output
2015	02				
2016	D3		OUT	2Ø	
2017	20				
2018	3E		MVI	A,FF	
2019	FF				
201A	17	LEFTCY	RAL		Move Display
201B	17	LEFT	RAL		Move Display
201C	D2		JNC	RIGHTCY	Test If Display Is OFF LED's
201D	25				
201E	20				
201F	CD		CALL	DISPLAY	Display Pattern
2020	30				
2021	20				
2022	C3		JMP	LEFT	Continue
2023	1B				
2024	20				
2025	1F	RIGHTCY	RAR		Move Display
2026	1F	RIGHT	RAR		Move Display
2027	D2		JNC	LEFTCY	Test If Display Is OFF LED's
2028	1A				
2029	20				
202A	CD		CALL	DISPLAY	Display Pattern
202B	30				
202C	20				
202D	C3		JMP	Right	Continue
202E	26				
202F	20				
2030	F5	DISPLAY	PUSH	PSW	Store LED Display
2031	D3		OUT	72	Display It
2032	22				
2033	1E		MVI	E,10	
2034	ØØ				
2035	DB		IN	21	Get Delay Time
2036	21				
2037	57		MOV	D,A	Put It Into DE
2038	1B	DELAY	DCX	D	Delay Routine
2039	7A		MOV	A,D	

MEMORY INFORMATION			INSTRUCTION		
ADDRESS	DATA	LABEL	OPCODE	OPERAND	COMMENT
203A	B3		ORA	E	} Delay Routine
203B	C2		JNZ	DELAY	
203C	38				
203D	20				
203E	F1		POP	PSW	Restore Display
203F	C9		RET		Return

7.15 PROJECT 48: ROTATING LIGHTS (NO BLANKS) WITH CONTROLLING SPEED

This program rotates the LEDs on output Port 22 back and forth. The switches on input Port 21 are employed to control the speed of the rotating lights.

After the program has been properly executed, the character E will appear in the Address Field. Also, one of the LEDs connected to OUT PORT 22 will begin rotating. The reader can vary the speed of the rotating LED by moving the switches on the DIP package.

MEMORY INFORMATION			INSTRUCTION		
ADDRESS	DATA	LABEL	OPCODE	OPERAND	COMMENT
2011	3E		MVI	A, 02	} Initialize Ports 21 and 22
2012	02				
2013	D3		OUT	20	
2014	20				
2015	31		LXI	SP, 2900	
2016	00				
2017	29				
2018	3E		MVI	A, 10	
2019	10				
201A	17	LOOP 1	RAL		Move LED
201B	D3		OUT	22	Display the New Position
201C	22				
201D	CD		CALL	SUB	Go to Time Delay Routine
201E	2F				
201F	20				
2020	D2		JNC	LOOP 1	Continue
2021	1A				
2022	20				
2023	1F	LOOP 2	RAR		Move LED
2024	D3		OUT	22	Display the New Position
2025	22				
2026	CD		CALL	SUB	Go to Time Delay Routine
2027	2F				

MEMORY INFORMATION			INSTRUCTION		
ADDRESS	DATA	LABEL	OPCODE	OPERAND	COMMENT
2028	20				
2029	D2		JNC	LOOP 2	Continue
202A	23				
202B	20				
202C	C3		JMP	LOOP 1	Reverse Direction
202D	1A				
202E	20				
202F	F5	SUB	PUSH	PSW	Store Display
2030	DB		IN	21	Read in Time Delay
2031	21				
2032	57		MOV	D,A	Load DE with the Delay Time
2033	5F		MOV	E,A	
2034	CD		CALL	DELAY	Delay to Slow Display
2035	F1				
2036	05				
2037	F1		POP	PSW	Restore Display
2038	C9		RET		

Note: This program requires Expansion RAM. (See Appendix)

7.16 PROJECT 49: ROTATING LIGHTS (NO SPEED CONTROL)

This program rotates the LEDs back and forth on output Port 22 without employing speed control.

MEMORY INFORMATION			INSTRUCTION		
ADDRESS	DATA	LABEL	OPCODE	OPERAND	COMMENT
2010	3E		MVI	A, 02	Initialize Port 22 For Output to LED's
2011	02				
2012	D3		OUT	20	
2013	20				
2014	31		LXI	SP, 2900	
2015	00				
2016	29				
2017	3E		MVI	A, 10	Set 1 Bit On
2018	10				
2019	17	LOOP 1	RAL		Move Display LED
201A	D3		OUT	22	Display LED Position
201B	22				
201C	CD		CALL	SUB	Call Delay Routine
201D	2E				
201E	20				
201F	D2		JNC	LOOP 1	Continue if No Carry
2020	19				

MEMORY INFORMATION			INSTRUCTION		
ADDRESS	DATA	LABEL	OPCODE	OPERAND	COMMENT
2021	20				
2022	1F	LOOP 2	RAR		Move Display LED
2023	D3		OUT	22	Display Position
2024	22				
2025	CD		CALL	SUB	Call Delay
2026	2E				
2027	20				
2028	D2		JNC	LOOP 2	Continue if No Carry
2029	22				
202A	20				
202B	C3		JMP	LOOP 1	Reverse Direction
202C	19				
202D	20				
202E	F5	SUB	PUSH	PSW	Store Display Value
202F	11		LXI	D, 8000	Load DE with Time Delay
2030	00				
2031	80				
2032	CD		CALL	DELAY	Call SDK-85 Delay Routine
2033	F1				
2034	05				
2035	F1		POP	PSW	Restore Display Value
2036	C9		RET		

Note: This Program Requires Expansion RAM.

7.17 PROJECT 50: ROTATING BLANK LIGHTS WITHOUT SPEED CONTROL

This program rotates the LEDs back and forth on output Port 22 with one blank LED, without employing speed control.

MEMORY INFORMATION			INSTRUCTION		
ADDRESS	DATA	LABEL	OPCODE	OPERAND	COMMENT
2011	31		LXI	SP, 20C2	
2012	C2				
2013	20				
2014	3E		MVI	A, 02	Initialize Port 22 for Output
2015	02				
2016	D3		OUT	20	
2017	20				
2018	3E		MVI	A, FF	Set all Bits ON Except CY
2019	FF				
201A	17	LEFTCY	RAL		Move Display
201B	17	LEFT	RAL		
201C	D2		JNC	RIGHTCY	Test if Display is OFF LED's
201D	25				

MEMORY INFORMATION ADDRESS	DATA	LABEL	INSTRUCTION OPCODE	OPERAND	COMMENT
201E	20				
201F	CD		CALL	DISPLAY	Display Pattern and Delay
2020	2E				
2021	20				
2022	C3		JMP	LEFT	Continue
2023	1B				
2024	20				
2025	1F	RIGHTCY	RAR		} Move Display
2026	1F	RIGHT	RAR		
2027	D2		JNC	LEFTCY	Test if Display is OFF LED's
2028	1A				
2029	20				
202A	CD		CALL	DISPLAY	Display Pattern and Display
202B	30				
202C	20				
202D	C3		JMP	RIGHT	Continue
202E	26				
202F	20				
2030	F5	DISPLAY	PUSH	PSW	Save Display Value
2031	D3		OUT	22	Display it
2032	22				
2033	11		LXI	D, 8ØØØ	Load DE with Delay Value
2034	00				
2035	80				
2036	1B	DELAY	DCX	D	} Delay Routine
2037	7A		MOV	A,D	
2038	B3		ORA	E	
2039	C2		JNZ	DELAY	
203A	36				
203B	20				
203C	F1		POP	PSW	Restore Display Value
203D	C9		RET		

7.18 PROJECT 51: DISPLAYING THE SEVEN SEGMENT ON THE SDK-85 WITH "INTEL 8085"

This program displays the phrase *INTEL 8085* on the SDK-85 trainer's seven segment display. The display codes for each letter to be displayed start at location 2050 in memory. The display will rotate across the seven segment display from right to left.

MEMORY INFORMATION ADDRESS	DATA	LABEL	INSTRUCTION OPCODE	OPERAND	COMMENT
2050	9F	I			
2051	BA	N			
2052	78	T			DATA for Project 51

MEMORY INFORMATION			INSTRUCTION		COMMENT
ADDRESS	DATA	LABEL	OPCODE	OPERAND	
2053	68	E			
2054	7C	L			
2055	FF				
2056	08	8	BLANK		DATA for Project 51
2057	0C	0			
2058	08	8			
2059	29	5			
205A	FF				
205B	FF		BLANK		
205C	FF		BLANK		
205D	FF		BLANK		
205E	FF		BLANK		
205F	FF		BLANK		
2010	3E		MVI	A, 02	
2011	02				
2012	DE		OUT	20	
2013	20				
2014	3E		MVI	A, 10	
2015	10				
2016	32		STA	1900	Initialize 8279 Display Chip
2017	00				
2018	19				
2019	3E		MVI	A, 90	
201A	90				
201B	32		STA	1900	
201C	00				
201D	19				
201E	31		LXI	SP, 20C2	Set Stack Pointer
201F	C2				
2020	20				
2021	06	LOOP 2	MVI	B, 15	Load Number of Characters to Display
2022	10				
2023	21		LXI	H, 2050	Point to Start of Data
2024	50				
2025	20				
2026	7E	LOOP 1	MOV	A,M	Get Character
2027	32		STA	1800	Send to Display
2028	00				
2029	18				
202A	CD		CALL	SUB	Call Time Delay
202B	35				
202C	20				
202D	23		INX	H	Point to Next Character
202E	05		DCR	B	Subtract One From Number of Characters

MEMORY INFORMATION			INSTRUCTION		
ADDRESS	DATA	LABEL	OPCODE	OPERAND	COMMENT
202F	C2		JNZ	LOOP 1	If Not Zero Get Next Character
2030	26				
2031	20				
2032	C3		JMP	LOOP 2	Restart Display
2033	21				
2034	20				
2035	F5	SUB	PUSH	PSW	Save Accumulator
2036	DB		IN	21	Get No. for Delay
2037	21				
2038	5F		MOV	E,A	
2039	57		MOV	D,A	Load DE with Delay
203A	CD		CALL	DELAY	Call ROM Delay Routine
203B	F1				
203C	05				
203D	F1		POP	PSW	Restore Accumulator
203E	C9		RET		

7.19 PROJECT 52: DISPLAYING THE SEVEN SEGMENT ON THE SDK-85 WITH "CHIP DISPLAY"

This program displays the phrase *CHIP DISPLAY* on the SDK-85 trainer's seven segment display. The display codes for each letter to be displayed start at location 2050 in memory. The display will rotate across the seven segment display from right to left.

MEMORY INFORMATION			INSTRUCTION		
ADDRESS	DATA	LABEL	OPCODE	OPERAND	COMMENT
2050	6C	C			
2051	98	H			
2052	9F	I			
2053	C8	P			Data for Project 52
2054	FF	BLANK			
2055	1A	D			
2056	9F	I			
2057	29	S			
2058	C8	P			
2059	7C	L			
205A	88	A			
205B	19	Y			
205C	FF	BLANK			
2010	3E		MVI	A, 02	
2011	02				
2012	DE		OUT	20	See Project 51
2013	20				
2014	3E		MVI	A, 10	for Comments

MEMORY INFORMATION			INSTRUCTION		
ADDRESS	DATA	LABEL	OPCODE	OPERAND	COMMENT
2015	10				
2016	32		STA	1900	
2017	00				
2018	19				
2019	3E		MVI	A, 90	
201A	90				
201B	32		STA	1900	
201C	00				
201D	19				
201E	31		LXI	SP, 20C2	
201F	C2				
2020	20				
2021	06	LOOP 2	MVI	B, 0C	
2022	0D				
2023	21		LXI	H, 2050	
2024	50				
2025	20				
2026	7E	LOOP 1	MOV	A,M	
2027	32		STA	1800	
2028	00				
2029	18				
202A	CD		CALL	SUB	
202B	35				
202C	20				
202D	23		INX	H	
202E	05		DCR	B	
202F	C2		JNZ	LOOP 1	
2030	26				
2031	20				
2032	C3		JMP	LOOP 2	
2033	21				
2034	20				
2035	F5	SUB	PUSH	PSW	
2036	DB		IN	21	
2037	21				
2038	5F		MOV	E,A	
2039	57		MOV	D,A	
203A	CD		CALL	DELAY	
203B	F1				
203C	05				
203D	F1		POP	PSW	
203E	C9		RET		

7.20 PROJECT 53: TWENTY FOUR HOUR CLOCK EMPLOYING MILITARY TIME

This program simulates a twenty four hour clock. The clock provides the hours, minutes, and seconds employing military time. The character E appears when the program executes. Pressing the VECT INTR button once advances the clock one second. Location 2000 displays HOURS, 2001 displays MINUTES, and 2002 displays SECONDS.

MEMORY INFORMATION			INSTRUCTION		
ADDRESS	DATA	LABEL	OPCODE	OPERAND	COMMENT
2010	31		LXI	SP, 2900	Load SP in the Expansion RAM
2011	00				
2012	29				
2013	3E	LOOP	MVI	A, 10	Clear 7.5 Interrupt
2014	1Ø				
2015	30		SIM		
2016	3E		MVI	A, 08	Unmask all Interrupts
2017	08				
2018	30		SIM		
2019	FB		EI		
201A	76		HLT		Wait for Interrupt
201B	11		LXI	D, FFFF	Time Delay for Key Debounce
201C	FF				
201D	FF				
201E	CD		CALL	DELAY	
201F	F1				
2020	05				
2021	C3		JMP	LOOP	Get Ready for Next Interrupt
2022	13				
2023	20				
20CE	C3		JMP	2050	
20CF	50				
20D0	20		LXI	H, 2002	
2050	21				
2051	02				
2052	20		MOV	A,M	Get Old Seconds Value
2053	7E		INR	A	Increment and Make Decimal
2054	3C		DAA		
2055	27		MOV	M,A	Put Back Into Memory
2056	77		CPI	60	Test for 60 Seconds
2057	FE				
2058	60				
2059	C0		RNZ		If Not Return
205A	36		MVI	M,ØØ	Put Zero in Seconds

MEMORY INFORMATION			INSTRUCTION		COMMENT
ADDRESS	DATA	LABEL	OPCODE	OPERAND	
205B	00		DCX	H	Point to Minutes
205C	2B		INX	M	Increment Minutes and Convent To Decimal
205D	34		MOV	A,M	
205E	7E		DAA		
205F	27		MOV	M,A	Store Decimal Number
2060	77		CPI	60	See if 60 Minutes are Up
2061	FE				
2062	60		RNZ		Return if Not
2063	C0		MVI	M,ØØ	Put Zero in Minutes
2064	36				
2065	00		DCX	H	Point to Hours
2066	2B		INR	M	Increment Hours and Convert to Decimal
2067	34		MOV	A,M	
2068	7E		DAA		
2069	27		MOV	M,A	Store Decimal Number
206A	77		CPI	24	Check if 24 Hours Are Up
206B	FE				
206C	24		RNZ		If Not Return
206D	C0		MVI	M,ØØ	Zero Hours
206E	36				
206F	00		RET		
2070	C9				
2000	00	HOURS			Set The Clock
2001	00	MIN			
2002	00	SECS			

7.21 PROJECT 54: VOLTAGE COMPARATOR

This program takes an external voltage and compares it to a voltage coded in memory. If the external voltage is greater than the voltage coded in memory, the left-most LED on Port 22 lights. If the external voltage is less than the voltage in memory, the right-most LED on Port 22 lights. If the external voltage is equal to the voltage in memory, the middle two LEDs on Port 22 light (the voltage in memory is written in octal format).

MEMORY INFORMATION			INSTRUCTION		COMMENT
ADDRESS	DATA	LABEL	OPCODE	OPERAND	
2010	3E		MVI	A,Ø2	Initialize Port 21 for Input and Port 22 for Output
2011	02				
2012	D3		OUT	2Ø	
2013	20				

MEMORY INFORMATION			INSTRUCTION		
ADDRESS	DATA	LABEL	OPCODE	OPERAND	COMMENT
2014	21		LXI	H,2000	Point HL at 2000
2015	00				
2016	20				
2017	DB	LOOP	IN	21	Get Value From Dip Switch
2018	21				
2019	BE		CMP	M	Compare With Number in 2000
201A	CA		JZ	EQUAL	
201B	25				
201C	20				
201D	DA		JC	GREATER	
201E	2A				
201F	20				
2020	3E		MVI	A, 80	Turn on Left LED if Less
2021	80				
2022	C3		JMP	EXIT	
2023	2C				
2024	20				
2025	3E	EQUAL	MVI	A,18	Turn on Middle LEDs if Equal
2026	18				
2027	C3		JMP	EXIT	
2028	2C				
2029	20				
202A	3E	GREATER	MVI	A, 01	Turn on Right LED if Greater
202B	01				
202C	D3	EXIT	OUT	22	
202D	22				
202E	C3		JMP	LOOP	
202F	17				
2030	20				

7.22 PROJECT 55: COUNT THE NUMBER OF BITS IN THE HIGH STATE

This program will count the number of bits in the HIGH ("1") or ON) state for the number stored in location 2000. The total number of bits stored in the HIGH state will be stored in location 2001.

MEMORY INFORMATION			INSTRUCTION		
ADDRESS	DATA	LABEL	OPCODE	OPERAND	COMMENT
2000		DATA			
2001		RESULT			
2010	21		LXI	H,2000	Point to the Number
2011	00				
2012	20				
2013	AF		XRA	A	Clear Counter

MEMORY INFORMATION ADDRESS	DATA	LABEL	INSTRUCTION OPCODE	OPERAND	COMMENT
2014	4F		MOV	C,A	Clear Counter
2015	06		MVI	B, 09	Set Loop Counter
2016	09				
2017	7E		MOV	A,M	Get the Number
2018	17	CONT	RAL		
2019	05		DCR	B	} Test if Loop Over
201A	CA		JNZ	EXIT 1	
201B	24				
201C	20				
201D	D2		JNC	CONT	Bit OFF, Continue
201E	18				
201F	20				
2020	0C		INR	C	Bit ON, Add to Count
2021	C3		JMP	CONT	
2022	18				
2023	20				
2024	2C	EXIT 1	INR	L	Point to Result
2025	71		MOV	M,C	Store It
2026	CF	EXIT	RST	1	

EXAMPLE:

ADDR	*DATA*
2000	OF
2001	04 Four "1"'s exist in Location 2000 for the Hex Number of (0000 1111)

7.23 PROJECT 56: ADJUSTABLE RANDOM NUMBER GENERATOR

This program will generate a random number between 00 and XX, where XX is in location 2001. The Vect. Intr. Key is pressed to begin the program, and the random Number appears in the Data Field.

MEMORY INFORMATION ADDRESS	DATA	LABEL	INSTRUCTION OPCODE	OPERAND	COMMENT
2000	12	RESULT			
2001	00	DATA			
2010	31	START	LXI	SP,20C2	
2011	C2				
2012	20				
2013	3E		MVI	A,1A	} Set Interrupt Mask
2014	1A				
2015	30		SIM		

MEMORY INFORMATION			INSTRUCTION		
ADDRESS	DATA	LABEL	OPCODE	OPERAND	COMMENT
2016	FB		EI		Enable Interrupts
2017	3A	LIMIT	LDA	2001	Get Limit for Random
2018	01				No. and Store
2019	20				
201A	47		MOV	B,A	
201B	21		LXI	H, 2000	Point to Storage Location
201C	00				
201D	20				
201E	AF		XRA	A	Clear Accumulator
201F	3C	GEN	INR	A	Increase Number
2020	B8		CMP	B	Jump if Number is Not
2021	C2		JNZ	GEN	Equal to the Limit
2022	1F				
2023	20				
2024	C3		JMP	LIMIT	Number is at Limit; Jump
2025	17				
2026	20				
2027	F3	NUM	D1		Service Routine
2028	77		MOV	M,A	Store Random Number
2029	D1		POP	DE	Remove Return Address
202A	CD		CALL	036E	Display Number
202B	6E				
202C	03				
202D	C3		JMP	START	Start Over
202E	10				
202F	20				
20CE	C3		JMP	NUM	Vector to Service Routine
20CF	27				
20D0	20				
20D1	00				

7.24 PROJECT 57: ELECTRONIC DICE NO. 1

This program simulates the throwing of dice. Everytime the Vect. Intr. Key is pushed a new roll of the dice will be displayed.

MEMORY INFORMATION			INSTRUCTION		
ADDRESS	DATA	LABEL	OPCODE	OPERAND	COMMENT
2010	31	START	LXI	SP,20C2	
2011	C2				
2012	20				
2013	3E		MVI	A, 1A	Set Interrupt Mask
2014	1A				
2015	30		SIM		

MEMORY ADDRESS	INFORMATION DATA	LABEL	INSTRUCTION OPCODE	OPERAND	COMMENT
2016	1E	AGAIN	MVI	E, 05	Set Limits for the Dice
2017	05				
2018	16	LSD	MVI	E, 05	
2019	05				
201A	FB	MSD	EI		
201B	00		NOP		Delay
201C	15		DCR	D	
201D	C2		JNZ	MSD	Jump if Number is Not Zero
201E	1A				
201F	20				
2020	1D		DCR	E	
2021	C2		JNZ	LSD	Jump if Number is Not Zero
2022	18				
2023	20				
2024	C3		JMP	AGAIN	Both Numbers Zero, Then
2025	16				Start Over
2026	20				
2027	F3	DISP	DI		Start of Interrupt Service Routine
2028	1C		INR	E	Increase D and E to Make
2029	14		INR	D	Numbers between 1 and 6
202A	7A		MOV	A,D	Move D to Left Side of Accumulator
202B	07		RLC		
202C	07		RLC		
202D	07		RLC		
202E	07		RLC		
202F	83		ADD	E	Put E Into Right Side of Accumulator
2030	CD		CALL	036EH	Display the Two Numbers
2031	6E				on the LEDs
2032	03				
2033	C1		POP	BC	Remove Return Address From Stack
2034	C3		JMP	START	Start Over Again
2035	10				
2036	20				
20CE	C3		JMP	DISP	Interrupt Vector To
20CF	27				Service Routine
20D0	20				

When the program is properly executed the character E will appear in the Address Field. Pressing the VECT INTR will cause a two digit number to be displayed in the Data Field. The two digit number will have values between 11 and 66 which represent two die values. If a 24 appears in the Data Field, this value represents a dice throw of SIX. Pressing of the VECT INTR key will randomly display other dice throws.

7.25 PROJECT 58-60: DIGITAL TO ANALOG (D/A) CONVERTER CIRCUIT (POWER SUPPLY, HARDWARE, AND MAIN PROGRAM)

PROJECT 58: PLUS AND MINUS 15 VOLT POWER SUPPLY FOR THE D/A CONVERTER CIRCUIT

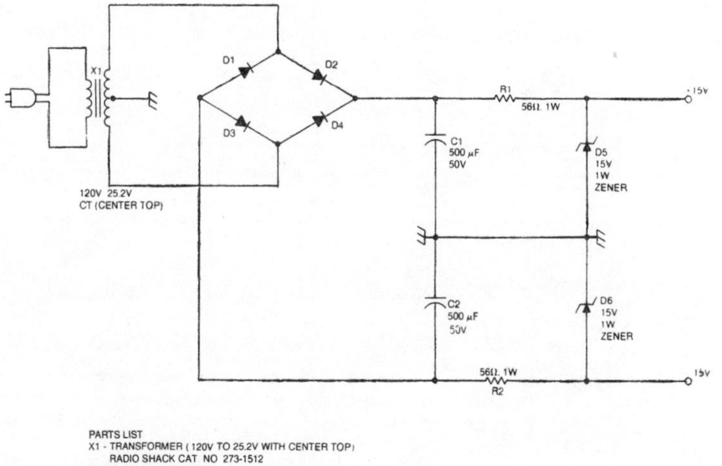

PARTS LIST
X1 - TRANSFORMER (120V TO 25.2V WITH CENTER TOP)
RADIO SHACK CAT NO 273-1512
D1, D2, D3, D4 - HEP R0056
D5, D6 - 15 V, 1W ZENER DIODES (RADIO SHACK NO 1N4744 CAT NO 276-564)
C1, C2 - 500 μF, 50V ELECTROLYTIC
R1, R2 - 56Ω, 1W
±15V POWER SUPPLY FOR D/A CONVERTER CIRCUIT

Fig. 7-1. The ±15V power supply for the D/A converter circuit.

The power supply that must be employed to furnish DC voltage to the D/A Converter Circuit and the complete parts list are shown in Fig. 7-1. The DC supply will furnish +15 V and −15 V at a very low current demand (about 50 mA) from the D/A Converter Circuit. The +5 V needed for the D/A Converter Circuit can be acquired from the SDK-85 Custom Power Supply shown in Project 1. The circuit components can be mounted on the Proto-Board or put together in a separate package.

This power supply is also employed in the projects of Chapter 9. The same voltages (+15 V, −15 V) are used at about a current demand of 100 mA. The reader is reminded to return to this section when needing a +15 V and −15 V DC supply in Chapter 9.

PROJECT 59: D/A CONVERTER HARDWARE FOR OSCILLOSCOPE DISPLAY

The circuit shown below must be employed to interface the SDK-85 trainer with an oscilloscope, in order to display a staircase voltage. The main program generates the staircase voltage, which is a software control voltage waveform.

Two chips are needed for the hardware. Both are Motorola chips, the MC 1408, and MC 1741. The 5 V power supply shown in Chapter 1 must be employed in the D/A Converter Circuit shown below.

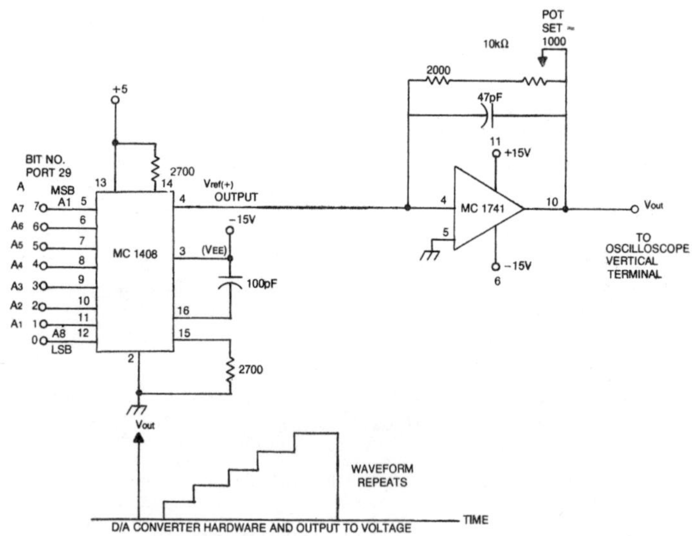

Fig. 7-2. D/A converter hardware and output voltage.

To test the D/A converter circuit, connect pins 5 through 12 on the MC 1408 chip to +5 V (HIGH). Then adjust the 10 kΩ potentiometer of the MC 1741 chip for an output of +5 V at pin 10 of the MC 1741 chip. In other words, turn the 10 kΩ potentiometer until you find the position when pin 10 of the MC 1741 chip reaches +5 V with respect to common (ground).

Next, remove the +5 V from pin 5 of the MC 1408 chip and connect pin 5 to common. If the output on pin 10 of the MC 1741 chip is +2.5 V with respect to common, then the D/A circuit is operating properly. Now disconnect +5 V from pins 5 through 12 on the MC 1408 chip, and connect pins 5 through 12 to the proper connections on Port 29 as indicated on Fig. 7-2.

If the procedure as outlined doesn't work, repeat the procedure once again to verify your first results. If +2.5 V is not measured at pin 10 of the MC 1741 chip the second time, then a wiring mistake may have been made, or one or both of the chips may not be operating properly.

PROJECT 60: MAIN PROGRAM FOR THE D/A CONVERTER

The main program that generates a software control voltage waveform (staircase voltage) is given below. The voltage can be displayed on the oscilloscope by employing Projects 58 and 59.

MEMORY INFORMATION			INSTRUCTION		COMMENT
ADDRESS	DATA	LABEL	OPCODE	OPERAND	
2010	31		LXI	SP, 20C2	Set Stack Pointer
2011	C2				
2012	20				
2013	2E		MVI	A, CD	Load Count Into Expansion RAM Timer
2014	CD				
2015	D3		OUT	2C	
2016	2C				
2017	3E		MVI	A,CØ	
2018	C0				
2019	D3		OUT	2D	
201A	2D				
201B	3E	BEGIN	MVI	A, D5	Load Expansion ROM Status Register
201C	D5				
201D	D3		OUT	28	
201E	28				
201F	3E		MVI	A,DD	Set Interrupt Mask
2020	00				
2021	30		SIM		
2022	3E		MVI	A,CB	Output Data To D/A Converter
2023	C8				
2024	D3		OUT	29	
2025	29				
2026	FB	BACK	EI		Enable And Wait For Interrupt
2027	76		HLT		
2028	3D		DCR	A	Decrement And Check For The End Of The Staircase
2029	FE		CPI	A,32	

MEMORY INFORMATION			INSTRUCTION		
ADDRESS	DATA	LABEL	OPCODE	OPERAND	COMMENT
202A	32				
202B	D3		OUT	29	Output Data
202C	29				
202D	C2		JNZ	BACK	Jump If Staircase Is Not Completed
202E	26				
202F	20				
2030	3E		MVI	A,CB	} Reset Staircase
2031	C8				
2032	D3		OUT	29	
2033	29				
2034	11		LXI	D, 2D00	} Pause Before Next Ramp
2035	00				
2036	20				
2037	CD		CALL	DELAY	
2038	F1				
2039	05				
203A	3E		MVI	A,55	
203B	55				
203C	D3		OUT	28	Reset Timer
203D	28				
203E	C3		JMP	BEGIN	Restart
203F	1B				
2040	20				
20C8	C9		RET		} Continue After Interrupt

7.26 PROJECT 61: RESET MEMORY (EXPANSION RAM)

This program will zero expansion RAM.

MEMORY INFORMATION			INSTRUCTION		
ADDRESS	DATA	LABEL	OPCODE	OPERAND	COMMENT
2010	3E		MVI	A,00	Number Of Locations Thru 0
2011	00				
2012	21		LXI	H,2800	Point To Start Of Expansion RAM
2013	00				
2014	28				
2015	47		MOV	B,A	Put 0 (256) Into B Register
2016	77	LOOP	MOV	M,A	Put Zero In
2017	23		INX	H	Point To Next Location
2018	05		DCR	B	Decrement Count
2019	C2		JNZ	LOOP	Loop If Not Done
201A	16				
201B	20				
201C	CF		RST	1	Back To Monitor

7.27 PROJECT 62: BINARY TO HEXADECIMAL NUMBER CONVERSION

This program will convert the binary input on the DIP switch at IN PORT 21 into a hexadecimal number which will be displayed in the Data Field. If the first four LEDs of IN PORT 21 are lit and the program is executed properly then OF should appear in the Data Field.

MEMORY INFORMATION			INSTRUCTION		COMMENT
ADDRESS	DATA	LABEL	OPCODE	OPERAND	
2010	DB		IN	21	} Get The Data From Port 21
2011	21				
2012	CD		CALL	036E	Display On Data Field
2013	6E				
2014	03				
2015	C3		JMP	GET BI	Start Over
2016	10				
2017	20				

7.29 PROJECT 63: THE GREATEST COMMON DIVISOR

The program shown below takes a number stored in location 2000 and compares it with a number stored in location 2001 and determines which number is the greatest common divisor. The answer is stored in location 2002. The reader must put the numbers in locations 2000 and 2001.

MEMORY INFORMATION			INSTRUCTION		COMMENT
ADDRESS	DATA	LABEL	OPCODE	OPERAND	
2000		No. 1			First Number In Hex
2001		No. 2			Second Number in Hex
2002		RESULT			Result
2010	21		LXI	M,2000	Points To Location 2000
2011	00				
2012	20				
2013	46		MOV	B,M	Moves Data In 2000 Into B Register
2014	23		INX	H	Increments HL To 2001
2015	7E		MOV	A,M	Moves 2001 Into A Register
2016	B8	LOOP	CMP	B	Compare A and B
2017	CA		JZ	EXIT 1	Exit Loop If A = B
2018	29				
2019	20				
201A	F2		JP	HIGHER	
201B	25				
201C	20				
201D	4F		MOV	C,A	Move A Into C Register
201F	78		MOV	A,B	
201F	91		SUB	C	

MEMORY INFORMATION			INSTRUCTION		
ADDRESS	DATA	LABEL	OPCODE	OPERAND	COMMENT
2020	47		MOV	B,A	
2021	79		MOV	A,C	
2022	C3		JMP	LOOP	
2023	16				
2024	20				
2025	90	HIGHER	SUB	B	
2026	C3		JMP	LOOP	
2027	16				
2028	20				
2029	23	EXIT 1	INX	H	
202A	77		MOV	M,A	
202B	CF		RST	1	

Chapter 8

Teletype (TTY) Projects

8.1 PROJECT 64: PURCHASE OF A TTY AND INTERFACING THE TTY WITH THE SDK-85

The authors have purchased used teletypes for one-fifth the cost of a printer or new teletype. The used teletypes are in perfect working order and have served us for the past four years without any need for repair; they are Teletype Corporation Model 33. They can be purchased from RCA Data Communication Service Groups which have offices in every large city throughout the United States. However, RCA has a toll free number you may call to order the used teletypes. The toll free number is 1-800-257-7784. The authors are not going to defend or criticize the use of a teletype, but only make the comment that the used teletype can be purchased for a few hundred dollars and it can be used as a printer or an input keyboard to a microcomputer system.

The authors recommend the purchase of any of the following Model 33's: 33 216 JA, 33 216 JB, 33 216 JE, 33 203 JE, 33 205 JA, and 33 205 JB. You can probably find other Model 33's that will operate satisfactorily compared to the models mentioned above.

After your TTY has arrived you must make the proper connections between the TTY and the SDK-85 trainer in order to perform the projects in this chapter. First refer to Sec. 1.9 and make sure your TTY switch assembly is wired according to the procedures outlined. Then look at the top right side of your SDK-85 trainer and find the ports marked RX+ (Port 12), RX– (Port 24), TX+ (Port 13), and TX– (Port 25). The RX ports are the receive ports and TX ports are the transmit ports. Four wires (one from each port) will connect the SDK-85 trainer to the TTY. The connection of the four wires is shown in the wiring diagram in Fig. 8-1A.

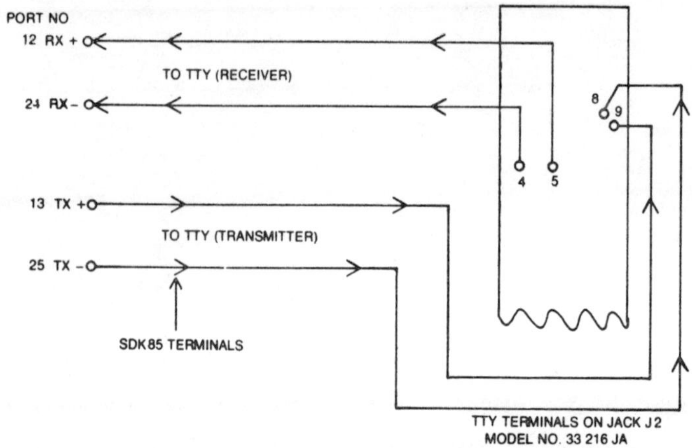

Fig. 8-1A. Wiring of TTY to SDK-85.

The wiring procedure up to this point seems simple. However, the location of Jack J2 in the back of the TTY and the physical connection of the four wires coming from the SDK-85 into the TTY may be extremely difficult but not impossible if the reader carefully looks at Fig. 8-2 and compares it with the back side of the TTY.

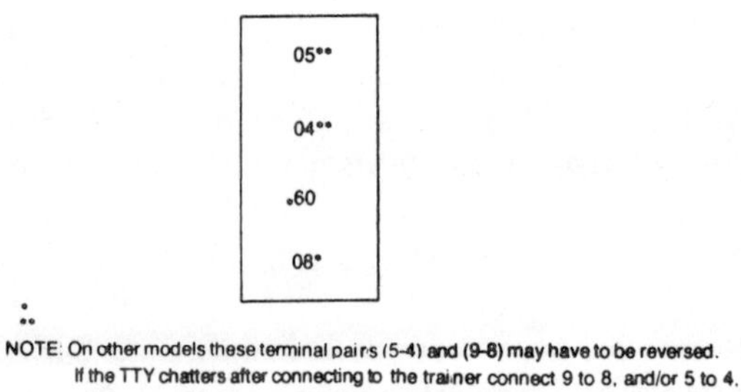

Fig. 8-1B. Terminal pairs which may have to be reversed.

Remove the cover of the TTY and then go to the back side and look in the upper left corner to find Jack J2. Now remove any wires connected to pins 4, 5, 8, and 9 and carefully tape the ends of the wire individually. Then connect the wires from the SDK-85 to the TTY pins as shown in Fig. 8-1 (if problems occur call INTEL Corp.). Make sure the TTY switch on the SDK-85 is pointing toward the display.

Now test to see if dialogue exists between the TTY and SDK-85 by pressing the RESET key on the SDK-85. If proper

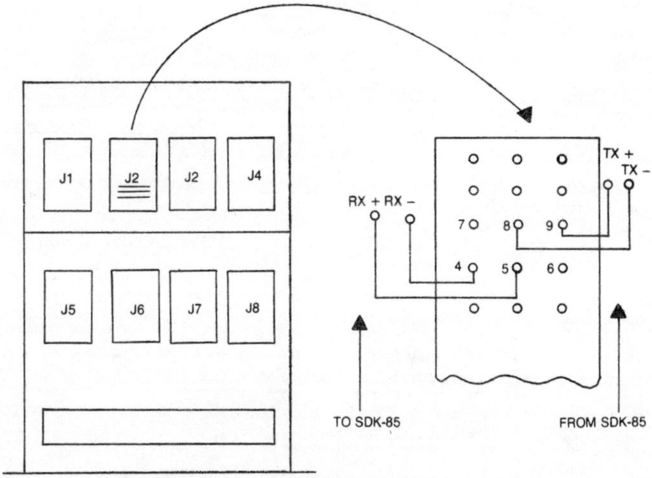

Fig. 8-2. Left backside view of TTY model 33 216 JA.

dialogue exists, one of the two messages should be printed on the TTY:

1. SDK-85 VER X.X"

2. MCS-85 Kit "."

If either of the two messages are printed, then the projects of this chapter can be performed.

8.2 PROJECT 65: TELETYPE PRINTING FROM SDK-85 MEMORY

This program takes data stored in the SDK-85 memory and displays it on a teletype (TTY).

MEMORY INFORMATION			INSTRUCTION		COMMENT
ADDRESS	DATA	LABEL	OPCODE	OPERAND	
2010	31		LXI	SP,20C2	
2011	C2				
2012	20				
2013	21		LXI	H,2030	Point to Start Of Message
2014	30				
2015	20				
2016	3E	LOOP	MVI	A,0D	
2017	0D				
2018	4E		MOV	C,M	Get Character and Compare It
2019	B9		CMP	C	With Carriage Return
201A	CA		J2	DONE	If It Is a CR the GOTO Is Done
201B	26				

MEMORY INFORMATION			INSTRUCTION		
ADDRESS	DATA	LABEL	OPCODE	OPERAND	COMMENT
201C	20				
201D	E5		PUSH	H	
201E	CD		CALL	07FA	If Not Display Character
201F	FA				
2020	07				
2021	E1		POP	H	
2022	23		INX	H	Point to Next Number
2023	C3		JMP	LOOP	Go Back Again
2024	16				
2025	20				
2026	CD	DONE	CALL	05EBH	Output a CR and Line Feed
2027	EB				
2028	05				
2029	CF		RST	1	
2030	48	45 4C	4C		Sample Message,
2034	4F	20 54	48		Considered to Be Data
2038	45	52 45	20		
203C	46	52 41	4E		
2040	4B	2C 20	48		
2044	4F	57 20	41		
2048	52	45 20	59		
204C	4F	55 3F	0D		
2030	48				Representation Or
2031	45				Explanation of Sample
2032	4C	2030	48 45	4C 4C	Message Considered to
2033	4C				Be Data From the
2034	4F				Previous Lines
2035	20	2034	4F	20 54 48	Data Will Be Shown In
2036	54				This Format In this Chapter
2037	48				

8.3 PROJECT 66: READ INTO THE SDK-85 AND PLAY BACK TO THE TELETYPE

This program will read in a line from the teletype (TTY) into the SDK-85, and once a character is entered it will display that character on the TTY.

MEMORY INFORMATION			INSTRUCTION		
ADDRESS	DATA	LABEL	OPCODE	OPERAND	COMMENT
2010	31		LXI	SP,20C2	
2011	C2				
2012	20				
2013	21		LXI	H,2040	Point to Message Storage
2014	40				

MEMORY INFORMATION		INSTRUCTION			
ADDRESS	DATA	LABEL	OPCODE	OPERAND	COMMENT
2015	20				
2016	CD	AGAIN	CALL	07FD	Get Character
2017	FD				
2018	07				
2019	E6		ANI	7F	Turn Into ASCII (TTY Code)
201A	7F				
201B	77		MOV	M,A	Store It
201C	23		INX	H	Point to Next Location
201D	FE		CPI	OD	Test If Character Is A CR
201E	OD				If Not Get Next Character
201F	C2		JNZ	AGAIN	
2020	16				
2021	20				
2022	21		LXI	H,2040	Point To Message For Play Back
2023	40				
2024	20				
2025	4E	LOOP	MOV	C,A	Put Character In C Register
2026	CD		CALL	07FA	And Output It
2027	FA				
2028	07				
2029	7E		MOV	A,M	Get Next Character
202A	FE		CPI	OD	
202B	OD				Test For CR Again
202C	23		INX	H	
202D	C2		JNZ	LOOP	
202E	25				
202F	20				
2030	4E		MOV	C,A	Output CR And Line Feed
2031	CD		CALL	05EB	
2032	EB				
2033	05				
2034	CF		RST	1	

8.4 PROJECT 67: TELETYPE ECHO AND PLAY BACK

This program will get a character from the teletype (TTY), echo it, and then display the whole message when the C/R key is pressed on the TTY.

MEMORY INFORMATION		INSTRUCTION			
ADDRESS	DATA	LABEL	OPCODE	OPERAND	COMMENT
2010	31		LXI	SP, 20C2	
2011	C2				
2012	20				
2013	21		LXI	H,2040	Point To Message Storage

MEMORY INFORMATION			INSTRUCTION		
ADDRESS	DATA	LABEL	OPCODE	OPERAND	COMMENT
2014	40				
2015	20				
2016	CD	AGAIN	CALL	07FD	Get Character
2017	FD				
2018	07				
2019	E6		ANI	7F	Convert To 7 Bit ASCII (TTY Code)
201A	7F				
201B	77		MOV	M,A	Store It
201C	F5		PUSH	PSW	
201D	4F		MOV	C,A	
201E	CD		CALL	07FA	Display It On TTY
201F	FA				
2020	07				
2021	F1		POP	PSW	
2022	23		INX	H	
2023	FE		CPI	OD	}
2024	OD				} Check To See If Completed
2025	C2		JNZ	AGAIN	}
2026	16				
2027	20				
2028	OE		MVI	C,OD	}
2029	OD				} Output CR And Line Feed
202A	CD		CALL	05EB	}
202B	EB				
202C	05				
202D	21				Point To Start Of message again
202E	40		LXI	H,2040	
202F	20				
2030	4E	LOOP 2	MOV	C,M	} Display Character On TTY
2031	CD		CALL	07FA	}
2032	FA				
2033	07				
2034	23		INX	H	
2035	7E		MOV	A,M	
2036	FE		CPI	OD	}
2037	OD				} Check If Character Is A CR
2038	C2		JNZ	LOOP 2	} If Not Loop Back
2039	30				
203A	20				
203B	4E		MOV	C,M	} Output A CR And Line Feed
203C	CD		CALL	05EB	}
203D	EB				
203E	05				
203F	CF		RST	1	

8.5 PROJECT 68: TELETYPE MESSAGE SHOWN ON THE SKD-85 SEVEN SEGMENT DISPLAY

This program takes characters from the teletype (TTY) and displays them on the seven segment of the SDK-85.

MEMORY INFORMATION			INSTRUCTION		COMMENT
ADDRESS	DATA	LABEL	OPCODE	OPERAND	
2010	31		LXI	SP,20C2	
2011	C2				
2012	20				
2013	CD	START	CALL	07FD	Get Character From TTY
2014	FD				(Hex 0 Through F)
2015	07				
2016	E6		ANI	7F	Turn Off Marking Or Parity
2017	7F				
2018	D6		SUI	30	
2019	30				Test If No. Is Less Than 30H,
201A	DA		JC	START	If So Go Back To Start
201B	13				
201C	20				
201D	FE		CPI	OA	
201E	OA				Test If No. Is Between 0 and 9;
201F	DA		JC	GO	If So Display It
2020	29				
2021	20				
2022	D6		SUI	07H	
2023	07				Test To See If Number Is A
2024	FE		CPI	10H	Character Between
2025	10				ASCII 9 and A,
2026	D2		JNC	START	If So Go Back
2027	13				
2028	20				
2029	CD	GO	CALL	036E	Display Character
202A	6E				
202B	03				
202C	C3		JMP	2013	Do It All Over Again
202D	13				
202E	20				

8.6 PROJECT 69: TELETYPE (TTY) LOOK UP TABLE

This program will take a hexadecimal number between 0 and F from the teletype (TTY) and display it on the SDK-85 seven segment display and then output a look up value on the TTY. The new data format and the previous data format are both shown below so that the reader can compare them.

MEMORY INFORMATION		INSTRUCTION			
ADDRESS	DATA	LABEL	OPCODE	OPERAND	COMMENT
2000	41	42 43	44		Data Look Up Table
2004	45	46 47	48		
2008	49	4A 4B	4C		
200C	4D	4E 4F	50		
2000	41				Data Look Up Table (Previous Data Format)
2001	42				
2002	43				
2003	44				
2004	45				
2005	46				
2006	47				
2007	48				
2008	49				
2009	4A				
200A	4B				
200B	4C				
200C	4D				
200D	4E				
200E	4F				
200F	50				
2010	31		LXI	SP,20C2	
2011	C2				
2012	20				
2013	CD	START	CALL	07FD H	Get Character From TTY
2014	FD				
2015	07				
2016	E6		ANI	7FH	Mask Off Parity Or Marking Bit
2017	7F				
2018	D6		SUI	30H	Test If No. Less Than Hex 30
2019	30				
201A	DA		JC	START	
201B	13				
201C	20				
201D	FE		CPI	OAH	Test If No. Is ASCII 0 Through 9
201E	OA				
201F	DA		JC	GO	
2020	29				
2021	20				
2022	D6		SUI	07H	
2023	07				
2024	FE		CPI	10H	Test If No. Greater Than ASCII F
2025	10				
2026	P2		JNC	START	

MEMORY INFORMATION			INSTRUCTION		
ADDRESS	DATA	LABEL	OPCODE	OPERAND	COMMENT
2027	13				
2028	20				
2029	F5	GO	PUSH	PSW	
202A	CD		CALL	036E H	} Display Characters On LEDs
202B	6E				
202C	03				
202D	F1		POP	PSW	
202E	26		MVI	H,20H	} Look Up No. In Table
202F	20				
2030	6F		MOV	L,A	
2031	4E		MOV	A,M	
2032	CD		CALL	07FA	Display No. On TTY
2033	FA				
2034	07				
2035	C3		JMP	START	Do It Again
2036	13				
2037	20				

8.7 PROJECT 70, 71: TTY PRINTING DESIGN (MAIN PROGRAM, AND DATA DESIGN)

This program will get data starting at location 2800. If the data represents an ASCII character, it will be printed. An OD message will output a carriage return and line feed. If bit 7 is set it will be masked off and the remaining number will cause that many spaces to be printed. The Data Design used as an example will display 8085 on the TTY. The data starts at location 2800 and ends at location 28FF which means every location of the expansion RAM is employed.

PROJECT 70: TTY PRINTING DESIGN MAIN PROGRAM

MEMORY INFORMATION			INSTRUCTION		
ADDRESS	DATA	LABEL	OPCODE	OPERAND	COMMENT
2010	31		LXI	SP,20C2	Set Stock Pointer
2011	C2				
2012	20				
2013	21		LXI	H,2800	Point To Data Storage
2014	00				
2015	28				
2016	7E	CTETcr	MOV	A,M	Get Data
2017	4F		MOV	C,A	Store Data In C
2018	23		INX	H	Point To Next Byte
2019	FE		CPI	00	} Test For End: If So Jump
201A	00				
201B	CA		JZ	EXIT	

MEMORY INFORMATION			INSTRUCTION		
ADDRESS	DATA	LABEL	OPCODE	OPERAND	COMMENT
201C	44				
201D	20				
201E	07		RLC		Shift Data And Check MSB
201F	DA		JC	TAB	For TAB: If Set Jump
2020	34				
2021	20				
2022	OF		RRC		Restore Accumulator And
2023	FE		CPI	OD	Check For Carriage Return
2024	OD				
2025	CA		JZ	CRET	If So Jump
2026	2E				
2027	20				
2028	CD		CALL	07FA	Print Character
2029	FA				
202A	07				
202B	C3		JMP	GETcr	Get Next Character
202C	16				
202D	20				
202E	CD	CRET	CALL	05EB	Output Carriage Return
202F	EB				And Line Feed
2030	05				
2031	C3		JMP	GETcr	Get the Next Character
2032	16				
2033	20				
2034	OF	TAB	RRC		Restore Accumulator
2035	E6		ANI	7F	Mask Off TAB Bit
2036	7F				
2037	57		MOV	D,A	Put No. Of Spaces In D Register
2038	OE	LOOP	MVI	C,20	Load Spare
2039	20				
203A	CD		CALL	07FA	Output Space
203B	FA				
203C	07				
203D	15		DCR	B	Loop If Not Done
203E	C2		JNZ	LOOP	
203F	38				
2040	20				
2041	C3		JMP	GETcr	Get the Next Character
2042	16				
2043	20				
2044	CF	EXIT	RST	1	Back To Monitor

PROJECT 71: DATA DESIGN (8085) FOR THE TTY PRINTING DESIGN

The data listed below will produce the Data Design 8085 on the TTY employing the characters 0 and 8 as shown below the data. The data is represented by the new data format explained in Sec. 8.2 of this chapter. This new format is used to save space and writing for the programmer. At this time the reader should be able to understand the efficiency of the new data format.

BEGIN ADDR	DATA (SIXTEEN ADDR; FROM BEGIN ADDR TO NEXT BEGIN ADDR)															
2800	89	38	38	38	38	38	8C	30	30	30	8B	38	38	38	38	38
2810	86	35	35	35	35	35	35	35	35	35	0D	87	38	38	85	38
2820	38	88	30	30	83	30	30	87	38	38	85	38	38	84	35	0D
2830	86	38	89	38	86	30	87	30	85	38	89	38	83	35	0D	86
2840	38	89	38	85	30	89	30	84	38	89	38	83	35	0D	86	38
2850	89	38	84	30	8B	30	83	38	89	38	83	35	0D	87	38	38
2860	85	38	38	85	30	8B	30	84	38	38	85	38	38	84	35	82
2870	35	35	35	0D	89	38	38	38	38	38	87	30	8B	30	86	38
2880	38	38	38	38	86	35	35	35	83	35	35	0D	87	38	38	85
2890	38	38	85	30	8B	30	84	38	38	85	38	38	84	35	87	35
28A0	0D	86	38	89	38	84	30	8B	30	83	38	89	38	8B	35	0D
28B0	86	38	89	38	85	30	89	30	84	38	89	38	8B	35	0D	86
28C0	38	89	38	86	30	87	30	85	38	89	38	83	35	87	35	0D
28D0	87	38	38	85	38	38	88	30	30	83	30	30	87	38	38	85
28E0	38	38	85	35	35	83	35	35	0D	89	38	38	38	38	38	8C
28F0	30	30	30	8B	38	38	38	38	38	89	35	35	35	0D	00	00

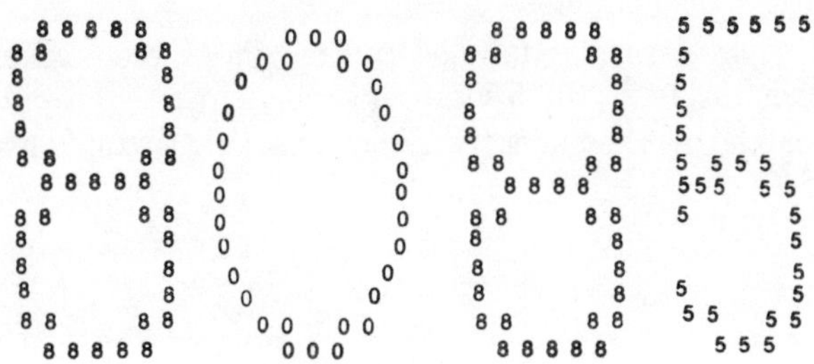

Chapter 9
Oscilloscope Projects

9.1 PROJECT 72: DIGITAL TO ANALOG (D/A) CONVERTER CIRCUITS FOR VERTICAL AND HORIZONTAL INPUTS OF THE OSCILLOSCOPE

The circuits that follow must be employed to interface the SDK-85 trainer with an oscilloscope in order to display the projects of this chapter on the CRT of the oscilloscope. The vertical and horizontal outputs of the D/A Converters go directly to the vertical and horizontal inputs of most oscilloscopes. The grounds of the oscilloscope, the D/A converters, and the SDK-85 trainer *MUST* be tied to a common point.

The power supplies for the D/A Converter Circuits are shown in earlier chapters. The 5 V power supply circuit is given in Ch. one, and the plus and minus 15 V power supply circuit is given in Sec. 7.25 of Ch. Seven.

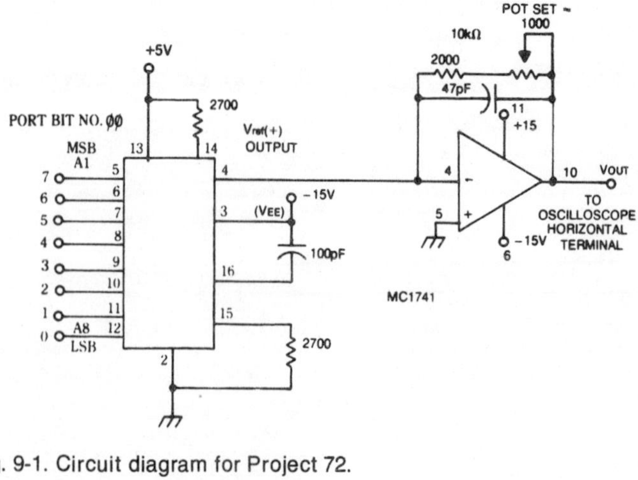

Fig. 9-1. Circuit diagram for Project 72.

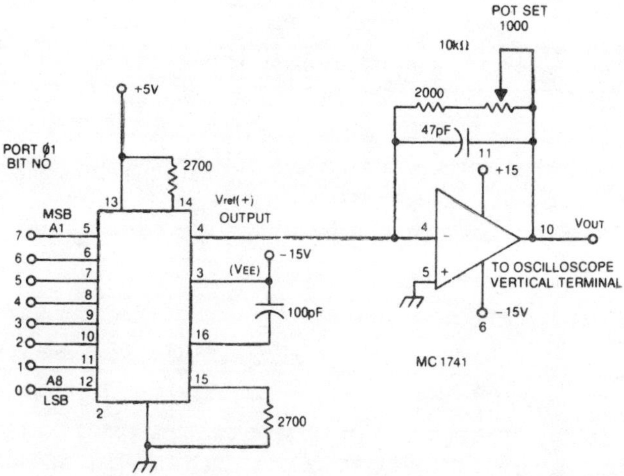

Fig. 9-1. Circuit diagram for Project 72 (continued from page 204).

9.2 PROJECTS 73, 74: STATIONARY DISPLAY ON THE OSCILLOSCOPE SCREEN (CRT) WITHOUT SWITCH CONTROL DELAY (MAIN PROGRAM, DATA DESIGN "8085")

PROJECT 73: MAIN PROGRAM FOR STATIONARY DISPLAY ON THE OSCILLOSCOPE CRT WITHOUT SWITCH CONTROL DELAY

The main program of this project displays on the CRT of the oscilloscope the second program of this section, which is the Data Design "8085." The D/A converter circuit must be connected to the oscilloscope and the SDK-85 trainer as indicated in Sec. 9.1 of this chapter.

The Data Design which is stored in the SDK-85 memory is displayed on the CRT by fast moving dots generated with the CRT electron beam. Since the electron beam is flashing the dots one at a time on the CRT at a very high speed, the Data Design appears to be a solid design to the observer.

The dots to be displayed on the CRT have their coordinates stored in memory starting at location 2800. The x-coordinates are stored in the even number memory locations and the y-coordinates are stored in the odd number memory locations. At the end of this section there is a graph of the dots indicating their memory location, and the position each dot should have in the Data Design "8085."

MEMORY INFORMATION			INSTRUCTION		
ADDRESS	DATA	LABEL	OPCODE	OPERAND	COMMENT
2010	31		LXI	SP,20CD	Load Stock Pointer
2011	C0				
2012	20				
2013	3E		MVI	A,FF	Set ports A (00) and B (01) Data Direction Registers
2014	FF				
2015	D3		OUT	Ø2	
2016	02				
2017	03		OUT	Ø3	
2018	03				
2019	04	BEGIN	INR	B	
201A	21		LXI	H,2800	Point To First Data Location
201B	00				
201C	28				
201D	7E	OUTPUT	MOV	A,M	Get Data If 0 Start Over Again
201E	B7		ORA	A	
201F	CA		JZ	BEGIN	
2020	19				
2021	20				
2022	D3		OUT	ØØ	Output Horizontal Position
2023	00				
2024	23		INX	H	Advance Memory Pointer
2025	7E		MOV	A,M	Get Vertical Position And Output It
2026	D3		OUT	Ø1	
2027	01				
2028	23		INX	H	Advance Pointer
2029	C2		JMP	OUTPUT	Continue With Display
202A	1D				
202B	20				

PROJECT 74: DATA DESIGN "8085" WITHOUT SWITCH CONTROL DELAY

The following program is for the design "8085". The data is stored in the SDK-85 memory as digital information, then is converted to analog information through the D/A converter circuit. The position in which the data will appear is shown on the last page of this section.

MEMORY INFORMATION			INSTRUCTION		
ADDRESS	DATA	LABEL	OPCODE	OPERAND	COMMENT
2800	0C				Data For 8085 Design
2801	58				The Position the Data Will
2802	0C				Appear On the Oscilloscope

MEMORY INFORMATION			INSTRUCTION		
ADDRESS	DATA	LABEL	OPCODE	OPERAND	COMMENT
2803	60				Is Shown On the Last Page
2804	0C				Of This Project
2805	68				
2806	14				
2807	70				
2808	1C				
2809	70				
280A	24				
280B	70				
280C	2C				
280D	68				
280E	2C				
280F	60				
2810	2C				
2811	58				
2812	24				
2813	50				
2814	1C				
2815	50				
2816	14				
2817	50				
2818	0C				
2819	48				
281A	0C				
281B	40				
281C	0C				
281D	38				
281E	14				
281F	30				
2820	1C				
2821	30				
2822	24				
2823	30				
2824	2C				
2825	38				
2826	2C				
2827	40				
2828	2C				
2829	48				
282A	3C				
282B	70				
282C	44				
282D	70				
282E	54				

MEMORY INFORMATION		INSTRUCTION			
ADDRESS	DATA	LABEL	OPCODE	OPERAND	COMMENT
282F	70				
2830	54				
2831	68				
2832	54				
2833	60				
2834	54				
2835	58				
2836	54				
2837	50				
2838	54				
2839	48				
283A	54				
283B	40				
283C	54				
283D	38				
283E	4C				
283F	30				
2840	44				
2841	30				
2842	3C				
2843	30				
2844	34				
2845	38				
2846	34				
2847	40				
2848	34				
2849	48				
284A	34				
284B	50				
284C	34				
284D	58				
284E	34				
284F	60				
2850	34				
2851	68				
2852	64				
2853	70				
2854	6C				
2855	70				
2856	74				
2857	70				
2858	7C				
2859	68				
285A	7C				

MEMORY INFORMATION		INSTRUCTION			
ADDRESS	DATA	LABEL	OPCODE	OPERAND	COMMENT
285B	60				
285C	7C				
287D	58				
285E	74				
285F	50				
2860	6C				
2861	50				
2862	64				
2863	50				
2864	5C				
2865	48				
2866	5C				
2867	40				
2868	5C				
2869	38				
286A	64				
286B	30				
286C	6C				
286D	30				
286E	74				
286F	30				
2870	7C				
2871	38				
2872	7C				
2873	40				
2874	7C				
2875	48				
2876	84				
2877	38				
2878	8C				
2879	30				
287A	94				
287B	30				
287C	9C				
285D	30				
287E	A4				
287F	38				
2880	A4				
2881	40				
2882	A4				
2883	48				
2884	A4				
2885	50				
2886	9E				

MEMORY INFORMATION			INSTRUCTION		
ADDRESS	DATA	LABEL	OPCODE	OPERAND	COMMENT
2887	56				
2888	94				
2889	58				
288A	8A				
288B	56				
288C	84				
288D	58				
288E	84				
288F	60				
2890	84				
2891	68				
2892	84				
2893	70				
2894	8C				
2895	70				
2896	94				
2897	70				
2898	9C				
2899	70				
289A	A4				
289B	70				
289C	00				

9.3 PROJECTS 75, 76: MOVING PICTURE DISPLAY ON THE OSCILLOSCOPE SCREEN (CRT) (MAIN PROGRAM, DATA DESIGN-MOVING TANK)

PROJECT 75: MAIN PROGRAM FOR MOVING DISPLAY

The second program of this section is the Data Design for a Tank. In fact, the main program will make the Tank move across the CRT. The D/A converter circuit must be connected to the oscilloscope and the SDK-85 trainer as indicated in Sec. 9.1 of this chapter.

The Data Design which is stored in the SDK-85 memory is displayed on the CRT by fast moving dots generated by the CRT electron beam. Since the electron beam is flashing the dots one at a time on the CRT at a very high speed, the Data Design appears to the observer to be a solid design. The Data Design will first appear stationary, then after a short pause will move off the CRT. This procedure keeps repeating.

The dots to be displayed on the CRT have their coordinates stored in memory starting at location 2800. The x-coordinates are stored in the even number memory locations and the y-coordinates

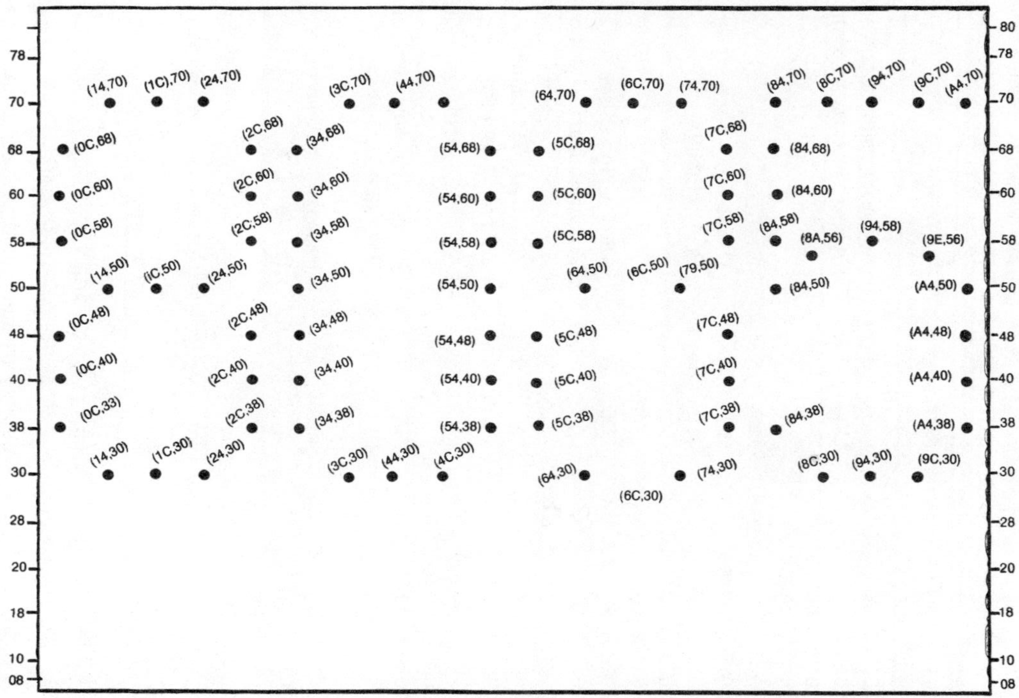

Fig. 9-4. 8085 Design.

are stored in the odd number memory locations. At the end of this section there is a graph of the dots indicating their memory location and the position each dot should have in the Data Design of the Tank.

MEMORY INFORMATION		INSTRUCTION			
ADDRESS	DATA	LABEL	OPCODE	OPERAND	COMMENT
2010	31		LXI	SP,20CO	Set the Stack Pointer
2011	C0				
2012	20				
2013	3E		MVI	A,FF	Set the Data Direction Registers For Ports 00 and 01
2014	FF				
2015	D3		OUT	Ø2	
2016	02				
2017	D3		OUT	Ø3	
2018	03				
2019	04	BEGIN	INR	B	Advance Position Counter
201A	21		LXI	H,2800	Point To First Data Location
201B	00				
201C	28				
201D	7E	OUTPUT	MOV	A,M	Get Data
201E	B7		ORA	A	If Data Is 00, Then Restart Picture
201F	CA		JZ	BEGIN	
2020	19				
2021	20				
2022	80		ADD	B	Add Position Offset
2023	D3		OUT	ØØ	Output Horizontal Position
2024	00				
2025	23		INX	H	Point To Next Location
2026	7E		MOV	A,M	Get and Output the Vertical Position
2027	D3		OUT	Ø1	
2028	01				
2029	23		INX	H	Point To the Next Location
202A	DB		IN	21	Get Value For Pause
202B	21				
202C	57		MOV	D,A	Pause Before Displaying the Next Dot
202D	CD		CALL	DELAY	
202E	F1				
202F	05				
2030	C3		JMP	OUTPUT	Continue With the Display
2031	1D				
2032	20				

PROJECT 76: DATA DESIGN FOR THE TANK

The following program is for the Tank design. The data is stored in the SDK-85 memory as digital information, then is converted to analog information through the D/A converter circuit. The position in which the data will appear on the CRT of the oscilloscope is shown on the last page of this section. The Tank will first appear stationary, then after a pause it will move off the CRT.

MEMORY INFORMATION			INSTRUCTION		COMMENT
ADDRESS	DATA	LABEL	OPCODE	OPERAND	
2800	6E				Data for Tank Design
2801	60				The Position In Which the Data Will
2802	6C				Appear On the Oscilloscope
2803	60				Is Shown On the Last Page
2804	6A				Of This Project
2805	60				
2806	68				
2807	60				
2808	66				
2809	60				
280A	64				
280B	60				
280C	60				
280D	60				
280E	5C				
280F	62				
2810	58				
2811	64				
2812	54				
2813	62				
2814	50				
2815	60				
2816	4C				
2817	5C				
2818	48				
2819	5A				
281A	44				
281B	58				
281C	40				
281D	54				
281E	44				
281F	50				
2820	48				
2821	4E				
2822	4C				
2823	4C				
2824	50				
2825	4C				

MEMORY INFORMATION			INSTRUCTION		
ADDRESS	DATA	LABEL	OPCODE	OPERAND	COMMENT
2826	54				
2827	4C				
2828	58				
2829	4C				
2830	5C				
2831	4C				
2832	60				
2833	4C				
2834	64				
2835	4C				
2836	68				
2837	4E				
2838	6C				
2839	50				
283A	70				
283B	54				
283C	6C				
283D	58				
283E	68				
283F	5A				
2840	64				
2841	5C				
2842	60				
2843	5C				
2844	5C				
2845	5C				
2846	58				
2847	5C				
2848	54				
2849	5C				
284A	50				
284B	5C				
284C	00				

9.4 PROJECT 77, 78: MOVING LETTER DISPLAY ON THE OSCILLOSCOPE SCREEN (CRT) (MAIN PROGRAM, DATA DESIGN

PROJECT 77: MAIN PROGRAM FOR MOVING LETTERS

For the explanation of the main program see Sec. 9.3. Instead of the Tank design the design for this program is "CSU".

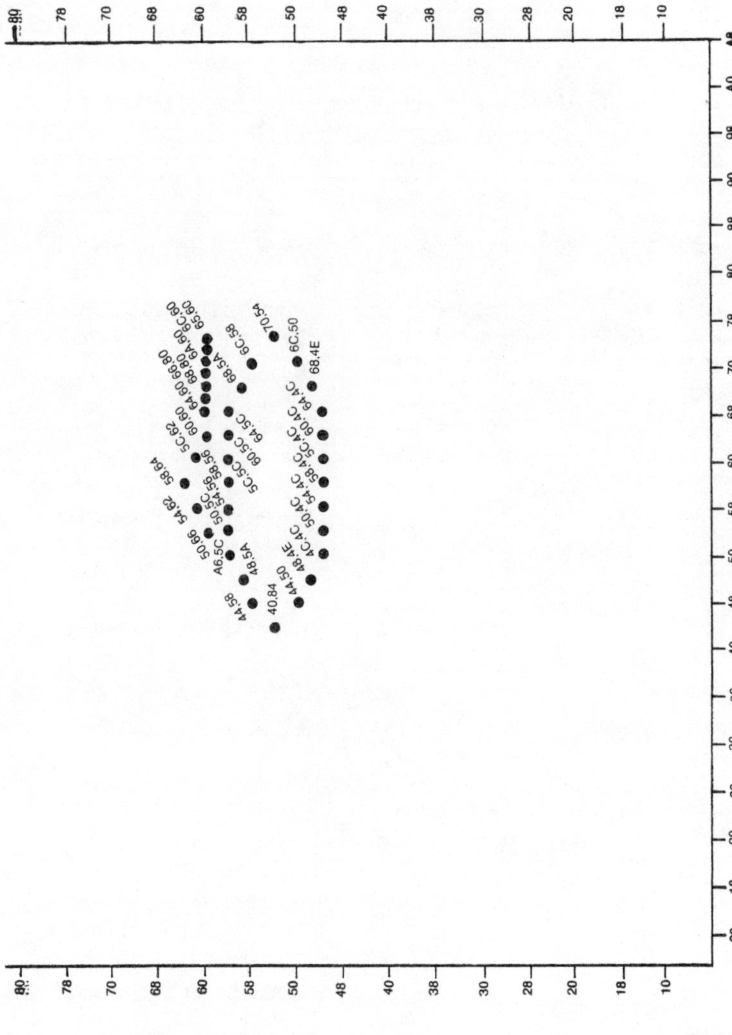

Fig. 9-7. Tank design.

MEMORY INFORMATION			INSTRUCTION		COMMENT
ADDRESS	DATA	LABEL	OPCODE	OPERAND	
2010	31		LXI	SP,20C0	Set Stack Pointer
2011	C0				
2012	20				
2013	3E		MUI	A,FF	Set the Data Direction Registers For Ports 00 and 01
2014	FF				
2015	D3		OUT	Ø2	
2016	02				
2017	D3		OUT	Ø3	
2018	03				
2019	04	BEGIN	INR	B	
201A	21		LXI	H,2800	Point To First Data Location
201B	00				
201C	28				
201D	7E	OUTPUT	MOV	A,M	
201E	B7		ORA	A	Get Data
201F	CA		JZ	BEGIN	If Data Is 00 Then Start Over
2020	19				
2021	20				
2022	D3		OUT	ØØ	Output Horizontal Position
2023	00				
2024	23		INX	H	Point To Next Location
2025	7E		MOV	A,M	Get and Output the Vertical Position
2026	D3		OUT	Ø1	
2027	01				
2028	23		INX	H	Point To the Next Location
2029	D8		IN	21	Get Value For the Delay
202A	21				
202C	57		MOV	D,A	Pause Before Displaying the Next Dot
202D	CD		CALL	DELAY	
202E	F1				
202F	05				
2030	C3		JMP	OUTPUT	Continue With the Display
2031	1D				
2032	20				

PROJECT 78: DATA DESIGN FOR CSU

MEMORY INFORMATION			INSTRUCTION		COMMENT
ADDRESS	DATA	LABEL	OPCODE	OPERAND	
2800	38				Data For CSU Design The Position In Which the Data Will Appear On the Oscilloscope Is Shown On the Last Page Of This Project
2801	70				
2802	30				
2803	78				
2804	28				

MEMORY INFORMATION			INSTRUCTION		COMMENT
ADDRESS	DATA	LABEL	OPCODE	OPERAND	
2805	78				
2806	20				
2807	78				
2808	18				
2809	70				
280A	18				
280B	68				
280C	18				
280D	60				
280E	18				
280F	58				
2810	18				
2811	50				
2812	18				
2813	48				
2814	18				
2815	40				
2816	18				
2817	38				
2818	18				
2819	30				
281A	20				
281B	28				
281C	28				
281D	28				
281E	30				
281F	28				
2820	38				
2821	30				
2822	48				
2823	30				
2824	50				
2825	28				
2826	58				
2827	28				
2828	60				
2829	28				
282A	68				
282B	30				
282C	68				
282D	38				
282E	68				
282F	40				
2830	60				

MEMORY INFORMATION			INSTRUCTION		COMMENT
ADDRESS	DATA	LABEL	OPCODE	OPERAND	
2831	48				
2832	58				
2833	50				
2834	58				
2835	48				
2836	60				
2837	48				
2838	68				
2839	48				
283A	70				
283B	50				
283C	78				
283D	58				
283E	78				
283F	60				
2840	78				
2841	68				
2842	70				
2843	78				
2844	78				
2845	78				
2846	70				
2847	78				
2848	68				
2849	78				
284A	60				
284B	78				
284C	58				
284D	78				
284E	50				
284F	78				
2850	48				
2851	78				
2852	40				
2853	78				
2854	38				
2855	78				
2856	30				
2857	80				
2858	28				
2859	88				
285A	28				
285B	90				

MEMORY INFORMATION		INSTRUCTION			COMMENT
ADDRESS	DATA	LABEL	OPCODE	OPERAND	
285C	28				
285D	98				
285E	30				
285F	98				
2860	38				
2861	98				
2862	40				
2863	98				
2864	48				
2865	98				
2866	50				
2867	98				
2868	58				
2869	98				
286A	60				
286B	98				
286C	68				
286D	98				
286E	70				
286F	98				
2870	78				
2871	00				

9.5 PROJECTS 79, 80: CONTROLLING SPEED OF MOVING PICTURE DISPLAY ON THE OSCILLOSCOPE SCREEN (CRT) EMPLOYING THE DIP SWITCHES FROM PORT 21 (MAIN PROGRAM, DATA DESIGN-MOVING "BOOM")

PROJECT 79: MAIN PROGRAM FOR CONTROLLING SPEED OF MOVING PICTURE DISPLAY ON THE CRT

For an explanation of the main program see Sec. 9.3. The design for this program is "BOOM". The design is programmed to move across the CRT, and the speed at which it moves can be varied by merely adjusting the DIP switches at Port 21. The reader should enjoy watching the BOOM design moving at different speeds as he/she adjusts the switches at Port 21.

MEMORY INFORMATION		INSTRUCTION			COMMENT
ADDRESS	DATA	LABEL	OPCODE	OPERAND	
2010	31		LXI	SP,20C0	
2011	C0				
2012	20				

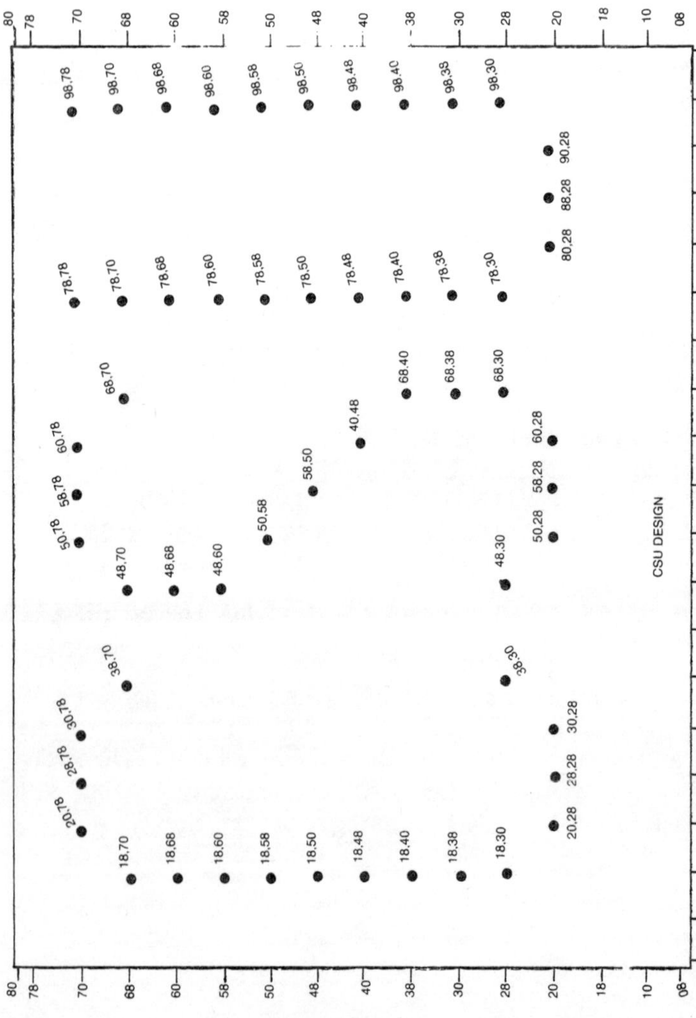

Fig. 9-10. CSU design.

MEMORY INFORMATION ADDRESS	DATA	LABEL	INSTRUCTION OPCODE	OPERAND	COMMENT
2013	3E		MVI	A,FF	
2014	FF				
2015	D3		OUT	Ø2	Set Ports A (00) and B Data (01) Direction Registers
2016	02				
2017	D3		OUT	Ø3	
2018	03				
2019	DB	BEGIN	IN	21	Get Speed Of Object From Port 21
201A	21				
201B	80		ADD	B	
201C	47		MOV	B,A	
201D	21		LXI	H,2850	Point To Location Of Data
201E	50				
201F	28				
2020	7E	OUTPUT	MOV	A,M	Get Data
2021	B7		ORA	A	If Data Is 0 Then Start Over
2022	CA		JZ	BEGIN	
2023	19				
2024	20				
2025	80		ADD	B	Add Offset
2026	D3		OUT	ØØ	Output Horizontal Position
2027	00				
2028	23		INX	H	
2029	7E		MOV	A,M	Get and Display Vertical Position
202A	D3		OUT	Ø1	
202B	01				
202C	23		INX	H	Point To Next Location
202D	16		MVI	D,02	
202E	20				
202F	CD		CALL	DELAY	Pause Before Next Data
2030	F1				
2031	05				
2032	C3		JMP	OUTPUT	Continue With Display
2033	20				
2034	20				

PROJECT 80: DATA DESIGN FOR BOOM

MEMORY INFORMATION ADDRESS	DATA	LABEL	INSTRUCTION OPCODE	OPERAND	COMMENT
2850	4C				Data For Boom Design
2851	48				The Position At Which the Data
2852	4C				Will Appear On the Oscilloscope
2853	4C				Is Shown On the Last Page
2854	4C				Of This Project
2855	50				

MEMORY INFORMATION		INSTRUCTION			
ADDRESS	DATA	LABEL	OPCODE	OPERAND	COMMENT
2856	4C				
2857	54				
2858	4C				
2859	58				
285A	50				
285B	58				
285C	54				
285D	58				
285E	58				
285F	54				
2860	54				
2861	50				
2862	50				
2863	50				
2864	58				
2865	4C				
2866	54				
2867	48				
2868	50				
2869	48				
286A	5C				
286B	4C				
286C	5C				
286D	50				
286E	5C				
286F	54				
2870	60				
2871	58				
2872	64				
2873	58				
2874	68				
2875	58				
2876	68				
2877	50				
2878	68				
2879	48				
287A	64				
287B	48				
287C	60				
287D	48				
287E	70				
287F	48				
2880	6C				

MEMORY INFORMATION		INSTRUCTION			
ADDRESS	DATA	LABEL	OPCODE	OPERAND	COMMENT
2881	4C				
2882	6C				
2883	50				
2884	6C				
2885	54				
2886	70				
2887	58				
2888	74				
2889	58				
288A	78				
288B	54				
288C	78				
288D	50				
288E	78				
288F	4C				
2890	74				
2891	48				
2892	7C				
2893	48				
2894	7C				
2895	4C				
2896	7C				
2897	50				
2898	7C				
2899	54				
289A	7C				
289B	58				
289C	80				
289D	54				
289E	84				
289F	50				
28A1	88				
28A2	54				
28A3	8C				
28A4	58				
28A5	8C				
28A6	54				
28A7	8C				
28A8	50				
28A9	8C				
28AA	4C				
28AB	8C				
28AC	48				

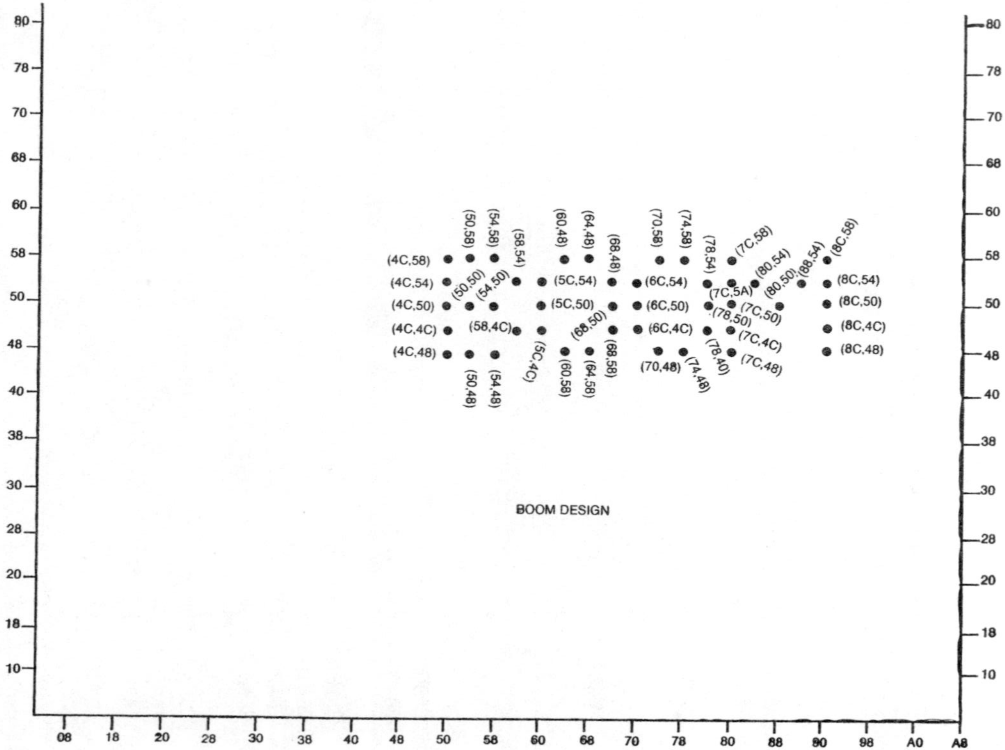

Fig. 9-12. Boom design.

9.6 PROJECTS 81, 82: SPACE SHUTTLE MOVING DISPLAY ON THE CRT (MAIN PROGRAM AND DATA DESIGN)

PROJECT 81: MAIN PROGRAM FOR SPACE SHUTTLE DISPLAY ON THE CRT

For the explanation of the main program see Sec. 9.3. The design for this program is a Space Shuttle. The design is programmed to move across the CRT, and the speed at which it moves can be varied by merely adjusting the DIP switches at Port 21.

MEMORY INFORMATION			INSTRUCTION		
ADDRESS	DATA	LABEL	OPCODE	OPERAND	COMMENT
2010	31		LXI	SP,20C0	Set the Stack Pointer
2011	C0				
2012	20				
2013	3E		MVI	A,FF	Set the Data Direction Register For Port (00) and (01)
2014	FF				
2015	D3		OUT	Ø2	
2016	02				
2017	D3		OUT	Ø3	
2018	03				
2019	04	BEGIN	INR	B	Advance Positive Counter
201A	21		LXI	H,2800	Point To the First Data Location
201B	00				
201C	28				
201D	7E	OUTPUT	MOV	A,M	Get Data
201E	B7		ORA	A	If Data = 00 Then Restart Picture
201F	CA		JZ	BEGIN	
2020	19				
2021	20				
2022	80		ADD	B	Add Position Offset
2023	D3		OUT		Output the Horizontal Position
2024	00				
2025	23		INX	H	Point To the Next Location
2026	7E		MOV	A,M	Get and Display the Vertical Position
2027	D3		OUT	Ø1	
2028	01				
2029	23		INX	H	Point To Next Data Location
202A	DB		IN	21	Get Value For Pause
202B	21				
202C	57		MOV	D,A	Pause Before Displaying the Next Dot
202D	CD		CALL	DELAY	
202E	F1				
202F	05				
2030	C3		JMP	OUTPUT	Continue With the Display
2031	1D				
2032	20				

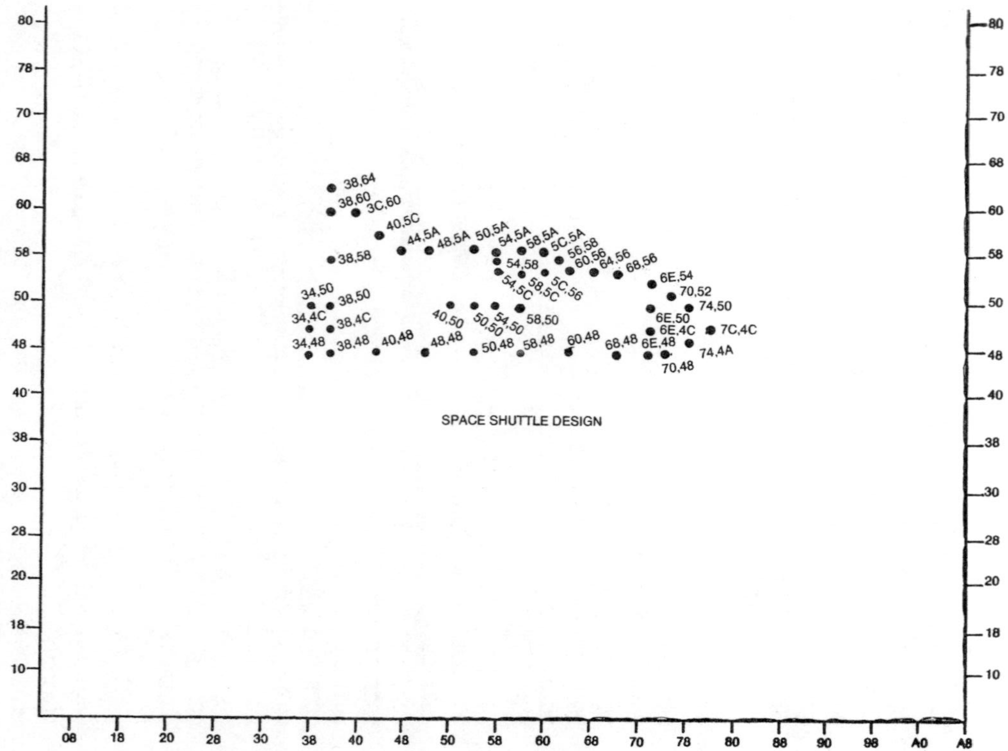

Fig. 9-14. Space Shuttle design.

PROJECT 82: DATA DESIGN FOR THE SPACE SHUTTLE

MEMORY INFORMATION			INSTRUCTION		
ADDRESS	DATA	LABEL	OPCODE	OPERAND	COMMENT
2800	7C				Data for Space Shuttle
2801	4C				
2802	74				
2803	50				
2804	70				
2805	52				
2806	6E				
2807	54				
2808	6E				
2809	50				
280A	6E				
280B	4C				
280C	6E				
280D	48				
280E	68				
280F	48				
2810	60				
2811	48				
2812	58				
2813	48				
2814	50				
2815	48				
2816	58				
2817	50				
2818	54				
2819	50				
281A	50				
281B	50				
281C	40				
281D	50				
281E	48				
281F	48				
2820	40				
2821	48				
2822	38				
2823	48				
2824	34				
2825	48				
2826	34				
2827	4C				
2828	34				
2829	50				

MEMORY INFORMATION		INSTRUCTION			
ADDRESS	DATA	LABEL	OPCODE	OPERAND	COMMENT
282A	38				Data for Space Shuttle
282B	50				
282C	38				
282D	4C				
282E	38				
282F	58				
2830	38				
2831	60				
2832	38				
2833	64				
2834	3C				
2835	60				
2836	40				
2837	5C				
2838	44				
2839	5A				
283A	48				
283B	5A				
283C	50				
283D	5A				
283E	54				
283F	5A				
2840	58				
2841	5A				
2842	5C				
2843	5A				
2844	5E				
2845	58				
2846	60				
2847	56				
2848	5C				
2849	56				
284A	58				
284B	5C				
284C	54				
284D	5C				
284E	54				
284F	58				
2850	64				
2851	56				
2852	68				
2853	56				
2854	00				

Chapter 10
Miscellaneous Projects

10.1 PROJECT 83: ELECTRONIC DICE NO. 2

The program begins by punching the machine language instructions for the main program and the interrupt service routine. First we set the program counter at location 2000, and then execute the program with the key sequence of Reset, Go, 2, 0, 0, 0. Then the Exec. key is employed.

The program continually loops until the Vect. Intr. key is pressed. At this time, the value of the two Dice is output at Port 22 in *binary coded decimal* (BCD) in the form shown in the following table.

Port 22 Bit Number	BCD Number	
0	BCD 1	First Die Value
1	BCD 2	
2	BCD 4	
3	BCD 8	
4	BCD 1	Second Die Value
5	BCD 2	
6	BCD 4	
7	BCD 8	

When the Vect. Intr. Key is pressed the second time, the output port is zeroed and the die values are removed. Additional keystrokes on the Vect. Intr. key will produce further die values.

MEMORY INFORMATION			INSTRUCTION		
ADDRESS	DATA	LABEL	OPCODE	OPERAND	COMMENT
2000	00		NOP		
2001	00				
2002	00				
2003	00				
2004	00				
2005	31		LXI	SP,20C2	
2006	C2				Load Stack Pointer
2007	20				
2008	3E		MVI	A,10	
2009	10				RESET 7.5 Flip Flop
200A	30		SIM		
200B	3E		MVI	A,0B	Unmask 7.5 Interrupt
200C	0B				And Drop Out 7.5
200D	30		SIM		Flip-Flop Reset
200E	00		NOP		
200F	00				
2010	00				
2011	3E		MVI	A,02	
2012	02				Define Port # 22
2013	D3		OUT	20	As Output Port
2014	20				
2015	AF		XRA	A	Zero Accumulator And Reset Carry Flags
2016	FB		EI		Enable Interrupt
2017	21	MAJOR	LXI	H,20A0	
2018	A0	LOOP			Load Memory Pointer
2019	20				
201A	06		MVI	B,23	Load Loop Counter
201B	23				
201C	00		NOP		
201D	00				
201E	00	MINOR			
201F	D2	LOOP	JNC	CONT	
2020	25				
2021	20				
2022	76		HLT		Wait For Interrupt
2023	00		NOP		
2024	00				
2025	23	CONT	INX	H	Increment Memory Counter
2026	05		DCR	B	Decrement Loop Counter
2027	00		NOP		
2028	00				
2029	00				

MEMORY INFORMATION			INSTRUCTION		
ADDRESS	DATA	LABEL	OPCODE	OPERAND	COMMENT
202A	00		NOP		
202B	C2		JNZ	MINOR	
202C	1E			LOOP	
202D	20				
202E	00				
202F	00				
2030	00				
2031	00				
2032	00				
2033	C3		JMP	MAJOR	
2034	17			LOOP	
2035	20				
2036					
2037					
2040	DA	ISR	JC	RESET	
2041	50				
2042	20				
2043	7E		MOV	A,M	Move Dice Value To Accumulator
2044	D3		OUT	22	Out Put Dice Value To Port 22
2045	22				
2046	00		NOP		
2047	00				
2048	00				
2049	00				
204A	AF		XRA	A	Reset Flags
204B	37	CONT	STC		Set Carry Flag
204C	FB		EI		Enable Interrupts
204D	C9		RET		
204E	00		NOP		
204F	00				
2050	AF	RESET	XRA	A	Cancel Out Dice Values
2051	D3		OUT	22	At Port 22
2052	22				
2053	C3		JMP	CONT	
2054	4C				
2055	20				
20CE	C3		JMP	ISR	
20CF	40				
20DO	20				

MEMORY INFORMATION			INSTRUCTION		
ADDRESS	DATA	LABEL	OPCODE	OPERAND	COMMENT
20A0	11				Note; These Numbers Are All The Possibilities Of 2 Dice
20A1	12				
20A2	13				
20A3	14				
20A4	15				
20A5	16				
20A6	21				
20A7	22				
20A8	23				
20A9	24				
20AA	25				
20AB	26				
20AC	31				
20AD	32				
20AE	33				
20AF	34				
20B0	35				
20B1	36				
20B2	41				
20B3	42				
20B4	43				
20B5	44				
20B6	45				
20B7	46				
20B8	51				
20B9	52				
20BA	53				
20BB	54				
20BC	55				
20BD	56				
20BE	61				
20BF	62				
20C0	63				
20C1	64				
20C2	65				
20C3	66				

10.2 PROJECT 84: RANDOM NUMBER GENERATOR NO. 2

The program begins by punching the machine language instructions into the SDK-85. The program is operated by positioning the program counter at location 2000 and executing the program with the key sequence of Reset, Go, 2, 0, 0, 0. Then the Exec. key is pressed.

The program continually loops until the Vect. Intr. key is pressed. At this time the decimal value of the loop counter is output at Port 22 in Binary Coded Decimal (BCD) in the form shown in the following table.

Port 22 Bit Number	BCD Number	
0	BCD 1	Least Significant Digit of Random Number
1	BCD 2	
2	BCD 4	
3	BCD 8	
4	BCD 1	Most Significant Digit of Random Number
5	BCD 2	
6	BCD 4	
7	BCD 8	

When the Vect. Intr. key is pressed the second time, the output port is zeroed. In the program many 00 instructions are included so that the reader can adapt this program to other applications.

MEMORY INFORMATION ADDRESS	DATA	LABEL	INSTRUCTION OPCODE	OPERAND	COMMENT
2000	00		NOP		
2001	00				
2002	00				
2003	00				
2004	31		LXI	SP,20C2	Load Stack Pointer
2005	C2				
2006	20				
2007	3E		MVI	A,10	Reset 7.5 Flip Flop (F/F)
2008	10				
2009	30		SIM		
200A	3E		MVI	A,0B	Drop Out 7.5 F/F Reset Unmask 7.5 Interrupt
200B	0B				
200C	30		SIM		
200D	00		NOP		
200E	00				
200F	00				
2010	00				
2011	3E		MVI	A,02	Define Port #22 As An Output Port
2012	02				
2013	D3		OUT	20	
2014	20				
2015	AF		XRA	A	Zero Accumulator & Reset Flags

MEMORY INFORMATION		INSTRUCTION			COMMENT
ADDRESS	DATA	LABEL	OPCODE	OPERAND	
2016	FB		EI		Enable Interrupts
2017	00		NOP		
2018	00				
2019	00				
201A	00				
201B	06	MAJOR	MVI	B,09	Bounds Of Random Number
201C	09				For 0-9 Load 09
201D	00		NOP		For 0-99 Load 63
201E	00	MINOR			
201F	00				
2020	D2		JNC	CONT	
2021	28				
2022	20				
2023	00		NOP		
2024	76		HLT		Wait For 2nd Interrupt
2025	00		NOP		
2026	00				
2027	00				
2028	05		DCR	B	Decrement Loop Counter
2029	00		NOP		
202A	00				
202B	00				
202C	00				
202D	C2		JNZ	MINOR	
202E	1E				
2030	20				
2031	00		NOP		
2032	00				
2033	00				
2034	C3		JMP	MAJOR	
2035	1B				
2036	20				
2050	DA	ISR	JC	RESET	
2051	61				
2052	20				
2053	00		NOP		
2054	AF		XRA	A	
2055	78		MOV	A,B	Move No. In Loop Counter
2056	00		NOP		To Acc.
2057	27		DAA		Decimal Adjust Accumulator
2058	00		NOP		
2059	D3		OUT	22	Output No. In Acc. To Port
205A	22				#22
205B	00		NOP		

MEMORY INFORMATION			INSTRUCTION		
ADDRESS	DATA	LABEL	OPCODE	OPERAND	COMMENT
205C	AF		XRA	A	Zero Accumulator, Clear Flags
205D	37		STC		Set Carry Flag
205E	FB		EI		Enable Interrupts
205F	C9		RET		
2060	00		NOP		
2061	00	RESET			
2062	00				
2063	AF		XRA	A	Zero Accumulator, Clear Flags
2064	D3		OUT	22	
2065	22				
2066	00		NOP		
2067	C3		JMP	CONT	
2068	5E				
2069	20				
20CE	C3		JMP	ISR	
20CF	50				
20DO	20				

10.3 PROJECTS 85-90: 24 HOUR CLOCK (MAIN PROGRAM, UPDATE TIME REGISTER ROUTINE, UNPACK ROUTINE, INTERRUPT SERVICE ROUTINE, DISPLAY ROUTINE, CIRCUIT FOR A 60 HZ SQUARE WAVE INTERRUPT)

PROJECT 85: MAIN PROGRAM OF 24 HOUR CLOCK

The machine language instructions are put into the memory locations and the circuit for the 60 Hz interrupt is connected to the SDK-85 as shown later in this section. To set the time, current time is put into memory locations 200A, 200B, and 200C employing the Subst. Mem. key. For example, if the time is 2:23 PM, the keystrokes used to set the time are as follows:
Reset, Subst. Mem., 2, 0, 0, A, Next, 1, 4.
Next, 2, 3. (This keystroke increments to memory location 200B, the minutes location of this program). Next, 0, 0. (This keystroke increments to memory location 200C, the seconds memory location).

Once the preset time is loaded, operation of the clock is started with the following sequence:
Reset, Go, 2, 0, 0, E, Exec. (This keystroke should display "E" in the left-most position of the SDK-85 display). Vect. Intr. (This keystroke starts the clock operation).

MEMORY INFORMATION			INSTRUCTION		
ADDRESS	DATA	LABEL	OPCODE	OPERAND	COMMENT
200E	31		LXI	SP,20C2	Load Stack Pointer
200F	C2				
2010	20				
2011	3E		MVI	A,10	Reset 7.5 F/F (Flip-Flop)
2012	10				
2013	30		SIM		
2014	3E		MVI	A,0B	Drop Out 7.5 F/F Reset Unmask 7.5 Interrupt
2015	0B				
2016	30		SIM		
2017	3E		MVI	A,02	Define Port 2A As Output Port
2018	02				
2019	D3		OUT	2A	
201A	28				
201B	FB		EI		Enable Interrupts
201C	76		HLT		Wait For 7.5 Interrupts
201D	76		HLT		Wait For 6.5 Interrupts
201E	AF		XRA	A	Set Output Bit That Resets Hardware 60 Hz. F/F
201F	3C		INR	A	
2020	D3		OUT	2A	
2021	2A				
2022	CD		CALL		Call Unpack Routine
2023	90				
2024	20				
2025	CD		CALL		Call Display Routine
2026	10				
2027	28				
2028	AF		XRA	A	Reset Output Bit, That Resets 60 Hz F/F
2029	D3		OUT	2A	
202A	2A				
202B	FB		EI		Enable Interrupts
202C	C3		JMP	201D	
202D	1D				
202E	20				
202F	00				
20C8	C3		JMP	ISR	Jump Update Time Routine
20C9	30				
20CA	20				
20CE	C3		JMP		Jump Start Time Routine
20CF	00				
20DO	2B				

Project 86: UPDATE TIME REGISTER ROUTINE

This program keeps track of seconds, minutes, and hours of this clock.

MEMORY INFORMATION			INSTRUCTION		
ADDRESS	DATA	LABEL	OPCODE	OPERAND	COMMENT
					(1/60 Second)
2030	21		LXI	H,200D	Point (HL) At 1/60 Sec Register
2031	0D				
2032	20				
2033	7E		MOV	A,M	Move 1/60 Sec Contents To Acc.
2034	3C		INR	A	Increment
2035	00		NOP		
2036	00				
2037	00				
2038	27		DAA		Decimal Adjust Accumulator
2039	FE		CPI	60	Acc. = 60?
203A	60				
203B	CA		JZ	2043	Jump Zero
203C	43				
203D	20				
203E	00		NOP		
203F	00				
2040	00				
2041	77		MOV	M,A	Move Updated 1/60 Sec. Contents
2042	C9		RET		Back To Memory
2043	00		NOP		
2044	00				
2045	AF		XRA	A	Place 0 In 1/60 Sec.
2046	77		MOV	M,A	Memory Location
2047	00		NOP		
2048	00				
2049	00				(Seconds)
204A	00				
204B	2B		DCX	H	Decrement Memory Pointer
204C	7E		MOV	A,M	Move Seconds Content To Acc.
204D	3C		INR	A	Increment
204E	27		DAA		Decimal Adjust Acc.
204F	FE		CPI	60	Acc = 60?
2050	60				
2051	CA		JZ		Jump Zero
2052	57				
2053	20				
2054	00		NOP		
2055	77		MOV	M,A	Move Updated Second Contents
2056	C9		RET		Back To Memory
2057	00		NOP		

MEMORY INFORMATION			INSTRUCTION		
ADDRESS	DATA	LABEL	OPCODE	OPERAND	COMMENT
2058	AF		XRA	A	Place 0 In Seconds
2059	77		MOV	M,A	Memory Location
205A	00		NOP		
205B	00				
205C	00				
205D	00				(Minutes)
205E	2B		DCX	H	Decrement Memory Pointer
205F	7E		MOV	A,M	Move Contents Of Minutes To Acc.
2060	3C		INR	A	Increment
2061	27		DAA		Decimal Adjust Acc.
2062	FE		CPI	60	Acc. = 60?
2063	60				
2064	CA		JZ		Jump Zero
2065	69				
2066	20				
2067	77		MOV	M,A	Move Updated Minutes Content
2068	C9		RET		Back To Memory
2069	00		NOP		
206A	AF		XRA	A	Place 0 In Minutes Memory
206B	77		MOV	M,A	Location
206C	00		NOP		
206D	00				
206E	00				(Hours)
206F	00				
2070	2B		DCX	H	Decrement Memory Pointer
2071	7E		MOV	A,M	Move Contents Of Hours To Acc.
2072	3C		INR	A	Increment
2073	27		DAA		Decimal Adjust Acc.
2074	FE		CPI	24	Acc = 24?
2075	24				
2076	CA		JZ		Jump Zero
2077	7B				
2078	20				
2079	77		MOV	M,A	Move Updated Hours Content
207A	C9		RET		Back To Memory
207B	AF		XRA	A	Place 0 In Hours Memory
207C	77		MOV	M,A	Location
207D	C9		RET		
207E					
207F					

PROJECT 87: UNPACK ROUTINE

To set the 24 hour clock, the current time is written into RAM memory in BCD form as follows:

Memory Location	Upper 4 bits of Memory	Lower 4 bits of Memory
200A	10's of hours digit	Unit hours digit
200B	10's of minutes digit	Unit minutes digit
200C	10's of seconds digit	Unit seconds digit
200D	10's of 1/60 sec. digit	Unit 1/60 sec. digit

The Unpack Routine takes the current time from memory locations 200A, 200B, 200C, and 200D, unpacks the two digits per memory location and arranges as a single digit with a leading zero. The routine locates the "Unpacked" time information as shown in the following table:

Memory Location	Upper 4 bits of Memory Word	Lower 4 bits of Memory Word
2000	0	10's of hours digit
2001	0	Unit hours digit
2002	0	10's of minutes digit
2003	0	Units minutes digit
2004	0	10's of second digit
2005	0	Unit seconds digit
2006	0	10's of 1/60 sec. digit
2007	0	Unit 1/60 sec. digit

MEMORY INFORMATION			INSTRUCTION		
ADDRESS	DATA	LABEL	OPCODE	OPERAND	COMMENT
2090	11		LXI	D,200A	
2091	0A				
2092	20				
2093	21		LXI	H,2000	
2094	00				
2095	20				
2096	06		MVI	B,04	
2097	04				
2098	00		NOP		
→2099	1A		LDAX	D	Load Acc. With Contents Of
209A	00		NOP		Memory Location Pointed To By DE
209B	0F		RRC		} Rotate Acc. Right So That
209C	0F		RRC		The Original Higher 4 Bits
209D	0F		RRC		Are Now In The Lower 4 Bit Location
209E	0F		RRC		
209F	E6		ANI	0F	} 0 Out The Higher 4 Bits
20A0	0F				Of The Accumulator

MEMORY INFORMATION			INSTRUCTION		
ADDRESS	DATA	LABEL	OPCODE	OPERAND	COMMENT
20A1	00		NOP		
20A2	77		MOV	M,A	Write To Unpacked Memory
20A3	00		NOP		Location
20A4	00		NOP		
20A5	23		INX	H	Increment Unpacked Memory Pointer
20A6	1A		LDAX		Reload Accumulator With
20A7	00		NOP		Packed Byte
20A8	E6		ANI	0F	} 0 Out The Higher 4 Bits
20A9	0F				Of The Accumulator
20AA	77		MOV	M,A	Write To Unpacked Memory Loc.
20AB	13		INX	D	Increment Packed Memory Pointer
20AC	23		INX	H	Increment Unpacked Memory Pointer
20AD	05		DCR	B	Decrement Loop Counter
20AE	C2		JNZ		Jump Not Zero
20AF	99				
20B0	20				
20B1	C9		RET		
20B2					
20B3					

PROJECT 88: INTERRUPT (7.5) SERVICE ROUTINE

This project must be used to start the clock running.

MEMORY INFORMATION			INSTRUCTION		
ADDRESS	DATA	LABEL	OPCODE	OPERAND	COMMENT
2800	3E		MVI	A, 1D	Unmask 6.5 Interrupt
2801	1D				
2802	30		SIM		
2803	3E		MVI	A,01	
2804	01				Set Bit At Port 2A
2805	D3		OUT	2A	To Reset 60Hz F/F
2806	2A				And Remove Reset Bit
2807	AF		XRA	A	
2808	D3		OUT	2A	
2809	2A				
280A	00		NOP		
280B	00				
280C	00				
280D	00				
280E	FB		EI		Enable Interrupts
280F	C9		RET		

PROJECT 89: DISPLAY ROUTINE

This project takes the current time information from memory locations 2000 through 2005, and displays the current time on the SDK-85 seven segment display.

MEMORY INFORMATION			INSTRUCTION		
ADDRESS	DATA	LABEL	OPCODE	OPERAND	COMMENT
2810	3E		MVI	A, 00	Write Into Address Field
2811	00				
2812	06		MVI	B, 00	No Decimal Point
2813	00				
2814	21		LXI	H, 2000	Point (HL) At Data To Be Displayed
2815	00				
2816	20				
2817	CD		CALL	OUT, 02B7	Call Routine In ROM Monitor
2818	B7				
2819	02				
281A	3E		MVI	A, 01	Write Into Data Field
281B	01				
281C	06		MVI	B, 00	No Decimal Point
281D	00				
281E	21		LXI	H, 2004	Point (HL) At Data To Be Displayed
281F	04				
2820	20				
2821	00		NOP		
2822	CD		CALL	OUT,02B7	Call Routine in ROM Monitor
2823	B7				
2824	02				
2825	C9		RET		
2826					
2827					

PROJECT 90: CIRCUIT FOR A 60 HZ SQUARE WAVE INTERRUPT (6.5)

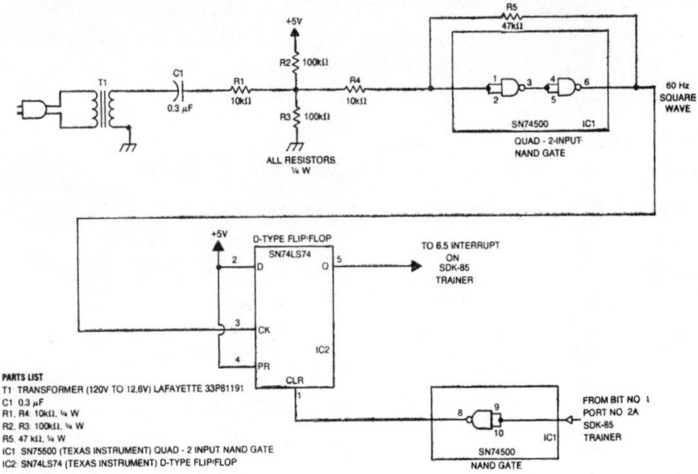

PARTS LIST
T1 TRANSFORMER (120V TO 12.6V) LAFAYETTE 33P81191
C1 0.3 µF
R1, R4 10kΩ, ¼ W
R2, R3 100kΩ, ¼ W
R5 47 kΩ, ¼ W
IC1 SN75500 (TEXAS INSTRUMENT) QUAD - 2 INPUT NAND GATE
IC2 SN74LS74 (TEXAS INSTRUMENT) D-TYPE FLIP/FLOP

10.4 PROJECTS 91-93: STOP CLOCK (MAIN PROGRAM, START TIME ROUTINE, DISPLAY ROUTINE)

PROJECT 91: MAIN PROGRAM OF STOP CLOCK

To operate the STOP Clock the following machine language instructions must be put into memory:

1. The main program, which immediately follows this discussion.

2. The "Update Time Register Routine" for the 24 HOUR Clock of Sec. 10.3. This routine begins at memory location 2030 and continues to memory location 207D.

3. The "Unpack Routine" for the 24 HOUR Clock of Sec. 10.3. This routine begins at memory location 2090 and continues to memory location 20B1.

4. The "Start Time Routine", which is the second project shown in this section.

5. The "Display Routine", which is the third project shown in this section.

6. Once the machine language instructions are loaded, the 60 Hz circuit interrupt, which is shown in Sec. 10.3 for the 24 HOUR Clock, must be connected to the SDK-85 trainer.

The following keystrokes operate the STOP Clock: Reset, Go, 2, 0, 0, E, Exec. (This keystroke should display "E" in the left most position of the SDK-85 display).

Vect. Intr. (This keystroke displays residual left in time memory locations at start up).

Vect. Intr. (This keystroke displays 00 (Min.) 00 (Sec.) 00 (1/60 Sec.)

Vect. Intr. (This keystroke starts the stop clock.)

Vect. Intr. (This keystroke stops the clock.)

MEMORY INFORMATION			INSTRUCTION		
ADDRESS	DATA	LABEL	OPCODE	OPERAND	COMMENT
200E	31		LXI	SP,20C2	Load Stack Pointer
200F	C2				
2010	20				
2011	3E		MVI	A,02	Define Port 2A As Output Port
2012	02				
2013	D3				
2014	2B				
2015	00		NOP		
2016	3E		MVI	A,0B	Unmask 7.5 Interrupt Only
2017	0B				

MEMORY INFORMATION			INSTRUCTION		
ADDRESS	DATA	LABEL	OPCODE	OPERAND	COMMENT
2018	30		SIM		Load Zero Into Memory Location 2009
2019	AF		XRA	A	
201A	32		STA	2009	
201B	09				
201C	20				
201D	FB		EI		Enable Interrupts; HLT And
201E	76		HLT		Wait For 7.5 or 6.5 Intr.
201F	AF		XRA	A	Set Bit At Output Port That Resets 60 Hz Flip Flop (F/F)
2020	3C		INR	A	
2021	D3		OUT	2A	
2022	2A				
2023	CD		CALL		Call Unpack Routine
2024	90				
2025	20				
2026	CD		CALL		Call Display Routine
2027	10				
2028	2B				
2029	AF		XRA	A	Reset Bit At Output Port That Resets 60 Hz F/F
202A	D3		OUT	2A	
202B	2A				
202C	FB		EI		Enable Interrupts
202D	C3		JMP		Jump To HLT.
202E	1E				
202F	20				
20C8	C3		JMP		Jump To Update Time Routine
20C9	30				
20CA	20				
20CE	C3				Jump To Start Time Routine
20CF	30				
20DO	28				

PROJECT 92: START TIME ROUTINE

MEMORY INFORMATION			INSTRUCTION		
ADDRESS	DATA	LABEL	OPCODE	OPERAND	COMMENT
2830	3A		LDA	2009	Load Acc. With Contents Of Memory Location 2009
2831	09				
2832	20				
2833	FE		CPI	00	Acc. = 0?
2834	00				
2835	C2		JNZ	2846	
2836	46				

MEMORY INFORMATION			INSTRUCTION		
ADDRESS	DATA	LABEL	OPCODE	OPERAND	COMMENT
2837	28				
2838	00		NOP		
2839	00				
283A	00				
283B	3E		MVI	A,0B	
283C	0B				Mask All But 7.5 Interrupt
283D	30		SIM		
283E	AF		XRA	A	Set Acc. = 0
283F	3C		INR	A	
2840	32		STA	2009	
2841	09				Load 01 Into Memory
2842	20				Location 2009
2843	00		NOP		
2844	C9		RET		Return
2845	00		NOP		
2846	FE		CPI	01	Acc. = 01?
2847	01				
2848	C2		JNZ	2866	
2849	66				
284A	28				
284B	00		NOP		
284C	00				
284D	00				
284E	3E		MVI	A,0B	
284F	0B				Mask All But 7.5 Interrupt
2850	30		SIM		
2851	00		NOP		
2852	AF		XRA	A	
2853	32		STA	200B	
2854	0B				
2855	20				
2856	32		STA	200C	0 Out Time
2857	0C				Display
2858	20				
2859	32		STA	200D	
285A	0D				
285B	20				
285C	00		NOP		
285D	AF		XRA	A	
285E	3C		INR	A	Set Acc = 02
285F	3C		INR	A	
2860	00		NOP		
2861	00				

MEMORY INFORMATION			INSTRUCTION		
ADDRESS	DATA	LABEL	OPCODE	OPERAND	COMMENT
2862	00				
2863	C3		JMP	2840	
2864	40				
2865	2B				
2866	00		NOP		
2867	3E		MVI	A,09	Unmask 7.5 & 6.5 Interrupt (Allow Time To Accumulate)
2868	09				
2869	30		SIM		
286A	3E		MVI	A,01	Set Bit At Output Port That Resets 60 Hz F/F Reset Bit At Output Port
286B	01				
286C	D3		Out	2A	
286D	2A				
286E	AF		XRA	A	
286F	D3		OUT	2A	
2870	2A				
2871	00		NOP		
2872	C3		JMP	2840	
2873	40				
2874	28				
2875					
2876					
2877					
2878					
2879					

PROJECT 93: DISPLAY ROUTINE

MEMORY INFORMATION			INSTRUCTION		
ADDRESS	DATA	LABEL	OPCODE	OPERAND	COMMENT
2810	3E		MVI	A,00	Write Into Address Field
2811	00				
2812	06		MVI	B,00	No Decimal Point
2813	00				
2814	21		LXI	H,2002	Point HL At Data To Be Displayed
2815	02				
2816	20				
2817	CD		CALL	OUTPUT	Call Subroutine In ROM Monitor
2818	B7				
2819	02				
281A	3E		MVI	A,01	Write Into Data Field
281B	01				
281C	06		MVI	B,00	No Decimal Point
281D	00				
281E	21		LXI	H,2006	Point HL At Data To Be Displayed
281F	06				
2820	20				

MEMORY INFORMATION			INSTRUCTION		
ADDRESS	DATA	LABEL	OPCODE	OPERAND	COMMENT
2821	00		NOP		
2822	CD		CALL	OUTPUT	Call Subroutine In ROM
2823	B7				Monitor
2824	02				
2825	C9		RET		
2826					

10.5 PROJECTS 94-97: METRONOME (MAIN PROGRAM, DISPLAY ROUTINE, LOOK UP TABLE, AND SOUND EFFECT AMPLIFIER)

To operate the Metronome the following steps must be followed:

1. The machine language instructions must be put in memory. That is, three programs must be put in memory: the Main Program, the Display Routine, and the Look Up Table.

2. The 60 Hz circuit interrupt, which is shown in Sec. 10.3 for the 24 HOUR Clock must be connected to the SDK-85 trainer.

3. The Sound Effect Amplifier for the Metronome must be connected to the SDK-85 trainer as indicated in the project of this section.

The following keystrokes operate the Metronome: Reset, Go, 2, 0, 1, 0, Exec (this keystroke should display "E" in the left most position of the SDK-85 display). 1, 2, 0, Vect. Intr (this keystroke starts the metronome at a rate of 120 beats/min., and the beats should be heard on the sound effect amplifier).

The software is designed to output 60 to 240 beats per minute in 10 beat increments (e.g., 60, 70, 80, etc.). The LED display indicates the number of beats per minute being output. Trying to enter a number outside the range of 60 to 240 beats per minute or a number not an integer increment of 10 beats per minute will cause the display to indicate "Err" and the processor to Halt operation. The second keystroke shown in the preceding paragraph is employed to load the desired beats per minute. For example, 60 beats/min would be loaded as 0, 6, 0, and 70 beats/min would be loaded as 0, 7, 0, etc.

PROJECT 94: MAIN PROGRAM FOR THE METRONOME

MEMORY INFORMATION			INSTRUCTION		
ADDRESS	DATA	LABEL	OPCODE	OPERAND	COMMENT
2010	31		LXI	SP,28F9	Load Stack Pointer
2011	F9				
2012	28				
2013	3E		MVI	A,10	Reset 7.5 Intr. F/F
2014	10				

MEMORY INFORMATION			INSTRUCTION		COMMENT
ADDRESS	DATA	LABEL	OPCODE	OPERAND	
2015	30		SIM		
2016	3E				Remove 7.5 Intr. F/F Reset
2017	0E				Unmask 5.5 Intr.
2018	30		SIM		
2019	3E		MVI	A,02	
201A	02				Define Port 2A As Output
201B	D3		OUT	28	Port
201C	28				
201D	21		LXI	H,2000	
201E	00				Point (HL) At 2000
201F	20				
2020	3E		MVI	A,FF	
2021	FF				Load Memory
2022	77		MOV	M,A	Locations
2023	23		INX	H	(HL) - 2001 — 2000, 2001
2024	77		MOV	M,A	
2025	23		INX	H	(HL) - 2002 — 2002, 2003
2026	77		MOV	M,A	With F/F
2027	23		INX	H	(HL) - 2003
2028	77		MOV	M,A	
2029	00		NOP		
202A	00				
202B	00				
202C	00				
202D	00				
202E	00				
202F	00				
2030	21		LXI	H,2000	
2031	00				Point (HL) At 2000
2032	20				
2033	3E		MVI	A,FF	
2034	FF				Write FF Into Location 2000
2035	77		MOV	M,A	
2036	23		INX	H	(HL) - 2001
2037	E5		PUSH	H	
2038	CD		CALL	RDKBD	Reads Keyboard To Accumulator
2039	E7				
203A	02				
203B	E1		POP	H	

MEMORY ADDRESS	INFORMATION DATA	LABEL	INSTRUCTION OPCODE	OPERAND	COMMENT
203C	77		MOV	M,A	
203D	E5		PUSH	H	
203E	CD		CALL	DISPLAY	Display Character Read From
203F	00				Keyboard
2040	28				
2041	00		NOP		
2042	00				
2043	00				
2044	E1		POP	H	
2045	23		INX	H	(HL) - 2002
2046	E5		PUSH	H	
2047	FB		EI		Enable Interrupt
2048	CD		CALL	RDKBD	Read Keyboard To Accumulator
2049	E7				
204A	02				
204B	E1		POP	H	
204C	77		MOV	M,A	
204D	E5		PUSH	H	
204E	CD		CALL	DISPLAY	Display Character Read From
204F	00				Keyboard
2050	28				
2051	00		NOP		
2052	00				
2053	00				
2054	E1		POP	H	
2055	23		INX	H	(HL) - 2003
2056	E5		PUSH	H	
2057	FB		EI		Enable Interrupts
2058	CD		CALL	RDKBD	Read Keyboard To Accumulator
2059	E7				
205A	02				
205B	E1		POP	H	
205C	77		MOV	M,A	
205D	E5		PUSH	H	
205E	CD		CALL	DISPLAY	Display Character Read From
205F	00				Keyboard
2060	28				
2061	00		NOP		
2062	00				
2063	00				
2064	00		NOP		
2065	E1		POP	H	(HL) - 2003
2066	4E		MOV	C,M	(2003) → (C)

MEMORY INFORMATION			INSTRUCTION		
ADDRESS	DATA	LABEL	OPCODE	OPERAND	COMMENT
2067	2B		DCX	H	(HL) - 2002
2068	7E		MOV	A,M	
2069	17		RAL		
206A	17		RAL		Rotate Lower Order Bits
206B	17		RAL		Of Acc. To Higher Order
206C	17		RAL		Position
206D	B1		ORA	C	So As Not To Wire Out Lower
206E	4F		MOV	C,A	Order Bits
206F	2B		DCX	H	(HL) - 2001
2070	46		MOV	B,M	
2071	00		NOP		
2072	00				
2073	00				
2074	00				
2075	00				
2076	00				
2077	00				
2078	21		LXI	H,2830	(HL) - 2830
2079	30				
207A	28				
207B	11		LXI	D,0060	(DE) - 0060
207C	60				
207D	00				
207E	7B		MOV	A,E	(A) - 60
207F	B9		CMP	C	
2080	CA		JZ	20B1	
2081	B1				
2082	20				
2083	C6		ADI	10	
2084	10				
2085	27		DAA		
2086	00		NOP		
2087	00				
2088	D2		JNC	208C	
2089	8C				
208A	20				
208B	14		INR	D	
208C	23		INX	H	
208D	F5		PUSH	PSW	
208E	7D		MOV	A,L	
208F	FE		CPI	43	
2090	43				
2091	C2		JNZ		
2092	AA				
2093	20				

MEMORY INFORMATION			INSTRUCTION		
ADDRESS	DATA	LABEL	OPCODE	OPERAND	COMMENT
2094	00		NOP		
2095	00				
2096	3E		MVI	A,0E	
2097	OE				
2098	32		STA	2001	
2099	01				
209A	20				
209B	3E		MVI	A 14	
209C	32		STA	2002	Flash Err In
209E	02				Address Field
209F	20				
20A0	32		STA	2003	
20A1	03				
20A2	20				
20A3	CD		CALL	DISPLAY	
20A4	00				
20A5	28				
20A6	76		HLT		
20A7	00		NOP		
20A8	00				
20A9	00				
20AA	F1		POP	PSW	
20AB	C3		JMP	207F	
20AC	7F				
20AD	20				
20AE	00		NOP		
20AF	00				
20B0	00				
20B1	F5		PUSH	PSW	
20B2	7A		MOV	A,D	
20B3	38		CMP	B	
20B4	C2		JNZ	20C2	
20B5	C2				
20B6	20				
20B7	4E		MOV	C,M	
20B8	AF		XRA	A	
209B	47		MOV	B,A	
20BA	3E		MVI	A, 0B	
20BB	0B				Unmask 7.5 Intr. Only
20BC	30		SIM		
20BD	FB		EI		Enable Interrupts
20BE	76		HLT		
20BF	C3		JMP	2843	
20C0	43				
20C1	28				
20C2	F1		POP	PSW	
20C3	C3		JMP	2083	
20C4	83				
20C5	20				
2843	AF		XRA	A	
2844	3C		INR	A	Set Bit To Reset 60 Hz
2845	D3		OUT	2A	F/F
2846	2A				Reset Bit

MEMORY INFORMATION			INSTRUCTION		
ADDRESS	DATA	LABEL	OPCODE	OPERAND	COMMENT
2847	AF		XRA	A	Set Bit
2848	D3		OUT	2A	To Reset 60 Hz F/F
2849	2A				Reset Bit
284A	3E		MVI	A,0D	
284B	0D				Mask All But 6.5 Intr.
284C	30		SIM		
284D	FB		EI		Enable Interrupts
284E	76		HLT		
284F	00				
2850	AF		XRA	A	
2851	D3		OUT	2A	Reset Speaker Bit
2852	2A				
2853	3C		INR	A	Set Bit To Reset
2854	D3		OUT	2A	60 Hz. F/F
2855	2A				
2856	04		INR	B	
2857	78		MOV	A,B	Increment B
2858	27		DAA		DAA And Store In B
2859	47		MOV	B,A	
285A	00		NOP		
285B	00				
285C	00				
285D	79		MOV	A,C	
285E	B8		CMP	B	
285F	CA		JZ	286F	
2860	6F				
2861	28				
2862	AF		XRA	A	Drop Out Set Bit
2863	D3		OUT	2A	To 60 Hz F/F
2864	2A				Drop Out Speaker Bit
2865	00		NOP		
2866	00				
2867	00				
2868	FB		EI		Enable Interrupts
2869	C3		JMP	284E	
286A	4E				
286B	28				
286C	00		NOP		
286D	00				
286E	00				
286F	AF		XRA	A	Clear B Register
2870	47		MOV	B,A	

MEMORY INFORMATION ADDRESS	DATA	LABEL	INSTRUCTION OPCODE	OPERAND	COMMENT
2871	D3		OUT	2A	Drop Out Bit That Resets 60 Hz F/F
2872	2A				
2873	3C		INR	A	Set Speaker Bit
2874	3C		INR	A	
2875	D3		OUT	2A	
2876	2A				
2877	00		NOP		
2878	00				
2879	00				
287A	C3		JMP	2868	
287B	68				
287C	28				
287D					

PROJECT 95: DISPLAY ROUTINE FOR THE METRONOME

MEMORY INFORMATION ADDRESS	DATA	LABEL	INSTRUCTION OPCODE	OPERAND	COMMENT
2800	3E		MVI	A,00	Write Into Address Field
2801	00				
2802	06		MVI	B,00	No Decimal Point
2803	00				
2804	21		LXI	H,2000	Point HL At Data To Be Displayed
2805	00				
2806	20				
2807	CD		CALL	OUTPUT	Using Routine In ROM Monitor
2808	B7				
2809	02				
280A	C9		RET		
2810	00		NOP		7.5 Intr. Service Routine
2811	00				
2812	00				
2813	C9		RET		
2817	00		NOP		6.5 Intr. Service Routine
2818	00				
2819	00				
281A	C9		RET		
20C8	C3		JMP	2817	Jump To 6.5 Intr. Service Routine
20C9	17				
20CA	28				
20CB					
20CE	C3		JMP	2810	Jump To 7.5 Intr. Service Routine
20CF	10				
20DO	28				

PROJECT 96: LOOK UP TABLE FOR THE METRONOME

MEMORY INFORMATION			INSTRUCTION		
ADDRESS	DATA	LABEL	OPCODE	OPERAND	COMMENT
2830	60			60	Corresponding Beats Per Minute
2831	51			70	
2832	45			80	
2833	40			90	
2834	36			100	
2835	33			110	
2836	30			120	
2837	28			130	
2838	26			140	
2839	24			150	
283A	22			160	
283B	21			170	
283C	20			180	
283D	19			190	
283E	18			200	
283F	17			210	
2840	16			220	
2841	16			230	
2842	15			240	

PROJECT 97: SOUND EFFECT AMPLIFIER FOR THE METRONOME

The circuit shown below is the amplifier used to simulate the sound of a metronome and it must be connected to the SDK-85 as indicated.

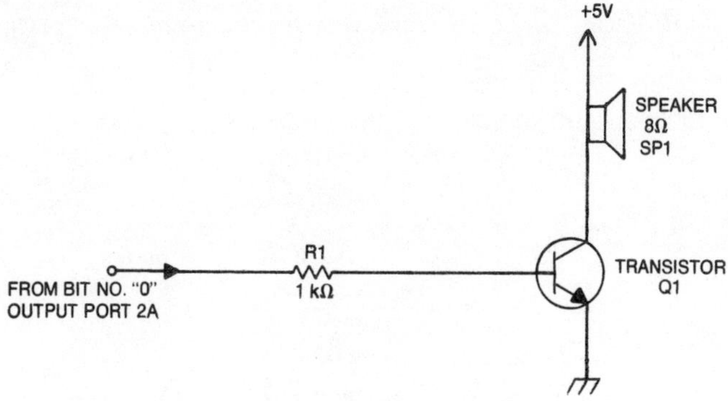

PARTS LIST

Q1: TRANSITOR, 2N2222
SP1: SPEAKER, 8Ω MINIATURE (RADIO SHACK CATALOG NO. 40-247)
R1: RESISTOR, 1 kΩ, ¼ W

10.6 PROJECT 98: PARALLEL DATA OUTPUT OR MEMORY DUMP TO LINE PRINTER

This program sends 200 characters per second to a printer. The program displays the output to the printer on the LEDs connected on Port 22.

MEMORY INFORMATION			INSTRUCTION		
ADDRESS	DATA	LABEL	OPCODE	OPERAND	COMMENT
2010	31		LXI	SP,20C2	Set Stock Pointer
2011	C2				
2012	20				
2013	3E		MVI	A,15	} Set Control Register In Expansion RAM
2014	15				
2015	D3		OUT	28	
2016	28				
2017	3E		MVI	A,02	} Initialize LED's
2018	02				
2019	D3		OUT	20	
201A	20				
201B	21		LXI	H,2800	Point To Data To Be Sent
201C	00				
201D	28				
201E	AF		XRA	A	Clear Accumulator
201F	4F		MOV	C,A	Clear C Register
2020	3E		MVI	A,0D	} Set Interrupt Mask
2021	0D				
2022	30		SIM		
2023	FB	BACK	EI		} Enable Interrupts And Wait For One
2024	76		HLT		
2025	22		INX	H	Point To Next Byte
2026	0D		DCR	C	Decrement Count
2027	C2		JNZ	BACK	Jump If Block Of Data Not Complete
2028	24				
2029	20				
202A	CF		RST	1	Back To Monitor Program
20C8	7E		MOV	A,N	Get Data
20C9	D3		OUT	22	Output Data To LEDs
20CA	22				
20CB	D3		OUT	29	Output Data To Parallel Port
20CC	29				
20CD	C9		RET		

10.7 PROJECT 99: SDK-85 USED AS A TRANSMITTER

This program runs at a 110 baud rate of transmitting data to another SDK-85 trainer. The SOD line is employed as the output for data transmission. The data to be transferred begins at location 2801. The words are sent out using even parity.

MEMORY INFORMATION			INSTRUCTION		COMMENT
ADDRESS	DATA	LABEL	OPCODE	OPERAND	
2010	31		LXI	SP,20C2	Load Stack Pointer
2011	C2				
2012	20				
2013	21		LXI	H,2801	Point To Data To Be Transmitted
2014	01				
2015	28				
2016	06	START	MVI	B,0	
2017	08				}
2018	3E		MVI	A,40	}Set Interrupt Mask
2019	40				}
201A	30		SIM		
201B	CD		CALL	DELAY	
201C	50				
201D	20				
201E	4E		MOV	C,M	
201F	79	SNDBT	MOV	A,C	Move Character Into Accumulator
2020	1F		RAR		Rotate Bit To Be Sent Into Carry
2021	4F		MOV	C,A	Save What Is Left In C
2022	3E		MVI	A,80	Set Mask
2023	80				
2024	1F		RAR		Rotate Bit Into SOD Bit
2025	30		SIM		Send Data
2026	CD		CALL	DELAY	
2027	50				
2028	20				
2029	05		DCR	B	
202A	C2		JNZ	SNDBT	
202B	1F				
202C	28				
202D	3E		MVI	A,C0	
202E	C0				
202F	30		SIM		
2030	CD		CALL	DELAY	
2031	50				
2032	20				
2033	CD		CALL	DELAY	
2034	50				

MEMORY INFORMATION			INSTRUCTION		COMMENT
ADDRESS	DATA	LABEL	OPCODE	OPERAND	
2035	20				
2036	7E		MOV	A,M	
2037	FE		CPI	1B	
2038	1B				
2039	CA		JZ	END	
203A	41				
203B	28				
203C	23		INX	H	
203D	C3		JMP	START	
203F	16				
2040	28				
2041	CF	END	RST	1	
2050	11	DELAY	LXI	D,048C	
2051	8C				
2052	04				
2053	1B	LOOP	DCX	D	
2054	7B		MOV	A,E	
2055	B2		ORA	D	
2056	C2		JNZ	LOOP	
2057	53				
2058	20				
2059	C9		RET		

10.8 PROJECT 100: SDK-85 USED AS A RECEIVER

This program receives series data from another SDK-85 trainer or 8085 CPU using the SID line to input the data. The words brought into the SDK-85 are stored sequentially starting at location 2080. When an odd parity is detected the parity error routine writes EE in location 2000. The program stops receiving once an ESC character code is received.

MEMORY INFORMATION			INSTRUCTION		COMMENT
ADDRESS	DATA	LABEL	OPCODE	OPERAND	
2010	31		LXI	SP,20C2	
2011	C2				
2012	20				
2013	21		LXI	H,2080	Point To Data Storage
2014	80				
2015	20				
2016	AF		XRA	A	Clear C And Accumulator

MEMORY INFORMATION			INSTRUCTION		COMMENT
ADDRESS	DATA	LABEL	OPCODE	OPERAND	
2017	4F		MOV	C,A	And Memory Location 2000H
2018	32		STA	2000	
2019	00				
201A	20				
201B	06	LOOP	MVI	B,08	Bit Counter
201C	08				
201D	11		LXI	D,06D2	Delay Time
201E	D2				
201F	06				
2020	20		RIM		Read SID Line
2021	17		RAL		Check For Data, Jump If
2022			JC	LOOP	None Found
2023	1B				
2024	20				
2025	CD		CALL	DELAY	Pause To Get To The Middle
2026	F1				Of Next Bit
2027	05				
2028	11	BACK	LXI	D,048C	Load Delay Value
2029	8C				
202A	04				
202B	20		RIM		Read Bit
202C	17				Save Bit
202D	1F			A,C	Add to Data in the C Register
202E	79				
202F	4F		MOV	C,A	
2030	CD		CALL	DELAY	Pause For 9.1 Milli-Seconds
2031	F1				
2032	05				
2033	05		DCR	B	Jump If Not Complete
2034	C2		JNZ	BACK	
2035	28				
2036	20				
2037	71		MOV	M,C	Store The Number
2038	7E		MOV	A,M	
2039	B7		ORR	A	Check Parity And Call Error
203A	E4		CPO	ERROR	If Parity Is Odd
203B	47				
203C	20				
203D	FE		CPI	1B	Check For ESC Character
203E	1B				
203F	CA		JZ	END	IF So Jump
2040	46				
2041	20				
2042	23		INX	H	Point To Next Storage Location

MEMORY INFORMATION			INSTRUCTION		COMMENT
ADDRESS	DATA	LABEL	OPCODE	OPERAND	
2043	C3		JMP	LOOP	Jump To Waiting For
2044	1B				Input Routine
2045	20				
2046	76	END	HLT		Program Done - Stop
2047	3E	ERROR	MVI	A,EE	Load Accumulator With Error
2048	EE				Message
2049	32		STA	2000	Store Error Flag
204A	00				
204B	20				
204C	C9		RET		Return To The Program

10.9 PROJECT 101: SDK-85 TRANSMITTING-RECEIVING CONNECTIONS

The diagram shown below illustrates the connections that must be made between two SDK-85 trainers in order that they may communicate between one another:

Now either can be used as a transmitter or receiver.

TO TEST YOUR PROGRAM:

a) Initialize SOD line to a stop bit on transmitter by executing these instructions:

```
MVI A, CØ
SIM
RST 1
```

b) Start the Receive Program
c) Start the Transmit Program
d) Check memory locations starting at 2080 to see if "message" was received.
e) Check location 2000 to make sure *no* parity error occurs. (No. EE there.)
f) Modify one character of your message in the transmitter by giving it odd parity.
g) Do parts (b) and (c) above again.
h) Check to see that your error detection routine has written an "EE" in location 2000.

Appendix
8355 16,384 Bit ROM with I/O

- 2048 Words + 8 Bits
- Single +5V Power Supply
- Internal Address Latch
- 2 General Purpose 8 Bit I/O Ports
- Each I/O Port Line Individually Programmable as Input or Output
- Multiplexed Address and Data Bus
- 40 Pin DIP

The 8355 is a ROM and I/O chip to be used in the MCS-85 microcomputer system. The ROM portion is organized as 2048 × 8. It has maximum access time of 400 ns to permit use with no wait states in 8085A CPU.

The I/O portion consists of two general purpose I/O ports. Each I/O port has 8 port lines, and each I/O port line is individually programmable as input or output.

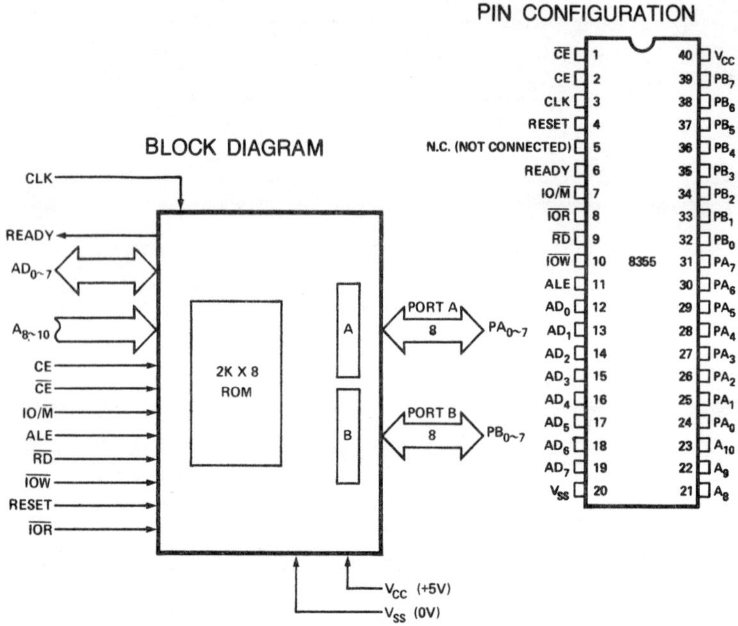

Fig. A-1. 8355 ROM with I/O.

8355 Functional Pin Definition

Symbol	Function
ALE	When ALE Address Latch Enable) is high, AD_{0-7}, $IO/\overline{M}$, A_{8-10}, CE, and $\overline{CE}$ enter address latched. The signals (AD, $IO/\overline{M}$, A_{8-10}, CE, $\overline{CE}$) are latched in at the trailing edge of ALE.
AD_{0-7}	Bi-directional Address/Data bus. The lower 8-bits of the ROM or I/O address are applied to the bus lines when ALE is high. During an I/O cycle, Port A or B are selected based on the latched value of AD_0. If $\overline{RD}$ or $\overline{IOR}$ is low when latched Chip Enables are active, the output buffers present data on the bus.
A_{8-10}	These are the high order bits of the ROM address. They do not affect I/O operations.
$\overline{CE}$	Chip Enable Inputs: $\overline{CE}$ is active *low* and CE is active *high*. The 8355 can be accessed only when *BOTH* Chip Enables are active at the time the ALE signal latches them up. If either Chip Enable input is not active, the AD_{0-7} and READY outputs will be in a high impedance state.
$IO/\overline{M}$	If the latched IO/M is high when $\overline{RD}$ is low, the output data comes from an I/O port. If it is low the output data comes from the ROM.

Symbol	Function
$\overline{RD}$	If the latched Chip Enables are active when $\overline{RD}$ goes low, the AD_{0-7} output buffers are enabled and output either the selected ROM location or I/O port. When both $\overline{RD}$ and $\overline{IOR}$ are high, the AD_{0-7} output buffers are tri-stated.
$\overline{IOW}$	If the latched Chip Enables are active, a low on $\overline{IOW}$ causes the output port pointed to by the latched value of AD_0 to be written with the data on AD_{0-7}. The state of $IO/\overline{M}$ is ignored.
$\overline{CLK}$	The CLK is used to force the READY into its high impedance state after it has been forced low by $\overline{CE}$ low, CE high and ALE high.
READY	Ready is a tri-state output controlled by $\overline{CE}$, CE, ALE and CLK. READY is forced low when the Chip Enables are active during the time ALE is high, and remains low until the rising edge of the next CLK (see Fig. 4)?
$\overline{PA_{0-7}}$	These are general purpose I/O pins. Their input/output direction is determined by the contents of Data Direction Register (DDR). Port A is selected for write operations when the Chip Enables are active and $\overline{IOW}$ is low and a 0 was previously latched from AD_0. Read operation is selected by $\overline{IOR}$ low when the Chip is enabled and AD_0 low. Alternately, $IO/\overline{M}$ high and $\overline{RD}$ low may be used in place of $\overline{IOR}$ when the chip is enabled and AD_0 is low to allow reading from a port.
$\overline{PB_{0-7}}$	This general purpose I/O port is identical to Port A except that it is selected by a 1 latched from AD_0.
$\overline{RESET}$	An input high on RESET causes all pins in Ports A and B to assume input mode.
$\overline{IOR}$	When the Chip Enables are active, a low on $\overline{IOR}$ will output the selected I/O port onto the AD bus. $\overline{IOR}$ low performs the same function as the combination $IO/\overline{M}$ high and $\overline{RD}$ low.
V_{cc}	+5 volt supply.
V_{ss}	0 volt supply.

8205 HIGH SPEED 1 OUT OF 8 BINARY DECODER

- I/O Port or Memory Selector
- Simple Expansion—Enable Inputs
- High Speed Schottky Bipolar Technology—18ns Max. Delay
- Directly Compatible with TTL Logic Circuits
- Low Input Load Current—.25 mA max., 1/6 Standard TTL Input Load
- Minimum Line Reflection—Low Voltage Diode Input Clamp

- Outputs Sink 10 mA min.
- 16-Pin Dual-In-Line Ceramic or Plastic Package

The 8205 decoder can be used for expansion of systems which utilize input ports, output ports, and memory components with active low chip select input. When the 8205 is enabled, one of its eight outputs goes "low", thus a single row of a memory system is selected. The 3 chip enable inputs on the 8205 allow easy system expansion. For very large systems, 8205 decoders can be cascaded such that each decoder can drive eight other decoders for arbitrary memory expansions.

The Intel 8205 is packaged in a standard 16 pin dual-in-line package; and its performance is specified over the temperature range of 0°C to +75°C, ambient. The use of Schottky barrier diode clamped transistors to obtain fast switching speeds results in higher performance than equivalent devices made with a gold diffusion process.

PIN CONFIGURATION

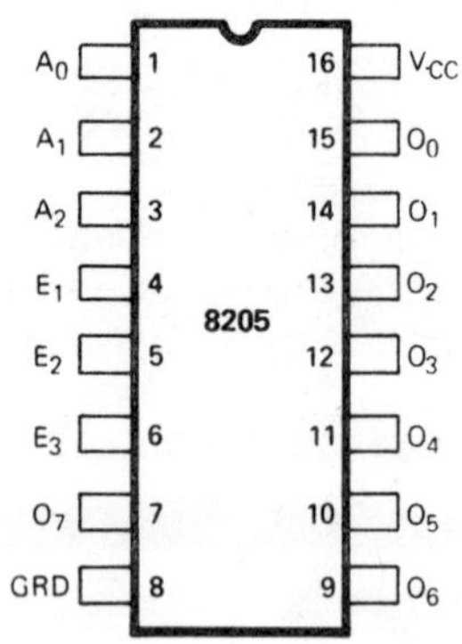

LOGIC SYMBOL

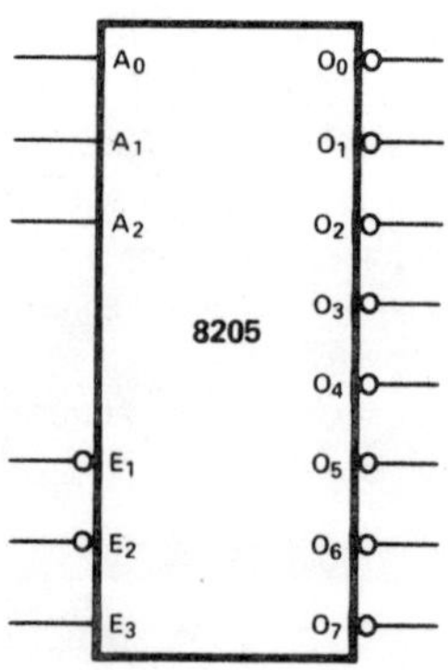

PIN NAMES

A_0- A_2	ADDRESS INPUTS
$\overline{E_1}$- $\overline{E_3}$	ENABLE INPUTS
$\overline{O_0}$- $\overline{O_7}$	DECODED OUTPUTS

ADDRESS			ENABLE			OUTPUTS							
A_0	A_1	A_2	E_1	E_2	E_3	0	1	2	3	4	5	6	7
L	L	L	L	L	H	L	H	H	H	H	H	H	H
H	L	L	L	L	H	H	L	H	H	H	H	H	H
L	H	L	L	L	H	H	H	L	H	H	H	H	H
H	H	L	L	L	H	H	H	H	L	H	H	H	H
L	L	H	L	L	H	H	H	H	H	L	H	H	H
H	L	H	L	L	H	H	H	H	H	H	L	H	H
L	H	H	L	L	H	H	H	H	H	H	H	L	H
H	H	H	L	L	H	H	H	H	H	H	H	H	L
X	X	X	L	L	L	H	H	H	H	H	H	H	H
X	X	X	H	L	L	H	H	H	H	H	H	H	H
X	X	X	L	H	L	H	H	H	H	H	H	H	H
X	X	X	H	H	L	H	H	H	H	H	H	H	H
X	X	X	H	L	H	H	H	H	H	H	H	H	H
X	X	X	L	H	H	H	H	H	H	H	H	H	H
X	X	X	H	H	H	H	H	H	H	H	H	H	H

Fig. A-2. 8205 decoder.

Functional Description

Decoder

The 8205 contains a one out of eight binary decoder. It accepts a three bit binary code and by gating this input, creates an exclusive output that represents the value of the input code.

For example, if a binary code of 101 was present on the A0, A1 and A2 address input lines, and the device was enabled, an active low signal would appear on the $\overline{05}$ output line. Note that all of the other output pins are sitting at a logic high, thus the decoded output is said to be exclusive. The decoders outputs will follow the truth table shown below in the same manner for all other input variations.

Enable Gate

When using a decoder it is often necessary to gate the outputs with timing or enabling signals so that the exclusive output of the decoded value is synchronous with the overall system.

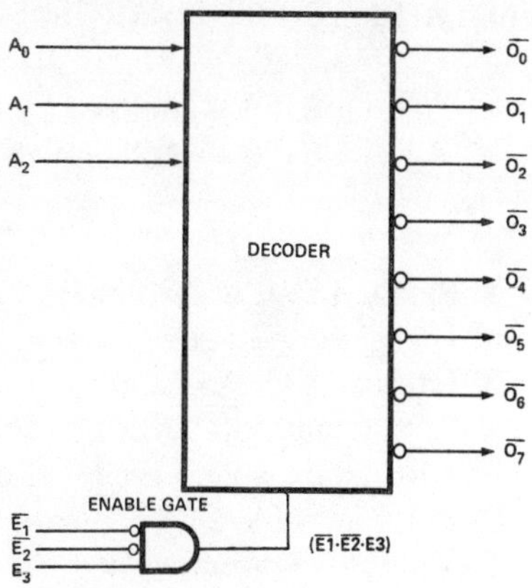

ADDRESS			ENABLE			OUTPUTS							
A_0	A_1	A_2	E_1	E_2	E_3	0	1	2	3	4	5	6	7
L	L	L	L	L	H	L	H	H	H	H	H	H	H
H	L	L	L	L	H	H	L	H	H	H	H	H	H
L	H	L	L	L	H	H	H	L	H	H	H	H	H
H	H	L	L	L	H	H	H	H	L	H	H	H	H
L	L	H	L	L	H	H	H	H	H	L	H	H	H
H	L	H	L	L	H	H	H	H	H	H	L	H	H
L	H	H	L	L	H	H	H	H	H	H	H	L	H
H	H	H	L	L	H	H	H	H	H	H	H	H	L
X	X	X	L	L	L	H	H	H	H	H	H	H	H
X	X	X	H	L	L	H	H	H	H	H	H	H	H
X	X	X	L	H	L	H	H	H	H	H	H	H	H
X	X	X	H	H	L	H	H	H	H	H	H	H	H
X	X	X	H	L	H	H	H	H	H	H	H	H	H
X	X	X	L	H	H	H	H	H	H	H	H	H	H
X	X	X	H	H	H	H	H	H	H	H	H	H	H

Fig. A-3. Diagram of decoder and enable gate.

The 8205 has a built-in function for such gating. The three enable inputs ($\overline{E1}$, $\overline{E2}$, E3) are ANDed together and create a single enable signal for the decoder. The combination of both active "high" and active "low" device enable inputs provides the designer with a powerfully flexible gating function to help reduce package count in his system.

Applications of the 8205

The 8205 can be used in a wide variety of applications in microcomputer systems. I/O ports can be decoded from the address bus, chip select signals can be generated to select memory devices and the type of machine state such as in 8008 systems can be derived from a simple decoding of the state lines (S0, S1, S2) of the 8008 CPU.

8155/8156 2048 BIT STATIC MOS RAM WITH I/O PORTS AND TIMER

8155 — Active Low Chip Enable ($\overline{CE}$)
8156 — Active High Chip Enable (CE)

- 256 Word × Bits
- Single +5V Power Supply
- Completely Static Operation
- Internal Address Latch
- 2 Programmable 8 Bit I/O Ports
- 1 Programmable 6 Bit I/O Port
- Programmable 14 Bit Binary Counter/Timer
- Multiplexed Address and Data Bus
- 40 Pin DIP

The 8155 and 8156 are RAM and I/O chips to be used in the MCS-85 microcomputer system. The RAM portion is designed with 2K bit static cells organized as 256 × 8. They have a maximum access time of 400ns to permit use with no wait states in 8085A CPU.

The I/O portion consists of three general purpose I/O ports. One of the three ports can be programmed to be status pins, thus allowing the other two ports to operate in handshake mode.

A 14 bit programmable counter/timer is also included on chip to provide either a square wave or terminal count pulse for the CPU system depending on timer mode.

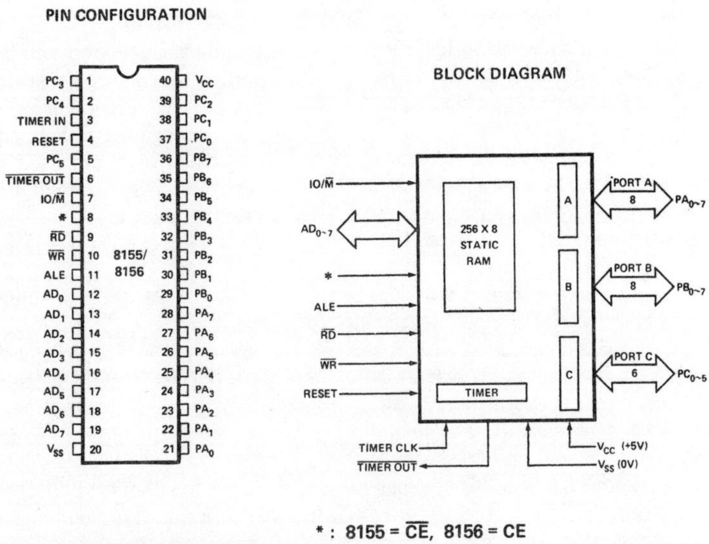

Fig. A-4. 8155/8156 RAM.

8155/8156 Functional Pin Definition

The following describes the functions of all of the 8155/8156 pins.

Symbol	Function
RESET	The Reset signal is a pulse provided by the 8085 to initialize the system. Input high on this line resets the chip and initializes the three I/O ports to input mode. The width of RESET pulse should typically be 600 nsec. (Two 8085A clock cycle times).
$AD_{0\text{-}7}$	These are 3-state Address/Data lines that interface with the CPU lower 8-bit Address/Data Bus. The 8-bit address is latched into the address latch on the falling edge of the ALE. The address can be either for the memory section or the I/O section depending on the polarity of the $IO/\overline{M}$ input signal. the 8-bit data is either written into the chip or Read from the chip depending on the status of $\overline{\text{WRITE}}$ or $\overline{\text{READ}}$ input signal.
CE or $\overline{\text{CE}}$	Chip Enable: On the *8155*, this pin is CE and is ACTIVE LOW. On the *8156*, this pin is CE and is ACTIVE HIGH.
$\overline{\text{RD}}$	Input low on this line with the Chip Enable active enables the $AD_{0\text{-}7}$ buffers. If $IO/\overline{M}$ pin is low, the RAM content will be read out to the AD bus. Otherwise the content of the selected I/O port will be read to the AD bus.

Symbol	Function
$\overline{WR}$	Input low on this line with the Chip Enable active causes the data on the AD lines to be written to the RAM or I/O ports depending on the polarity of IO/$\overline{M}$.
ALE	Address Latch Enable: This control signal latches both the address on the AD_{0-7} lines and the state of the Chip Enable and IO/$\overline{M}$ into the chip at the falling edge of ALE.
IO/$\overline{M}$	IO/$\overline{Memory}$ Select: This line selects the memory if low and selects the IO if high.
PA_{0-7}(8)	These 8 pins are general purpose I/O pins. The in/out direction is selected by programming the Command/Status Register.
PB_{0-7}(8)	These 8 pins are general purpose I/O pins. The in/out direction is selected by programming the Command/Status Register.
PC_{0-5}(6)	These 6 pins can function as either input port, output port, or as control signals for PA and PB. Programming is done through the C/S Register. When PC_{0-5} are used as control signals, they will provide the following: PC_0 — A INTR (Port A Interrupt) PC_1 — A BF (Port A Buffer full) PC_2 — $\overline{A\ STB}$ (Port A Strobe) PC_3 — B INTR (Port B Interrupt) PC_4 — B BF (Port B Buffer Full) PC_5 — $\overline{B\ STB}$ (Port B Strobe)
TIMER IN	This is the input to the counter timer.
$\overline{TIMER\ OUT}$	This pin is the timer output. This output can be either a square wave or a pulse depending on the timer mode.
V_{CC}	+5 volt supply.
V_{SS}	Ground Reference.

Operational Description

The 8155/8156 includes the following operational features:

- 2K Bit Static RAM organized as 256 × 8
- Two 8-bit I/O ports (PA & PB) and one 6-bit I/O port (PC)
- 14-bit down counter

The I/O portion contains four registers (Command/Status, PA_{0-7}, PB_{0-7}, PC_{0-5}). The IO/M (IO/Memory Select) pin selects the I/O or the memory (RAM) portion. Detailed descriptions of memory, I/O ports and timer functions will follow.

The 8-bit address on the AD lines, the Chip Enable input, and IO/$\overline{M}$ are all latched on chip at the falling edge of ALE. A low on the IO/$\overline{M}$ must be provided to select the memory section.

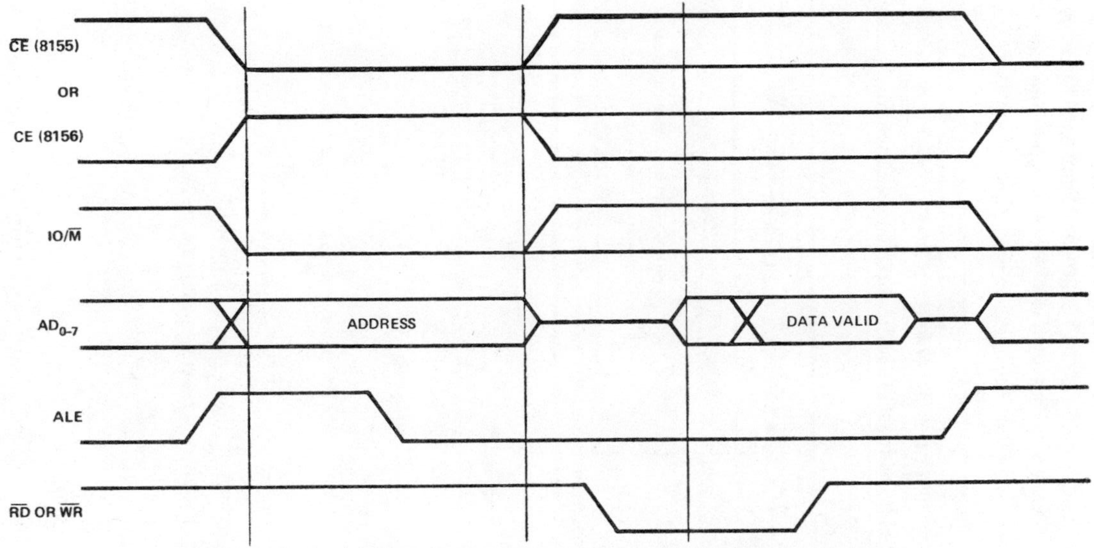

NOTE: FOR DETAILED TIMING DIAGRAM INFORMATION, SEE FIGURE 7 AND A.C. CHARACTERISTICS.

Fig. A-5. Memory read/write cycle.

Programming of the Command/Status Register

The command register consists of eight latches one for each bit. Four bits (0-3) define the mode of the ports, two bits (4-5) enable or disable the interrupt from port C when it acts as control port, and the last two bits (6-7) are for the timer.

The C/S register contents can be altered at any time by using the I/O address XXXXX000 during a WRITE operation. The meaning of each bit of the command byte is defined as follows:

Reading the Command/Status Register

The status register consists of seven latches one for each bit; six (0-5) for the status of the ports and one (6) for the status of the timer.

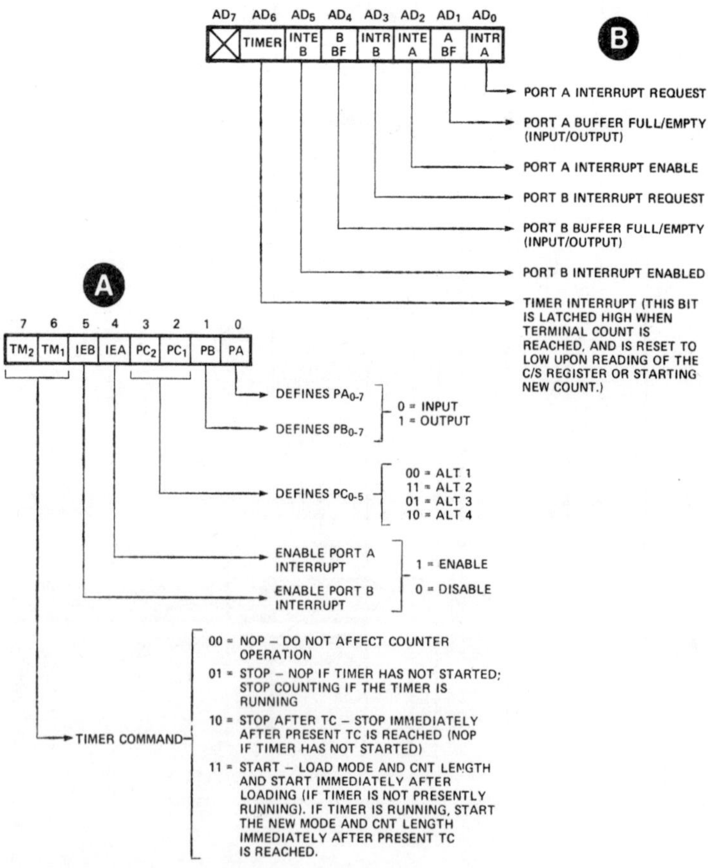

Fig. A-6. Command/Status register. Register bit assignment (A). Status word format (B).

CONTROL	INPUT MODE	OUTPUT MODE
BF	Low	Low
INTR	Low	High
$\overline{STB}$	Input Control	Input Control

TABLE 1. TABLE OF PORT CONTROL ASSIGNMENT.

Pin	ALT 1	ALT 2	ALT 3	ALT 4
PC0	Input Port	Output Port	A INTR (Port A Interrupt)	A INTR (Port A Interrupt)
PC1	Input Port	Output Port	A BF (Port A Buffer Full)	A BF (Port A Buffer Full)
PC2	Input Port	Output Port	A $\overline{STB}$ (Port A Strobe)	A $\overline{STB}$ (Port A Strobe)
PC3	Input Port	Output Port	Output Port	B INTR (Port B Interrupt)
PC4	Input Port	Output Port	Output Port	B BF (Port B Buffer Full)
PC5	Input Port	Output Port	Output Port	B $\overline{STB}$ (Port B Strobe)

The set and reset of INTR and BF with respect to $\overline{STB}$, $\overline{WR}$ and $\overline{RD}$ timing is shown in Figure 8.

To summarize, the registers' assignments are:

Address	Pinouts	Functions	No. of Bits
XXXXX000	Internal	Command/Status Register	8
XXXXX001	PA0-7	General Purpose I/O Port	8
XXXXX010	PB0-7	General Purpose I/O Port	8
XXXXX011	PC0-5	General Purpose I/O Port or Control Lines	6

Fig. A-7. Table of port control assignment.

8212 EIGHT-BIT INPUT/OUTPUT PORT

- Fully Parallel 8-Bit Data Register and Buffer
- Service Request Flip-Flop for Interrupt Generation
- Low Input Load Current—.25 mA Max.
- Three State Outputs
- Outputs Sink 15 mA
- 3.65V Output High Voltage for Direct Interface to 8008, 8080A, or 8085A CPU
- Asynchronous Register Clear
- Replaces Buffers, Latches and Multiplexers in Microcomputer Systems
- Reduces System Package Count

The 8212 input/output port consists of an 8-bit latch with 3-state output buffers along with control and device selection logic. Also included is a service request flip-flop for the generation and control of interrupts to the microprocessor.

The device is multimode in nature. It can be used to implement latches, gated buffers or multiplexers. Thus, all of the principal peripheral and input/output functions of a microcomputer system can be implemented with this device.

Functional Description

Data Latch

The 8 flip-flops that make up the data latch are of a "D" type design. The output (Q) of the flip-flop will follow the data input (D) while the clock input (C) is high. Latching will occur when the clock (C) returns low.

The data latch is cleared by an asynchronous reset input ($\overline{CLR}$). (Note: Clock (C) Overrides Reset ($\overline{CLR}$).)

Output Buffer

The outputs of the data latch (Q) are connected to 3-state, non-inverting output buffers. These buffers have a common control line (EN); this control line either enables the buffer to transmit the data from the outputs of the data latch (Q) or disables the buffer, forcing the output into a high impedance state. (3-state)

This high-impedance state allows the designer to connect the 8212 directly onto the microprocessor bi-directional data bus.

LOGIC DIAGRAM

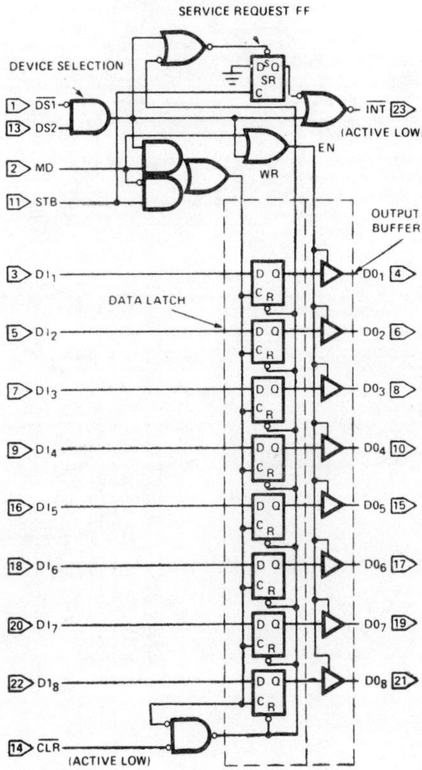

PIN CONFIGURATION

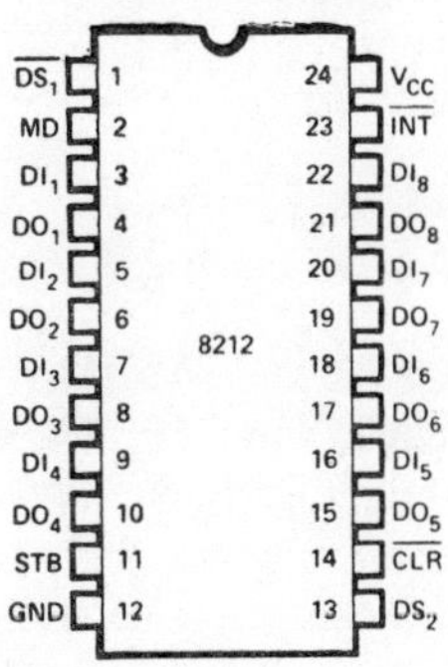

PIN NAMES

DI_1-DI_8	DATA IN
DO_1-DO_8	DATA OUT
$\overline{DS_1}$-DS_2	DEVICE SELECT
MD	MODE
STB	STROBE
$\overline{INT}$	INTERRUPT (ACTIVE LOW)
$\overline{CLR}$	CLEAR (ACTIVE LOW)

Fig. A-8. 8212 input/output port.

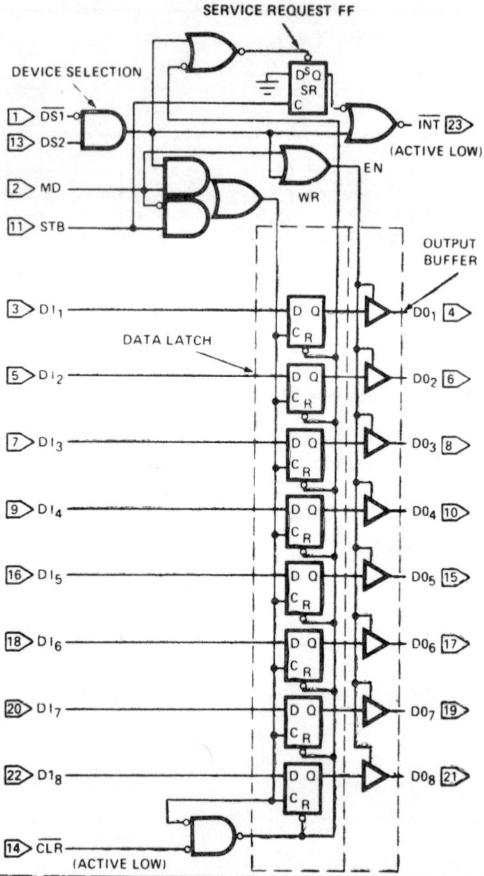

STB	MD	$(\overline{DS_1} \cdot DS_2)$	DATA OUT EQUALS
0	0	0	3-STATE
1	0	0	3-STATE
0	1	0	DATA LATCH
1	1	0	DATA LATCH
0	0	1	DATA LATCH
1	0	1	DATA IN
0	1	1	DATA IN
1	1	1	DATA IN

$\overline{CLR}$ – RESETS DATA LATCH
SETS SR FLIP-FLOP
(NO EFFECT ON OUTPUT BUFFER)

CLR	$(\overline{DS_1} \cdot DS_2)$	STB	*SR	INT
0	0	0	1	1
0	1	0	1	0
1	1	‾_	0	0
1	1	0	1	0
1	0	0	1	1
1	1	‾_	1	0

*INTERNAL SR FLIP-FLOP

Fig. A-9. Functional diagram.

Control Logic

The 8212 has control inputs $\overline{DS1}$, DS2, MD and STB. These inputs are used to control device selection, data latching, output buffer state and service request flip-flop.

$\overline{DS1}$, DS2 (Device Select)

These 2 inputs are used for device selection. When $\overline{DS1}$ is low and DS2 is high ($\overline{DS1}$ • DS2) the device is selected. In the selected state the output buffer is enabled and the service request flip-flop (SR) is asynchronously set.

MD (Mode)

This input is used to control the state of the output buffer and to determine the source of the clock input (C) to the data latch.

When MD is high (output mode) the output buffers are enabled and the source of clock (C) to the data latch is from the device selection logic ($\overline{DS1}$ • DS2).

When MD is low (input mode) the output buffer state is determined by the device selection logic ($\overline{DS1}$ • DS2) and the source of clock (C) to the data latch is the STB (Strobe) input.

STB (Strobe)

This input is used as the clock (C) to the data latch for the input mode MD = 0) and to synchronously reset the service request flip-flop (SR).

Note that the SR flip-flop is negative edge triggered.

Service Request Flip-Flop

The (SR) flip-flop is used to generate and control interrupts in microcomputer systems. It is asynchronously set by the $\overline{CLR}$ input (active low). When the (SR) flip-flop is set it is in the non-interrupting state.

The output of the (SR) flip-flop (Q) is connected to an inverting input of a "NOR" gate. The other input to the "NOR" gate is non-inverting and is connected to the device selection logic ($\overline{DS1}$ • DS2). The output of the "NOR" gate ($\overline{INT}$) is active low (interrupting state) for connection to active low input priority generating circuits.

8216/8226 4-BIT PARALLEL BI-DIRECTIONAL BUS DRIVER

- Data Bus Buffer Driver for 8080 CPU
- Low Input Load Current — .25 mA Maximum
- High Output Drive Capability for Driving System Data Bus
- 3.65V Output High Voltage for Direct Interface to 8080 CPU
- Three State Outputs
- Reduces System Package Count

The 8216/8226 is a 4-bit bi-directional bus driver/receiver.

PIN CONFIGURATION

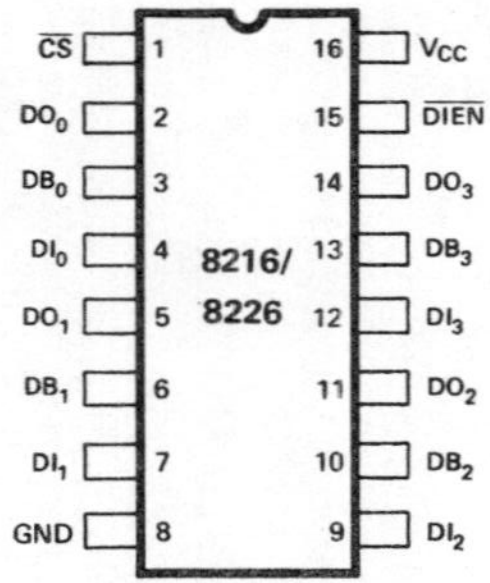

PIN NAMES

DB_0-DB_3	DATA BUS BI-DIRECTIONAL
DI_0-DI_3	DATA INPUT
DO_0-DO_3	DATA OUTPUT
$\overline{DIEN}$	DATA IN ENABLE DIRECTION CONTROL
$\overline{CS}$	CHIP SELECT

LOGIC DIAGRAM 8216

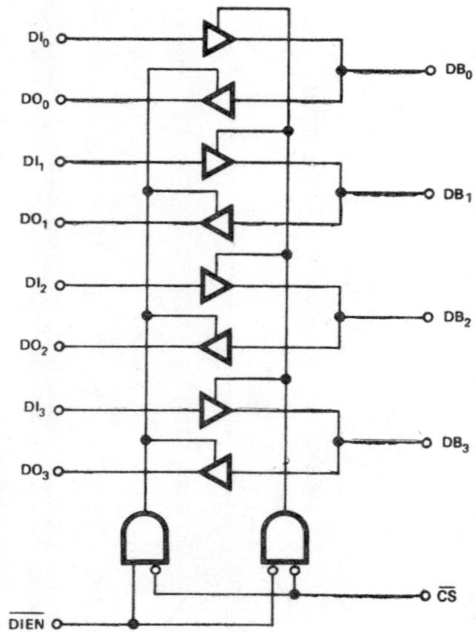

LOGIC DIAGRAM 8226

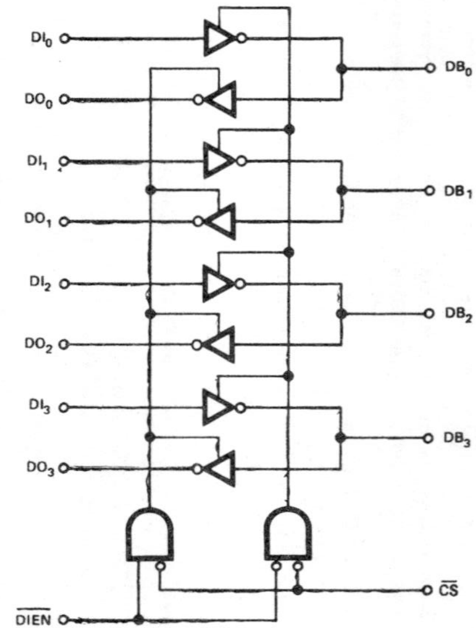

Fig. A-10. 8216/8226 bus driver.

All inputs are low power TTL compatible. For driving MOS, the DO outputs provide a high 3.65V V_{OH}, and for high capacitance terminated bus structures, the DB outputs provide a high 50mA I_{OL} capability.

A non-inverting (8216) and an inverting (8226) are available to meet a wide variety of applications for buffering in microcomputer systems.

Functional Description

Microprocessors like the 8080 are MOS devices and are generally capable of driving a single TTL load. The same is true for MOS memory devices. While this type of drive is sufficient in small systems with few components, quite often it is necessary to buffer the microprocessor and memories when adding components or expanding to a multi-board system.

The 8216/8226 is a four bit bi-directional bus driver specifically designed to buffer microcomputer system components.

Bi-Directional Driver

Each buffered line of the four bit driver consists of two separate buffers that are tri-state in nature to achieve direct bus interface and bi-directional capability. On one side of the driver the output of one buffer and the input of another are tied together (DB), this side is used to interface to the system side components such as memories, I/O, etc., because its interface is direct TTL compatible and it has high drive (50mA). On the other side of the driver the inputs and outputs are separated to provide maximum flexibility. Of course, they can be tied together so that the driver can be used to buffer a true bi-directional bus such as the 8080 Data Bus. The DO outputs on this side of the driver have a special high voltage output drive capability (3.65V) so that direct interface to the 8080 and 8008 CPUs is achieved with an adequate amount of noise immunity (350mV worst case).

Control Gating $\overline{\text{DIEN}}$, $\overline{\text{CS}}$

The CS input is actually a device select. When it is "high" the output drivers are all forced to their high-impedance state. When it is at "zero" the device is selected (enabled) and the direction of the data flow is determined by the $\overline{\text{DIEN}}$ input.

The DIEN input controls the direction of data flow (see Fig. A-11.) for complete truth table. This direction control is ac-

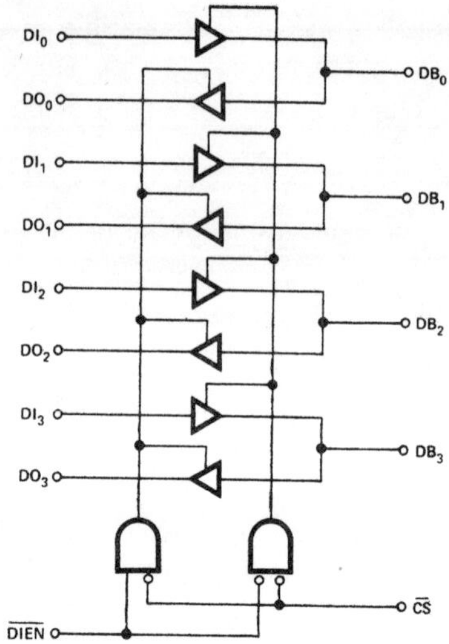

(a) 8216

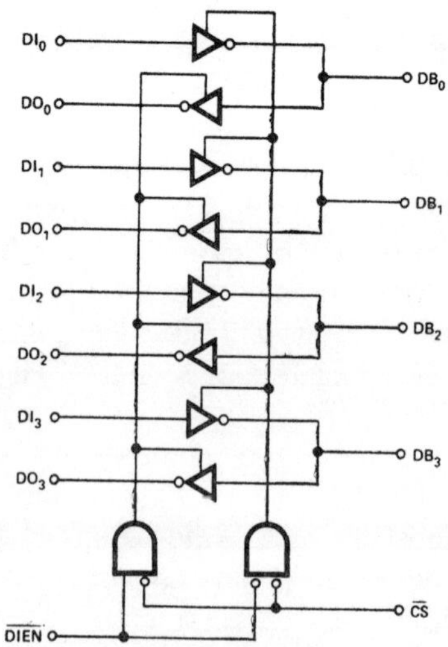

$\overline{DIEN}$	$\overline{CS}$	
0	0	DI → DB
1	0	DB → DO
0	1	HIGH IMPEDANCE
1	1	HIGH IMPEDANCE

(b) 8226

Fig. A-11. 8216-8226 logic diagram.

complished by forcing one of the pair of buffers into its high impedance state and allowing the other to transmit its data. A simple two gate circuit is used for this function.

The 8216/8226 is a device that will reduce component count in microcomputer systems and at the same time enhance noise immunity to assure reliable, high performance operation.

8279, 8279-5 PROGRAMMABLE KEYBOARD/DISPLAY INTERFACE

- MCS-85 Compatible 8279-5
- Simultaneous Keyboard Display Operations
- Scanned Keyboard Mode
- Scanned Sensor Mode
- Strobed Input Entry Mode
- 8 Character Keyboard FIFO
- 2 Key Lockout or N Key Rollover with Contact Debounce
- Dual 8 or 16 Numerical Display
- Single 16 Character Display
- Right or Left Entry 16 Byte Display RAM
- Mode Programmable from CPU
- Programmable Scan Timing
- Interrupt Output on Key Entry

The 8279 is a general purpose programmable keyboard and display I/O interface device designed for use with Intel microprocessors. The keyboard portion can provide a scanned interface to a 64 contact key matrix which can be expanded to 128. The keyboard portion will also interface to an array of sensors or a strobed interface keyboard, such as the Hall effect and Ferrite variety. Key depressions can be 2 key lockout or N key rollover. Keyboard entries are debounced and strobed in an 8 character FIFO. If more than 8 characters are entered, over run status is set. Key entries set the interrupt output line to the CPU.

The display portion provides a scanned display interface for LED, incandescent and other popular display technologies. Both numeric and alphanumeric segment displays may be used as well as simple indicators. The 8279 has a 16×8 display RAM which can be organized into a dual 16×4. The RAM can be loaded or interrogated by the CPU. Both right entry, calculator and left entry typewriter display formats are possible. Both read and write of the display RAM can be done with auto-increment of the display RAM address.

8279 Basic Functional Description

Introduction

Since data input and display are an integral part of many microprocessor designs, the system designer needs an interface that can control these functions without placing a large load on the CPU. The 8279 provides this function for 8-bit microprocessors.

PIN CONFIGURATION

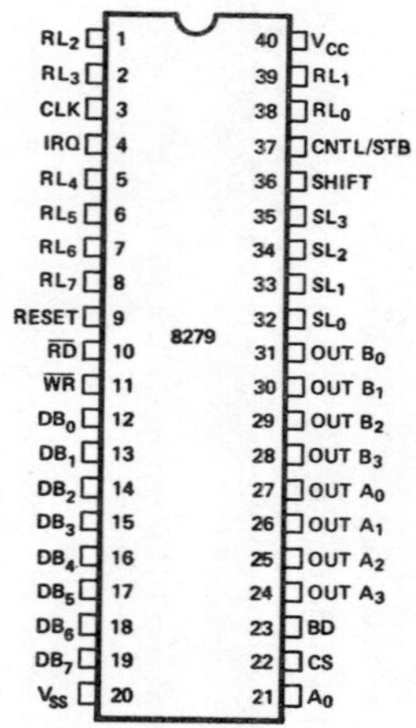

PIN NAMES

NAME	I/O	FUNCTION
DB_{0-7}	I/O	DATA BUS (BI-DIRECTIONAL)
CLK	I	CLOCK INPUT
RESET	I	RESET INPUT
$\overline{CS}$	I	CHIP SELECT
$\overline{RD}$	I	READ INPUT
$\overline{WR}$	I	WRITE INPUT
A_0	I	BUFFER ADDRESS
IRQ	O	INTERRUPT REQUEST OUTPUT
SL_{0-3}	O	SCAN LINES
RL_{0-7}	I	RETURN LINES
SHIFT	I	SHIFT INPUT
CNTL/STB	I	CONTROL/STROBE INPUT
OUT A_{0-3}	O	DISPLAY (A) OUTPUTS
OUT B_{0-3}	O	DISPLAY (B) OUTPUTS
$\overline{BD}$	O	BLANK DISPLAY OUTPUT

LOGIC SYMBOL

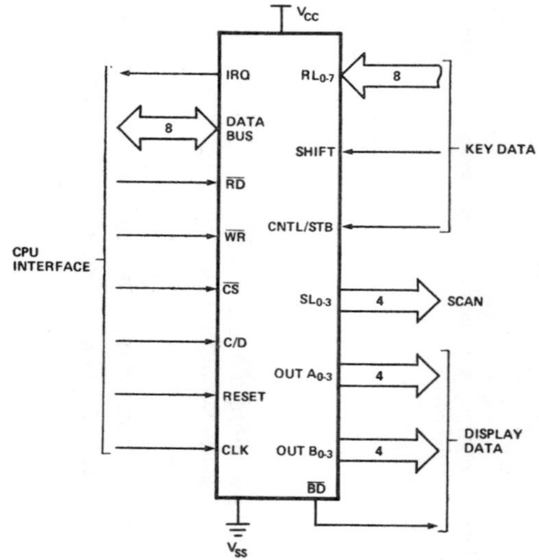

Fig. A-12. 8279/8279-5 Interface.

The 8279 has two sections: keyboard and display. The keyboard section can interface to regular typewriter style keyboards or random toggle or thumb switches. The display section drives alphanumeric displays or a bank of indicator lights. Thus the CPU is relieved from scanning the keyboard or refreshing the display.

The 8279 is designed to directly connect to the microprocessor bus. The CPU can program all operating modes for the 8279. These modes include:

Input Modes

- Scanned Keyboard — with encoded (8×8×4 key keyboard) or decoded (4×8×4 key keyboard) scan lines. A key depression generates a 6-bit encoding of key position. Position and shift and control status are stored in the FIFO. Keys are automatically debounced with 2-key lockout or N-key rollover.
- Scanned Sensor Matrix — with encoded (8×8 matrix switches) or decoded (4×8 matrix switches) scan lines. Key status (open or closed) stored in RAM addressable by CPU.
- Strobed Input — Data on return lines during control line strobe is transferred to FIFO.

Output Modes

- 8 or 16 character multiplexed displays that can be organized as dual 4-bit or single 8-bit.
- Right entry or left entry display formats.

Other features of the 8279 include:

- Mode programming from the CPU.
- Programmable clock to match the 8279 scan times to the CPU cycle time.
- Interrupt output to signal CPU when there is keyboard or sensor data available.
- An 8 byte FIFO to store keyboard information.
- 16 byte internal Display RAM for display refresh. This RAM can also be read by the CPU.

Hardware Description

The 8279 is packaged in a 40 pin DIP. The following is a functional description of each pin.

No. Of Pins	Designation	Function
8	DB_0-DB_7	Bi-directional data bus. All data and commands between the CPU and the 8279 are transmitted on these lines.
1	CLK	Clock from system used to generate internal timing.
1	RESET	A high signal on this pin resets the 8279.
1	$\overline{CS}$	Chip Select. A low on this pin enables the interface functions to receive or transmit.
1	A_0	Buffer Address. A high on this line indicates the signals in or out are interpreted as a command or status. A low indicates that they are data.
2	$\overline{RD}$, $\overline{WR}$	Input/Output read and write. These signals enable the data buffers to either send data to the external bus or receive it from the external bus.
1	IRQ	Interrupt Request. In a keyboard mode, the interrupt line is high when there is data in the FIFO/Sensor RAM. The interrupt line goes low with each FIFO/Sensor RAM read and returns high if there is still information in the RAM. In a sensor mode, the interrupt line goes high whenever a change in a sensor is detected.
2	V_{SS}, V_{CC}	Ground and power supply pins.
4	SL_0-SL_3	Scan Lines which are used to scan the key switch or sensor matrix and the display digits. These lines can be either encoded (1 of 16) or decoded (1 of 4).

No. Of Pins	Designation	Function
8	RL_0-RL_7	Return line inputs which are connected to the scan lines through the keys or sensor switches. They have active internal pullups to keep them high until a switch closure pulls one low. they also serve as an 8-bit input in the Strobed Input mode.
1	SHIFT	The shift input status is stored along with the key position on key closure in the Scanned Keyboard modes. It has an active internal pullup to keep it high until a switch closure pulls it low.
1	CNTL/STB	For keyboard modes this line is used as a control input and stored like status on a key closure. The line is also the strobe line that enters the data into the FIFO in the Strobed Input mode. (Rising Edge). It has an active internal pullup to keep it high until a switch closure pulls it low.
4 4	OUT A_0-OUT A_3 OUT B_0-OUT B_3	These two ports are the outputs for the 16 × 4 display refresh registers. The data from these outputs is synchronized to the scan lines (SL_0-SL_3) for multiplexed digit displays. The two 4 bit ports may be blanked independently. These two ports may also be considered as one 8 bit port.
1	$\overline{BD}$	Blank Display. This output is used to blank the display during digit switching or by a display blanking command.

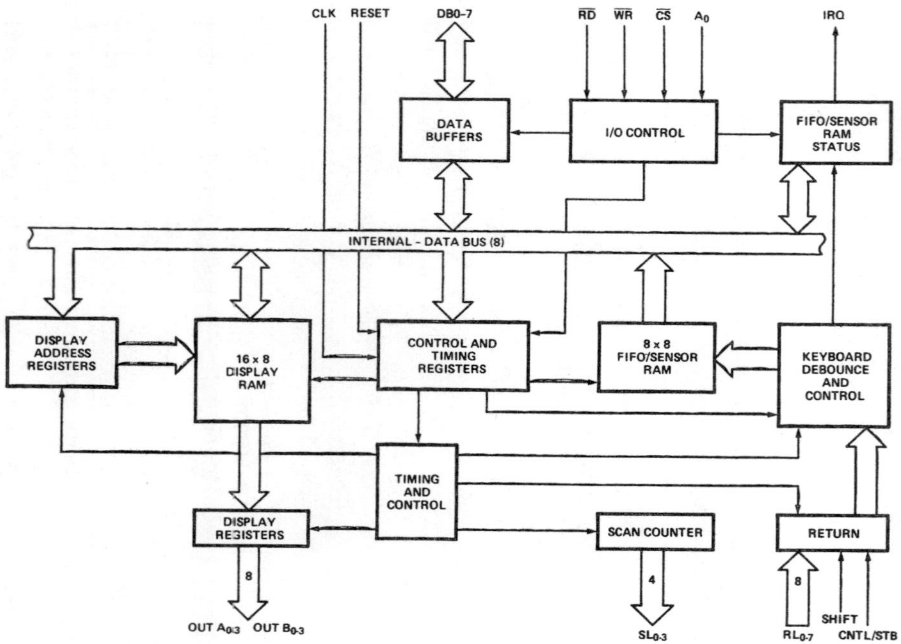

Fig. A-13. 8279 block diagram.

Principles of Operation

The following is a description of the major elements of the 8279 Programmable Keyboard/Display interface device. Refer to the block diagram in Fig. 13.

I/O Control and Data Buffers

The I/O control section uses the $\overline{CS}$, A_0, $\overline{RD}$ and $\overline{WR}$ lines to control data flow to and from the various internal registers and buffers. All data flow to and from the 8279 is enabled by $\overline{CS}$. The character of the information, given or desired by the CPU, is identified by A_0. A logic one means the information is a command or status. A logic zero means the information is data. $\overline{RD}$ and $\overline{WR}$ determine the direction of data flow through the Data Buffers. The Data Buffers are bi-directional buffers that connect the internal bus to the external bus. When the chip is not selected ($\overline{CS}$ = 1), the devices are in a high impedance state. The drivers input during WR • $\overline{CS}$ and output during RD • $\overline{CS}$.

Control and Timing Registers and Timing Control

These registers store the keyboard and display modes and other operating conditions programmed by the CPU. The modes are programmed by presenting the proper command on the data lines with A_0 = 1 and then sending a $\overline{WR}$. The command is latched on the rising edge of $\overline{WR}$.

The command is then decoded and the appropriate function is set. The timing control contains the basic timing counter chain. The first counter is a ÷ N prescaler that can be programmed to match the CPU cycle time to the internal timing. The prescaler is software programmed to a value between 2 and 31. A value which yields an internal frequency of 100 kHz gives a 5.1 ms keyboard scan time and a 10.3 ms debounce time. The other counters divide down the basic internal frequency to provide the proper key scan, row scan, keyboard matrix scan, and display scan times.

Scan Counter

The scan counter has two modes. In the encoded mode, the counter provides a binary count that must be externally decoded to provide the scan lines for the keyboard and display. In the decoded mode, the scan counter decodes the least significant 2 bits and provides a decoded 1 of 4 scan. Note than when the keyboard is in decoded scan, so is the display. This means that only the first 4 characters in the Display RAM are displayed.

In the encoded mode, the scan lines are active high outputs. In the decoded mode, the scan lines are active low outputs.

Return Buffers and Keyboard Debounce and Control

The 8 return lines are buffered and latched by the Return Buffers. In the keyboard mode, these lines are scanned, looking for key closures in that row. If the debounce circuit detects a closed switch, it waits about 10 msec to check if the switch remains closed. If it does, the address of the switch in the matrix plus the status of SHIFT and CONTROL are transferred to the FIFO. In the scanned Sensor Matrix modes, the contents of the return lines is directly transferred to the corresponding row of the Sensor RAM (FIFO) each key scan time. In Strobed Input mode, the contents of the return lines are transferred to the FIFO on the rising edge of the CNTL/STB line pulse.

FIFO/Sensor RAM and Status

This block is a dual function 8 × 8 RAM. In Keyboard or Strobed Input modes, it is a FIFO. Each new entry is written into successive RAM positions and each is then read in order of entry. FIFO status keeps track of the number of characters in the FIFO and whether it is full or empty. Too many reads or writes will be recognized as an error. The status can be read by an $\overline{RD}$ with $\overline{CS}$ low and A_0 high. The status logic also provides an IRQ signal when the FIFO is not empty. In Scanned Sensor Matrix mode, the memory is a Sensor RAM. Each row of the Sensor RAM is loaded with the status of the corresponding row of sensor in the sensor matrix. In this mode, IRQ is high if a change in a sensor is detected.

Display Address Registers and Display RAM

The Display Address Registers hold the address of the word currently being written or read by the CPU and the two 4-bit nibbles being displayed. The read/write addresses are programmed by CPU command. They also can be set to auto increment after each read or write. The Display RAM can be directly read by the CPU after the correct mode and address is set. The addresses for the A and B nibbles are automatically updated by the 8279 to match data entry by the CPU. The A and B nibbles can be entered independently or as one word, according to the mode that is set by the CPU. Data entry to the display can be set to either left or right entry. See Interface Considerations for details.

Software Operation

8279 Commands

The following commands program the 8279 operating modes. The commands are sent on the Data Bus with $\overline{CS}$ low and A_0 high and are loaded to the 8279 on the rising edge of $\overline{WR}$.

Keyboard/Display Mode set

	MSB							LSB
Code:	0	0	0	D	D	K	K	K

Where DD is the Display Mode and KKK is the Keyboard Mode.

DD

0 0 8 8-bit character display — Left entry
0 1 16 8-bit character display — Left entry*
1 0 8 8-bit character display — Right entry
1 1 16 8-bit character display — Right entry

For description of right and left entry, see Interface Considerations. Note that when decoded scan is set in keyboard mode, the display is reduced to 4 characters independent of display mode set.

KK

0 0 0 Encoded Scan Keyboard — 2 Key Lockout
0 0 1 Decoded Scan Keyboard — 2-Key Lockout
0 1 0 Encoded Scan Keyboard — N-Key Rollover
0 1 1 Decoded Scan Keyboard — N-Key Rollover
1 0 0 Encoded Scan Sensor Matrix
1 0 1 Decoded Scan Sensor Matrix
1 1 0 Strobed Input, Encoded Display Scan
1 1 1 Strobed Input, Decoded Display Scan

Program Clock

Code:	0	0	1	P	P	P	P	P

Where PPPPP is the prescaler value 2 to 31. The programmable prescaler divides the external clock by PPPPP to get the basic internal frequency. Choosing a divisor that yields 100 kHz will give the specified scan and debounce times. Default after a reset pulse (but not a program clear) is 31.

Read FIFO/Sensor RAM

Code:	0	1	0	A1	X	A	A	A	X = Don't Care

Where A1 is the Auto-Increment flag for the Sensor RAM and AAA is the row that is going to be read by the CPU. A1 and AAA are used only if the mode is set to Sensor Matrix. This command is used to specify that the source of data reads ($\overline{CS} \cdot RD \cdot \overline{A_0}$) by the CPU is

**Default after reset.*

the FIFO/Sensor RAM. No additional commands are necessary as long as data is desired from the FIFO/Sensor RAM. Another command is necessary if reading is desired from a different row than has been selected. If A1 is a one, the row select counter will be incremented after each read so the next read will be from the next Sensor RAM row.

In the Auto Increment mode for reading data from the FIFO/Sensor RAM, each read advances the address by one so that the next read is from the next character. This Auto Incrementing has no effect on the display.

Read Display RAM

Code:

0	1	1	AI	A	A	A	A

Where AI is the Auto-Increment flag for the Display RAM and AAAA is the character that the CPU is going to read next. Since the CPU uses the same counter for reading and writing, this command also sets the next write location and Auto-Increment mode. This command is used to specify the display RAM as the data source for CPU data reads. If AI is set, the character address will be incremented after each read (or write) so that the next read (or write) will be from (to) the next character.

Write Display RAM

Code:

1	0	0	AI	A	A	A	A

Where AI is the Auto-Increment flag for the Display RAM and AAAA is the character that the CPU is going to write next. The addressing and Auto-Increment are identical to Read Display RAM. The difference is that Write Display RAM does not affect the source of CPU reads. The CPU will read from whichever RAM (Display or FIFO/Sensor) was last specified. This command will, however, change the location the next Display RAM read will be from if that source was specified.

Display Write Inhibit/Blanking

Code:

1	0	1	X	IW	IW	BL	BL
				A	**B**	**A**	**B**

Where IW is Inhibit Writing (nibble A or B) and BL is Blanking (nibble A or B). If the display is being used as a dual 4-bit display, then it is necessary to mask one of the 4-bit halves so that entries to the Display from the CPU do not affect the other half. The IW flags allow the programmer to do this. It is also useful to be able to blank either half when that half is not to be displayed. The BL flags blank the display. The next command sets the output code to be used as a "blank". Default after reset is all zeros. Note that to blank a display formatted as a single 8-bit output, it is necessary to set both BL flags to entirely blank the display. A "1" sets the flag. Reissuing the command with a "0" resets the flag.

Clear

Code: | 1 | 1 | 0 | C_D | C_D | D_D | C_F | C_A |

Where C_D is Clear Display, C_F is Clear FIFO Status (including interrupt), and C_A is Clear All. C_D is used to clear all positions of the Display RAM to a programmable code. All ones, all zeros and hexadecimal 20 are possible. The 2 least significant bits of C_D are also used to specify the blanking code (see below).

C_D	C_D	C_D	
	0	X	All Zeros (X = Don't Care)
	1	0	AB = Hex 20 (0010 0000)
	1	1	All Ones

(C_D, first bit:) Enable clear display when = 1 (or by C_A = 1)

Clearing the display takes one display scan. During this time the CPU cannot write to the Display RAM. The MSB of the FIFO status word will be set during this time.

C_F set the FIFO status to empty and resets the interrupt output line. After execution of a clear command and C_F set, the Sensor Matrix mode RAM pointer will be set to row 0.

C_A has the combined effect of C_D and C_F. C_A uses the C_D clearing code to determine how to clear the Display RAM. C_A also resets the internal timing chain to resynchronize it.

End Interrupt/Error Mode Set

Code: | 1 | 1 | 1 | E | X | X | X | X | X | = Don't Care

For the sensor matrix modes this command lowers the IRQ line and enables further writing into RAM. (The IRQ line would have been raised upon the detection of a change in a sensor value. This would have also inhibited further writing into the RAM until reset).

For the N-key rollover mode—if the E bit is programmed to "1" the chip will operate in the special Error mode. (For further details, see Interface Considerations Section.)

Status Word

The status word contains the FIFO status, error, and display unavailable signals. This word is read by the CPU when A_0 is high

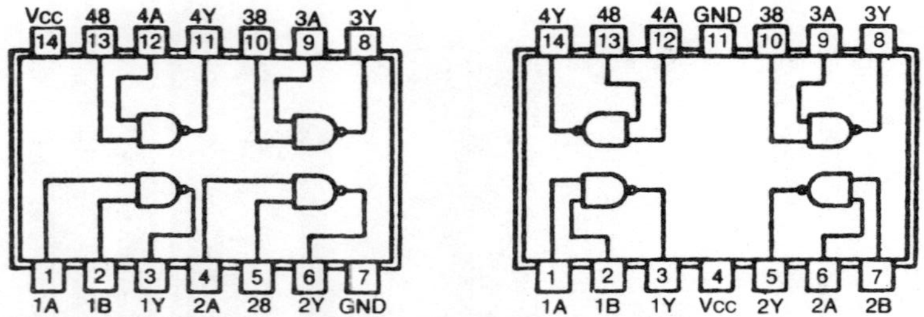

PIN ASSIGNMENTS FOR THE SN74S00: QUAD 2-INPUT NAND GATE (POSITIVE)

Fig. A-14.

FUNCTION TABLE

INPUTS				OUTPUTS	
PRESET	CLEAR	CLOCK	D	Q	$\overline{Q}$
L	H	X	X	H	L
H	L	X	X	L	H
L	L	X	X	H*	H*
H	H	↑	H	H	L
H	H	↑	L	L	H
H	H	L	X	Q0	$\overline{Q}$0

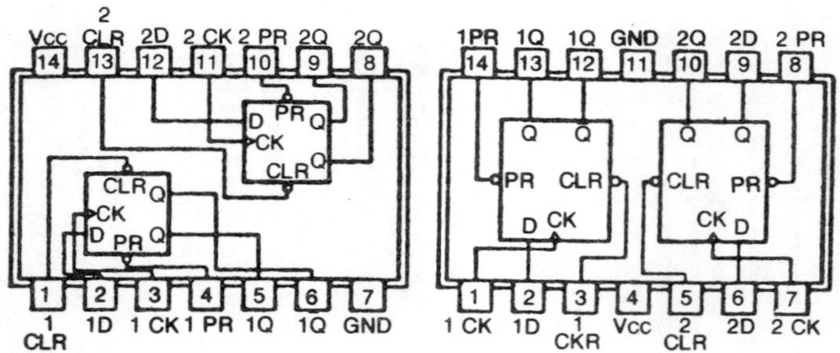

PIN ASSIGNMENTS FOR THE SN74LS74: DUAL D-TYPE POSITIVE EDGE TRIGGERED FLIP-FLOPS WITH PRESET AND CLEAR

Fig. A-15.

DUAL 2- TO 4-LINE DECODER
DUAL 1- TO 4-LINE DEMULTIPLEXER
3- TO 8-LINE DECODER
1- TO 8-LINE DEMULTIPLEXER

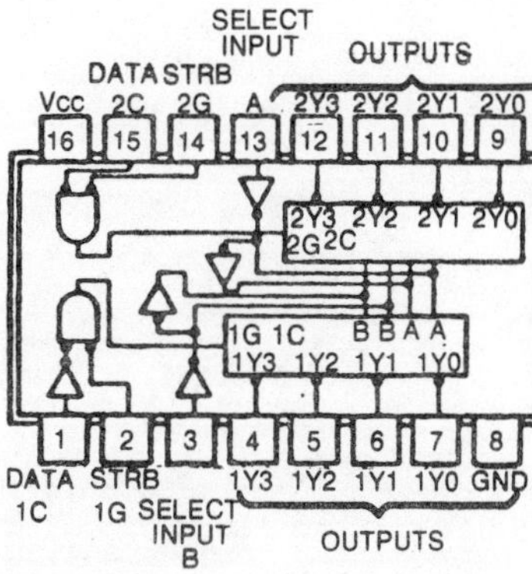

Fig. A-16.

PIN ASSIGNMENTS FOR THE SN74LS156: DECODERS/DEMULTIPLEXERS OPEN-COLLECTOR OUTPUTS

positive logic: Y = A

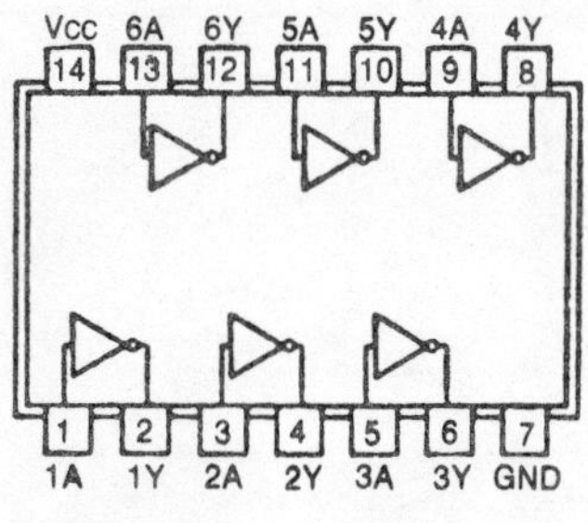

Fig. A-17. SN5416 (J,W) SN7416 (,N)

PIN ASSIGNMENTS FOR THE SN7416: HEX INVERTER BUFFERS/DRIVERS WITH OPEN-COLLECTOR HIGH VOLTAGE OUTPUTS

and $\overline{CS}$ and $\overline{RD}$ are low. See Interface Considerations for more detail on status word.

Data Read

Data is read when A_0, $\overline{CS}$ and $\overline{RD}$ are all low. The source of the data is specified by the Read FIFO or Read Display commands. The trailing edge of RD will cause the address of the RAM being read to be incremented if the Auto-Increment flag is set. FIFO reads always increment (if no error occurs) independent of AI.

Data Write

Data that is written with A_0, $\overline{CS}$ and $\overline{WR}$ low is always written to the Display RAM. The address is specified by the latest Read Display or Write Display command. Auto-Incrementing on the rising edge of $\overline{WR}$ occurs if AI set by the latest display command.

Index

Index